Public Relations For Dummies®

D0506592

Nine Marketing Problems that PR Can Help You Solve

- ✔ Your competitors are bigger than you and can outspend you in advertising. PR, because of its low cost, can level the playing field.

- ✔ Your product or service is the best — and nobody knows about it. PR can get the word out in a more believable way than paid advertising.

- ✔ Your product isn't better than anyone else's. PR can help set you apart and convince buyers to see you as the leader in your field.

- ✔ Management cuts your marketing budget. PR can make up the shortfall, at a fraction of the cost.

- ✔ Management demands tangible results. PR results can be monitored and measured.

- ✔ Traditional marketing isn't working anymore. PR overcomes the skepticism that consumers have built up against paid promotion.

- ✔ Your competitors are getting all the good press. PR can help reverse the situation.

- ✔ You need venture capital or are planning an initial public offering (IPO). PR gains you the visibility to make both of these propositions more viable.

- ✔ You are media-genic. Some organizations, causes, products, and individuals have natural appeal to the media. If that describes you, why not take advantage of it?

See Chapters 1 and 2 for more PR solutions.

Three Important PR Principles

- ✔ You have to be different. Conventional publicity strategies get lost in the noise. You have to find a creative way to stand out from the crowd and get noticed.

- ✔ Getting publicity is fun, but it's a waste of time and money if it doesn't help you achieve your marketing objective. If getting on the front page of *The Wall Street Journal* doesn't help you make more money or increase your firm's market share, is it really worth the trouble?

- ✔ You don't have to have media contacts to get big-time publicity. You don't have to know Joe TV star to get on his TV show; you just have to come up with an idea that will interest his producer.

Chapters 22 and 23 expand these ideas.

Three Indispensable Media Resources

Bacon's Information, Inc.
332 S. Michigan Avenue
Chicago, IL 60604
Phone: 800-621-0561
Media lists for print and broadcast — directories, labels, disk, and distribution of press releases via mail and fax

All in One Dictionary
Gebbie Press
P.O. Box 1000
New Paltz, NY 12561-0017
Phone: 914-255-7560
Web site: wwwgebbieinc.com
Popular media directory, published annually

PR Newswire
810 Seventh Avenue, 32nd Floor
New York, NY 10019
Phone: 888-PRNEWS7
Web site: www.prnewswire.com
Press release distribution service

Public Relations Kit For Dummies®

Cheat Sheet

Eight Fundamentals of Dealing with Media

- Build a personal contact file. Keep at it until you have a list of at least 100 media contacts who know you personally and take your call when you have a story you want to publicize.

- Follow up. Call everyone to whom you send your press release — several times each, if necessary. Do this and you will get coverage.

- Become the "go-to guy." Show the press that you're the one to call for expert interviews in your particular field. For example, Alan Dershowitz is the go-to guy for law.

- Don't limit yourself. Broaden your outreach. A CEO reads *Forbes,* but he also watches the evening TV news.

- Offer an exclusive. If it's important for you to get into a particular publication, offer the editor an exclusive on the story (meaning you won't send out a press release to other media until that publication has run it first).

- Go where the cameras already are. Instead of trying to get media to cover your event, make noise at an event they're already covering. Domino's Pizza gets national TV coverage by bringing free pizza to the post office on April 15 to feed last-minute taxpayers standing in line.

- Don't expect interest from media in you or your product. They care only whether your story will interest their readers or viewers.

- Remember: Media are your customers. They are buying stories, and you are selling. Meet their needs, and they will run your stories.

Check out Chapter 12 for more ideas.

Eight "Hooks" that Get Editors to Print Your Press Releases

- Offer a free booklet or report. Readers love freebies, and editors love to offer them.

- Set up a hotline for people to call for information or advice.

- Stage a special or timely event or gimmick. A manufacturer of juice machines gained media coverage by holding "juicing seminars" in major cities.

- Introduce a new product or service. Many magazines have special sections featuring new products and services.

- Offer new literature. Many trade journals have sections featuring new sales literature (brochures and catalogs, for example).

- Tie in with a current trend, fad, or news issue and piggyback on that coverage.

- Sound a call to action. Ask people to participate in a boycott, for example.

- Tie your publicity to your high-visibility advertising if it received a lot of attention and created some buzz.

See Chapter 15 for details on how to use these hooks.

For Dummies™: Bestselling Book Series for Beginners

Praise for Eric Yaverbaum

"Eric Yaverbaum has captured the essence of public relations and communications, and distilled it down to the simplest terms. Any manager can grasp these concepts and put them to use in their own strategies."

— William Lauder, President, Clinique Laboratories, Inc.

"Eric taught me how to sell books on Letterman, Oprah, Larry King, The Today Show, Jay Leno, and 5,000 other FREE media outlets. If you don't use his wisdom, you don't want to sell."

— Matthew Lesko, *New York Times* Best Selling Author

"PR For Dummies is the single best resource I have ever read about how the PR process really works! For many years my company has employed PR firms and spent many dollars on PR programs to enhance our brand. I wish I had read Eric's book before I ever spent a dime on this vital part of the marketing mix. Eric has made it simple, yet incredibly insightful. No wonder his agency has won so many awards in the past decade!"

— Irwin D. Simon, CEO, The Hain Celestial Group

"Eric Yaverbaum is a first-class public relations professional whose entertaining and illuminating book benefits from his years of success in the PR business. The book is full of good and thoughtful counsel on how to practice the profession successfully, but Eric is especially instructive and wise in his chapter on those things that should never be done in the name of PR."

— Howard G. Paster, CEO, Hill and Knowlton

"I have been a client of Eric's agency for 17 years...from 300 million Wacky Wallwalkers sold...to a highly rated children's television show...to my Shaker Furniture Collection which tours museums throughout the world...to my current website. From Oprah to *Time* magazine to being profiled on *60 Minutes,* I've seen how effective public relations can translate to the bottom line! Eric's book is the secret weapon I'd always hoped none of my competitors would see. The book is extremely well written and a totally understandable road map to use PR in the same ways I have been benefiting from for two decades!

— Ken "Dr. Fad" Hakuta

"Eric Yaverbaum's book *PR Kit For Dummies* proves there is a place for creativity in your company. His simple team oriented approach will not only give you a plan for improving PR, but also make for a more cohesive involved organization."

> — Alexandra Lebenthal, CEO, Lebenthal and Company, Inc.

"With a master's degree in public relations from Boston University, I can't tell you how many PR books I've read over the years. What a pleasant surprise to see a book that is understandable to both the average CEO and the average reader."

> — Marcy Syms, CEO, Syms Corporation

"PR is not, nor ever will be, a rocket science, and it's great to find a book which debunks some of the highfalutin language, to tell it like it is."

> — Adam Leyland, Editor-in-Chief, *PR Week*

Public Relations Kit

FOR

DUMMIES®

Public Relations Kit

FOR

DUMMIES®

by Eric Yaverbaum
with Bob Bly

IDG BOOKS WORLDWIDE

IDG Books Worldwide, Inc.
An International Data Group Company

Foster City, CA ◆ Chicago, IL ◆ Indianapolis, IN ◆ New York, NY

Public Relations Kit For Dummies®

Published by
IDG Books Worldwide, Inc.
An International Data Group Company
919 E. Hillsdale Blvd.
Suite 300
Foster City, CA 94404
www.idgbooks.com (IDG Books Worldwide Web Site)
www.dummies.com (Dummies Press Web Site)

Library of Congress Control Number: 00-108216

ISBN: 0-7645-5277-5

Printed in the United States of America

10 9 8 7 6 5 4 3 2 1

1O/RT/RS/QQ/IN

Distributed in the United States by IDG Books Worldwide, Inc.

Distributed by CDG Books Canada Inc. for Canada; by Transworld Publishers Limited in the United Kingdom; by IDG Norge Books for Norway; by IDG Sweden Books for Sweden; by IDG Books Australia Publishing Corporation Pty. Ltd. for Australia and New Zealand; by TransQuest Publishers Pte Ltd. for Singapore, Malaysia, Thailand, Indonesia, and Hong Kong; by Gotop Information Inc. for Taiwan; by ICG Muse, Inc. for Japan; by Intersoft for South Africa; by Eyrolles for France; by International Thomson Publishing for Germany, Austria and Switzerland; by Distribuidora Cuspide for Argentina; by LR International for Brazil; by Galileo Libros for Chile; by Ediciones ZETA S.C.R. Ltda. for Peru; by WS Computer Publishing Corporation, Inc., for the Philippines; by Contemporanea de Ediciones for Venezuela; by Express Computer Distributors for the Caribbean and West Indies; by Micronesia Media Distributor, Inc. for Micronesia; by Chips Computadoras S.A. de C.V. for Mexico; by Editorial Norma de Panama S.A. for Panama; by American Bookshops for Finland.

For general information on IDG Books Worldwide's books in the U.S., please call our Consumer Customer Service department at 800-762-2974. For reseller information, including discounts and premium sales, please call our Reseller Customer Service department at 800-434-3422.

For information on where to purchase IDG Books Worldwide's books outside the U.S., please contact our International Sales department at 317-572-3993 or fax 317-572-4002.

For consumer information on foreign language translations, please contact our Customer Service department at 1-800-434-3422, fax 317-572-4002, or e-mail rights@idgbooks.com.

For information on licensing foreign or domestic rights, please phone +1-650-653-7098.

For sales inquiries and special prices for bulk quantities, please contact our Order Services department at 800-434-4322 or write to the address above.

For information on using IDG Books Worldwide's books in the classroom or for ordering examination copies, please contact our Educational Sales department at 800-434-2086 or fax 317-572-4005.

For press review copies, author interviews, or other publicity information, please contact our Public Relations department at 650-653-7000 or fax 650-653-7500.

For authorization to photocopy items for corporate, personal, or educational use, please contact Copyright Clearance Center, 222 Rosewood Drive, Danvers, MA 01923, or fax 978-750-4470.

is a registered trademark under exclusive license to IDG Books Worldwide, Inc. from International Data Group, Inc.

About the Authors

Eric Yaverbaum is co-founder of Jericho Communications, a New York City–based PR firm, and has served as its president for the past 16 years. He brings more than 20 years of experience to the practice of public relations and has earned a reputation for his unique expertise in strategic media relations, crisis communications, and media training. Eric has amassed extensive experience in counseling a wide range of clients in corporate, consumer, retail, technology, and professional services markets and building brands such as Sony, IKEA, Domino's Pizza, Bell Atlantic, and American Express, among many others.

With partner Jonathan Sawyer, Eric works diligently to maintain Jericho's creative caliber and foster the level of "out-of-the-box" thinking for which the agency has become synonymous. On a day-to-day basis, Eric serves as managing director for the agency's overall operations in both New York City and Seattle, new business development efforts, and client programs in five main practice areas: Corporate, Business-to-Business, Consumer Product, Food, and Publishing, as well as the agency's media relations, creative services, and communications training specialties. A hands-on manager and strategist, he is regularly called upon by the nation's most prominent chief executive officers and presidents for his counsel on all aspects of strategic planning, media relations, and crisis preparedness.

Eric has acted as corporate spokesperson on behalf of dozens of clients, including Domino's Pizza, Hain Food Group, Prince Tennis Rackets, and Camp Beverly Hills Clothing. He is a regular on the lecture circuit, speaking to professional organizations across the country on the art of public relations. He has been a guest on many national and regional television and radio programs, including *CBS This Morning,* CNN, and *Larry King Live.*

Eric has written many articles for trade journals on various topics in public relations and co-authored the best-selling book *I'll Get Back to You* (McGraw-Hill). A graduate of The American University, Eric is an active member of the highly selective Young President's Organization and the Public Relations Society of America.

Eric can be reached at:

Eric Yaverbaum
Jericho Communications
304 Hudson Street
New York, NY 10013
Phone 212-645-6900
Fax 212-645-5880
www.jerichopr.com

Bob Bly is an independent copywriter specializing in traditional and Internet direct marketing. He has written lead-generating sales letters, direct-mail packages, ads, scripts, Web sites, Internet direct mail, and PR materials for more than 100 clients, including IBM, AT&T, The BOC Group, EBI Medical Systems, Associated Air Freight, CoreStates Financial Corp., PSE&G, Alloy Technology, M&T Chemicals, ITT, Phillips Publishing, Nortel Networks, Fala Direct Marketing, Citrix Systems, and Grumman Corp.

Bob is the author of more than 45 books, including *The Copywriter's Handbook* (Henry Holt), *Selling Your Services* (Henry Holt & Co.), *Business-to-Business Direct Marketing* (NTC), *The Advertising Manager's Handbook* (Prentice Hall), and *Internet Direct Mail: The Complete Guide to Successful e-mail Marketing Campaigns* (NTC). His articles have appeared in *Direct, Business Marketing, Computer Decisions, Chemical Engineering, Direct Marketing, Writer's Digest, Amtrak Express, DM News, Cosmopolitan, New Jersey Monthly, City Paper,* and many other publications. A winner of the Direct Marketing Association's Gold Echo Award, Bob has presented seminars on direct marketing and related business topics to numerous organizations, including IBM, Foxboro Company, Arco Chemical, Thoroughbred Software Leaders Conference, Cambridge Technology Partners, Haht Software, and Dow Chemical.

Bob Bly can be reached at:

Bob Bly
22 E. Quackenbush Avenue
Dumont, NJ 07628
Phone 201-385-1220
Fax 201-385-1138
E-mail: rwbly@bly.com
Web site: www.bly.com

Dedication

To George Steinbrenner, Patrick Ewing, and Pat Riley: You've all made being a New York sports fan tougher. I beg you to read my book. —Eric Yaverbaum

To the Howards — Scott, Leslie, Brandon, and Zack. —Bob Bly

Authors' Acknowledgments

First and foremost, I must acknowledge that every "I" in the book should have been "we." Nothing I have ever accomplished in my career would have been remotely possible without some of the great staff I have at our offices on both the east and west coasts. I thank them from the very bottom of my heart. My office is filled with superstars, but only one of that great team got his name on the cover.

Every once in a while, you meet a business associate whose chemistry with you is akin to catching lightning in a bottle. My relationship with my coauthor, Bob Bly, was just that. Not a word that you read in this book was untouched by Bob. I've been around this industry long enough to know that I got seriously lucky to have chosen Bob to work with. Professional 110 percent of the time . . . just like I like it! I'll pass on winning the lottery . . . Bob was just that.

Thank you to my idol, partner, and smartest person I know (besides my parents!), Jonathan Sawyer. Much of what you read in this book and on many days in your daily newspaper is my humble and "behind-the-scenes" partner's brilliant opinions or concepts. I am grateful to have been exposed to Jon's intellectual presence for the past 20 years.

At Jericho, thanks so much to those of you who contributed time and materials to this book, including Sherri Candel, Ian Madover, Greg Mowery, Maryann Palumbo, Tim Schramm, Michelle Frankfort, Lauren Weinberg, Kathy Bell, Lara Hauptman, Beth Scheffer, and Marisa DiGrazia. Thanks to some of my other longtime valued staff who had a lot less of my time while I was working on this project, including Felicitas Pardo, Finley Shaw, Marc Wasserman, Saideh Brown, Dawn Kanaan, Eric Rayvid, Heather Johnson, Jennifer Foisy, Windy Lopez, Dana Wigdor, Erica Kestenbaum, Ilyse Berkinow, Jeanette Chin, Michelle Quivey, Rob Grossman, Alison Prakin, Angela Yu, Tiffany Hofmann, Leydi Bautista, Daniel Rodriguez, Vanessa Losada, Christopher Russo, Daniel Teboul, Santa Rando, and Ursala Cuevas. I wish I could list everyone!

Thanks to Susan Halligan for introducing me to my agent, Mark Reiter, the best of the best!

Thanks to the clients who have honored me with their permissions to let us use work we did on their dime as examples in this book.

Thank you to event planner extraordinare Jen Madover and to incredible media trainer Michael Klepper for materials they produced and are used in this book.

Always a big thank you for never ending support to my parents, Harry and Gayle Yaverbaum; to Dana, David, Remy, and Logan Zais; Lori Yaverbaum; Bernie, Noreen, Craig, and Merrill Nisker; Freda, Bessie, and Nan.

Last but far from least, my never ending appreciation and gratitude to the "Best Friends Club," my greatest and most fulfilling joy in life — my wife Suri and kids, Cole and Jace, who gave me up for five months while I wrote the book that will make you (the reader) famous. We can unlock the attic door now!

—Eric Yaverbaum

Eric and I would like to thank the editorial and production teams at IDG Books for doing the hard work of turning a draft into an acceptable manuscript, and a manuscript into a published book. Their dedicated effort and attention to detail showed us why the Dummies series is so spectacularly successful. Of these folks, we'd like to single out our editor, Norm Crampton, whose knowledge and insight in book writing and PR significantly improved the text as we incorporated his ideas in our revisions, and our copy editors, Tina Sims and Patricia Pan, who made the words flow much better.

—Bob Bly

ABOUT IDG BOOKS WORLDWIDE

Welcome to the world of IDG Books Worldwide.

IDG Books Worldwide, Inc., is a subsidiary of International Data Group, the world's largest publisher of computer-related information and the leading global provider of information services on information technology. IDG was founded more than 30 years ago by Patrick J. McGovern and now employs more than 9,000 people worldwide. IDG publishes more than 290 computer publications in over 75 countries. More than 90 million people read one or more IDG publications each month.

Launched in 1990, IDG Books Worldwide is today the #1 publisher of best-selling computer books in the United States. We are proud to have received eight awards from the Computer Press Association in recognition of editorial excellence and three from Computer Currents' First Annual Readers' Choice Awards. Our best-selling *...For Dummies*® series has more than 50 million copies in print with translations in 31 languages. IDG Books Worldwide, through a joint venture with IDG's Hi-Tech Beijing, became the first U.S. publisher to publish a computer book in the People's Republic of China. In record time, IDG Books Worldwide has become the first choice for millions of readers around the world who want to learn how to better manage their businesses.

Our mission is simple: Every one of our books is designed to bring extra value and skill-building instructions to the reader. Our books are written by experts who understand and care about our readers. The knowledge base of our editorial staff comes from years of experience in publishing, education, and journalism — experience we use to produce books to carry us into the new millennium. In short, we care about books, so we attract the best people. We devote special attention to details such as audience, interior design, use of icons, and illustrations. And because we use an efficient process of authoring, editing, and desktop publishing our books electronically, we can spend more time ensuring superior content and less time on the technicalities of making books.

You can count on our commitment to deliver high-quality books at competitive prices on topics you want to read about. At IDG Books Worldwide, we continue in the IDG tradition of delivering quality for more than 30 years. You'll find no better book on a subject than one from IDG Books Worldwide.

John Kilcullen
Chairman and CEO
IDG Books Worldwide, Inc.

Eighth Annual Computer Press Awards ≥1992

Ninth Annual Computer Press Awards ≥1993

Tenth Annual Computer Press Awards ≥1994

Eleventh Annual Computer Press Awards ≥1995

IDG is the world's leading IT media, research and exposition company. Founded in 1964, IDG had 1997 revenues of $2.05 billion and has more than 9,000 employees worldwide. IDG offers the widest range of media options that reach IT buyers in 75 countries representing 95% of worldwide IT spending. IDG's diverse product and services portfolio spans six key areas including print publishing, online publishing, expositions and conferences, market research, education and training, and global marketing services. More than 90 million people read one or more of IDG's 290 magazines and newspapers, including IDG's leading global brands — Computerworld, PC World, Network World, Macworld and the Channel World family of publications. IDG Books Worldwide is one of the fastest-growing computer book publishers in the world, with more than 700 titles in 36 languages. The "...For Dummies®" series alone has more than 50 million copies in print. IDG offers online users the largest network of technology-specific Web sites around the world through IDG.net (http://www.idg.net), which comprises more than 225 targeted Web sites in 55 countries worldwide. International Data Corporation (IDC) is the world's largest provider of information technology data, analysis and consulting, with research centers in over 41 countries and more than 400 research analysts worldwide. IDG World Expo is a leading producer of more than 168 globally branded conferences and expositions in 35 countries including E3 (Electronic Entertainment Expo), Macworld Expo, ComNet, Windows World Expo, ICE (Internet Commerce Expo), Agenda, DEMO, and Spotlight. IDG's training subsidiary, ExecuTrain, is the world's largest computer training company, with more than 230 locations worldwide and 785 training courses. IDG Marketing Services helps industry-leading IT companies build international brand recognition by developing global integrated marketing programs via IDG's print, online and exposition products worldwide. Further information about the company can be found at www.idg.com.   1/26/00

Publisher's Acknowledgments

We're proud of this book; please register your comments through our IDG Books Worldwide Online Registration Form located at http://my2cents.dummies.com.

Some of the people who helped bring this book to market include the following:

Acquisitions, Editorial, and Media Development

Project Editor: Norm Crampton

Acquisitions Editor: Holly McGuire

Associate Acquisitions Editor: Jill Alexander

Copy Editors: Tina Sims, Patricia Pan

Technical Editor: David Zitlow

Permissions Editor: Carmen Krikorian

Associate Media Development Specialist: Megan Decraene

Editorial Manager: Pam Mourouzis

Media Development Manager: Laura Carpenter

Editorial Assistant: Carol Strickland

Production

Project Coordinator: Leslie Alvarez

Layout and Graphics: Amy Adrian, Heather Pope, Julie Trippetti, Brian Torwelle, Jeremey Unger, Erin Zeltner

Proofreaders: Jennifer Mahern, Dwight Ramsey, Charles Spencer, York Production Services, Inc.

Indexer: York Production Services, Inc.

General and Administrative

IDG Books Worldwide, Inc.: John Kilcullen, CEO; Bill Barry, President and COO

IDG Books Consumer Reference Group

Business: Kathleen A. Welton, Vice President and Publisher; Kevin Thornton, Acquisitions Manager

Cooking/Gardening: Jennifer Feldman, Associate Vice President and Publisher

Education/Reference: Diane Graves Steele, Vice President and Publisher; Greg Tubach, Publishing Director

Lifestyles: Kathleen Nebenhaus, Vice President and Publisher; Tracy Boggier, Managing Editor

Pets: Dominique De Vito, Associate Vice President and Publisher; Tracy Boggier, Managing Editor

Travel: Michael Spring, Vice President and Publisher; Suzanne Jannetta, Editorial Director; Brice Gosnell, Managing Editor

IDG Books Consumer Editorial Services: Kathleen Nebenhaus, Vice President and Publisher; Kristin A. Cocks, Editorial Director; Cindy Kitchel, Editorial Director

IDG Books Consumer Production: Debbie Stailey, Production Director

IDG Books Packaging: Marc J. Mikulich, Vice President, Brand Strategy and Research

◆

The publisher would like to give special thanks to Patrick J. McGovern, without whom this book would not have been possible.

◆

Contents at a Glance

Cartoons at a Glance

By Rich Tennant

page 7

page 279

"Tarzan's paintings good, but no one come to gallery. Need to put buzz on street. That when Tarzan call in elephant stampede down Bleeker Street."

page 245

"The Queen says if the people have no bread, let them eat cake that's baked here at the castle and distributed free of charge. That's a little wordy. We need to sound bite it. Let's hear ideas..."

page 91

page 161

page 57

Fax: 978-546-7747
E-mail: richtennant@the5thwave.com
World Wide Web: www.the5thwave.com

Table of Contents

Foreword

∙ ∙

"*W*hat is more likely to make you spend your money at a certain restaurant — a good ad or a good review?" This question was posed to me by Eric Yaverbaum, president of Jericho Communications, my company's public relations firm of the last six years.

Public relations in Sweden, where I am from and IKEA was started, is different than in the United States. I was quick to understand this once I met Eric. We discussed what was the true value of a good public relations program and Eric challenged me to think about this question, which seemed fairly innocuous at first. But, now that I've seen it work, I see the significance. In today's world, where consumers are so savvy to how companies market themselves, and we all know that anyone can run an ad and say just about anything they want, having the media say it for you breaks down consumers' defenses and can convince and motivate them. Just one obvious reason to have a great PR program!

Nothing in this country is more effective at driving consumers' spending habits than the media. There is nothing that molds opinion to its degree, nothing as trusted, nothing more powerful, as the nation's press and broadcast that we all see and read daily. Plain and simple, to harness even a small portion of that power is to succeed in business. It is the difference between winners and losers, category leaders and followers, and because it is so cost-effective, it can be the great equalizer between entrepreneurial Davids and corporate Goliaths. To be able to take your business message and translate it into news, so that the media reports on it, allows you to communicate to your customer in a trusted, motivating, effective, and credible manner. Eric Yaverbaum is a master translator.

If Eric is the master translator, *Public Relations Kit For Dummies* is the official "English to Public Relations Dictionary." It has allowed me to see all the methods behind the madness that allows Eric to get such strong results for his clients. It even makes me more effective at managing him and his agency as our PR representatives. The lessons in this book are so insightful, so easy to follow, that it is clear to see how a national public relations campaign can be created by either a one-person business or a multinational corporation with similar ease and equal success.

This book is successful at taking you from the first basic question of whether you should you use public relations, through building effective strategies, up to the use of the newest technologies. After reading the book, we no longer need Eric's agency and we'll take this opportunity to fire them! So as you can see . . . the book will not only help you develop winning PR programs . . . it will save you money!

Jan Kjellman

President, IKEA North America

Introduction

· ·

*W*hoever you are, wherever you are, public relations makes a difference in your life — believe it or not.

If you're a small-business owner or manager or a wannabe entrepreneur, PR helps level the playing field between you and your bigger, wealthier competitors. You may not be able to afford a 60-second commercial during the Super Bowl, but if you offer a free session at your health club to people who come in *during* the Super Bowl, you can get front-page publicity based on your PR event.

If you're a corporate manager or executive, you've seen ad budgets decline while ad costs skyrocket. With an effective public relations program, you can communicate with your target market *more* often, not less, without increasing ad spending.

And if you're a consumer, public relations plays a role in your education and the formation of your opinions without your even being aware of it. Did you know that half or more of everything you read, see, and hear in the media was put there through the actions of a public relations manager or a PR firm? PR has an enormous effect on the information you get every day of your life.

About This Book

You can think of *Public Relations Kit For Dummies* as "your PR agency in a box." Between the book and the CD-ROM, all the tools you need to do your own PR — ideas, checklists, forms, documents, and resources — are in your hands right now, presented in a clear, easy-to-use package. By using the book and CD, you can get your product or service featured whenever and wherever you wish — in newspapers, magazines, and trade journals; on TV, radio, and the Web — so that people learn about what you are offering and come to you to buy it. The result? More fame, recognition, awareness, inquiries, orders, sales — money!

Can you do your own PR? Yes. Thousands of small- and medium-sized businesses conduct very successful PR campaigns every day, for pennies on the dollar compared to what they'd pay for a similar amount of advertising. Large corporations also are doing an increasing amount of PR in-house. This book is written to help you succeed on your own. You don't need me, my PR agency, or any other PR agency, if you're willing to put in the effort and follow the simple guidelines presented in *Public Relations Kit For Dummies*.

Who Needs This Book

Whether you want to put out a single press release to announce your grand opening, or plan an ongoing PR campaign, *Public Relations Kit For Dummies* can show you how to get the maximum results for your efforts. If you want to do your own public relations, you'll find enough examples, samples, and techniques to keep your product name in the public eye for many years to come. If you prefer to have someone do your PR for you, this book can help you find and hire the right PR counselor or agency and then make informed judgments about and contributions to the work they do for you.

The tactics covered in *Public Relations Kit For Dummies* have been proven to work well for average business owners and managers all over the country. You don't need a big budget or special contacts with the media. No previous experience or training is required. All you need is a telephone, a desk, a word processor, and your wits. The book-CD set supplies most of the rest or tells you where to get it.

On the other hand, some of you may have substantial PR experience or even be public relations professionals. If you're in this category, don't despair! Although I've made *Public Relations Kit For Dummies* accessible to the novice, I've also packed it with successful ideas, techniques, and campaigns that my own clients have paid tens of thousands of dollars for, and I show you how to adapt them to your own clientele, product, or service. To hire my firm costs $10,000 just for a month. But with *Public Relations Kit For Dummies,* you get me as your personal PR adviser and coach for the price of a paperback book. What could be fairer than that?

How to Use This Book

You can read through *Public Relations Kit For Dummies* start to finish, or you can start with the chapters that interest you most. It's up to you.

If you want to see quick, immediate results, go to Chapter 9. Follow the press release strategies presented there, and write a release for your own product following the sample in the chapter. Then distribute the press release to the media by using one of the publicity outlet resources listed on the CD-ROM, and follow up according to the guidelines in Chapter 11. The press release is one of the fastest, easiest techniques in this book, and you'll see results fast. I like that because you receive tangible proof that PR works — press clippings.

My hope is that your newfound enthusiasm for the PR process spurs you to try more and more of the ideas and strategies presented throughout *Public Relations Kit For Dummies.* When you do, you'll magnify your results, make your company famous, and get more business than you can handle. What a nice problem to have!

How This Book Is Organized

The *For Dummies* series was conceived as books for smart people who are absolute beginners, and that's the approach I use in *Public Relations Kit For Dummies.* Part I covers the basics. Part II discusses the process we use to create successful PR campaigns. Part III covers the PR materials you need and how to create them. In Part IV, you learn how to work with the media to get your material published. Part V gives you power techniques for getting the media to notice and cover you. And Part VI is a collection of useful tips. The Appendix introduces you to the many useful forms and other resources on the CD-ROM.

The breakdown of each part follows.

Part I: PR: What It Is, How It Works

Everybody has heard of PR but surprisingly few people have a clear picture of what it really is and what it involves. Part I supplies the big picture overview of the public relations field. Chapter 1 defines what public relations is and how it fits into an overall marketing campaign. Chapter 2 examines PR uses and applications, answering the questions "Who needs PR?" and "How can it benefit me and my company?" The chapter also debunks common PR myths and misperceptions. Chapter 3 covers the process of planning a campaign from initial concept through implementation and evaluation. Chapter 4 deals with the "make or buy" issue: Should you always do your own PR or does it ever make sense to hire outside help? It also covers the alternatives available (PR firms, ad agencies, graphic design services, and freelancers), including where to find them and how to evaluate and hire them.

Part II: Brainstorming and Thinking Creatively

PR is largely a business of creative ideas, and this section shows you how to think more creatively about PR and get breakthrough ideas that make your product or service stand out and get media attention. In Chapter 5, I show you how to set up your own in-house PR capabilities, so you can do just what the big PR agencies do, only without the big PR agency bills. Chapter 6 gives you a technique for producing PR ideas. Chapter 7 is my arsenal of PR "weapons" — tactics we have used with extraordinary success to publicize my firm's clients.

Part III: Laying the Groundwork

Sitting around cooking up ideas for PR campaigns is fun, but there's a lot of hard work involved to turn the plans into a working campaign that gets your name in the papers and your company on the evening news in a favorable light. Chapter 8 covers the details of setting up that workhorse of PR programs, the company newsletter. In Chapter 9, you see how to churn out press releases and media kits. Chapter 10 explores writing and placing feature articles. And Chapter 11 shows you how to deliver your message in person with confidence and persuasiveness at interviews, press conferences, media tours, and other presentations.

Part IV: Implementing Your PR Strategy

The ideas you come up with and the PR materials you produce won't generate one thin dime of extra revenues or profits if you don't get the media to run them. Part IV shows you how to pitch your ideas to the media so that you get the coverage you want. Chapter 12 is a crash course on how to deal with media types effectively. Chapters 13 through 16 focus on specific media: radio, TV, print, and the Internet.

Part V: Creating Buzz

If things about your business aren't exciting enough to get the media's attention, you have to stir things up a bit — to create "buzz," as PR professionals are fond of saying. Chapter 17 shows how to create events that generate tons of free publicity for you and your organization. Chapter 18 shows you how to exploit events and activities originated by others. Chapter 19 covers how to handle events when things don't go your way and a crisis pops up, whether it's a toxic spill at your plant or a defect in your product. Chapter 20 suggests ways to monitor and measure PR results, so you can determine the return on your PR investment.

Part VI: The Part of Tens

Here you can find a large amount of very useful little items, arranged in groups of ten: the ten greatest PR coups of all time (Chapter 21); the top ten situations in which PR can help you achieve better business results (Chapter 22); ten tips for coming off to media and colleagues as a true PR pro (Chapter 23); the ten things you should never do in the quest for more publicity because they are illegal, unethical, immoral, or in the long run unproductive (Chapter 24); and ten steps to writing better PR materials (Chapter 25).

Appendix: About the CD

Lots of resources exist to help you with your do-it-yourself PR efforts, and this section puts them at your fingertips. The appendix tells you all about the dozens of resources you'll find waiting for you on the CD-ROM supplied with this book.

Icons Used in This Book

The Win/Win Medal highlights best practices — things you should regularly do as a PR practitioner.

The bomb warns you about potential mistakes you want to avoid.

String around the finger marks important items you don't want to forget.

This icon is a flag for special tips and insights.

The zinger gives you tricks and twists that you may not find in standard PR texts.

This icon points out a valuable resource you can find on the CD-ROM.

Where to Go from Here

Some of you will use *Public Relations Kit For Dummies* to create the one or two PR programs you want to do, execute them, and get great results — and that may be it. That's okay, and it's the beauty of PR. With its low cost and the ease with which you can do your own PR without professional help, even a single PR effort can generate tremendous returns, paying back your investment in this kit 100 times over.

But I hope you aggressively embrace and pursue the many PR opportunities available to your organization on a regular basis. Why pay the media a fortune every time you want them to carry your message with a paid advertisement, when in essence you can get them to do all your advertising for you absolutely free?

The bottom line: PR can communicate your company's message and achieve your marketing objectives at a fraction of the cost of paid advertising. Any business or organization that sells or markets but doesn't take advantage of the incredible leverage of free publicity is pouring marketing dollars down the drain. But it's never too late to start. So dip into *Public Relations Kit For Dummies,* put the ideas to work, make your organization or product famous, and get rich. If you become a millionaire or celebrity in the process, more power to you!

Part I

PR: What It Is, How It Works

The 5th Wave   By Rich Tennant

YOU CAN ALWAYS TRUST A FOWLER DITCH

LOOK FOR MY OTHER DITCHES ALONG RTE 682

ANOTHER BEAUTIFUL DITCH DUG BY **BILL FOWLER**

In this part . . .

Everybody has heard of PR but surprisingly few people have a clear picture of what it really is and how it works. Part I supplies the "big picture" overview of the public relations field. Chapter 1 defines what public relations is and how it fits into an overall marketing campaign. Chapter 2 examines PR uses and applications, answering the questions "Who needs PR?" and "How can it benefit me and my company?" Chapter 3 demonstrates a process you can use to plan your own PR, from a single press release to a complete national campaign. Chapter 4 deals with the "make or buy" issue: Should you always do your own PR or does it ever make sense to hire outside help? It also covers the alternatives available (staff PR director, freelancers, counselors, agencies), including where to find them and how to evaluate and hire them.

Chapter 1

The Power of PR

In This Chapter

▶ Discovering the meaning of public relations

▶ Exploring what a PR person does

▶ Looking at the differences between PR and advertising

*W*hen I was a young man of 24 and almost a complete beginner at public relations, I got myself on the front page of *USA Today* with a feature story and a color photograph of my partner and myself. That piece put my then-fledgling PR firm "on the map," so to speak, and helped advance my career in the PR business.

At the time, no one had heard of my agency or me, and I had no press contacts with *USA Today* — or any other major media. That lack of contacts could easily have become a major stumbling block for our PR firm in getting new clients: The agency did good work, but larger corporate prospects would naturally — and in my opinion, naively — ask, "Who are your key media contacts?" When I confessed that I didn't know the editor-in-chief of *The New York Times* and wasn't invited to Oprah's dinner parties, potential clients could have easily lost interest and chosen other firms. This was a problem I wanted to solve as quickly as possible.

So how did I get *USA Today* to put my picture on the cover? At the time, a major league baseball strike was the news of the day. My partner and I sent out a press announcement and called the media to announce that we had formed a new organization, called "Strike Back," to protest the baseball strike. The premise was simple: For every day the major league players refused to play, we would boycott their games for one day when the players did return to work.

Did I do this for the love of the game? Yes — partially. But it certainly wasn't lost on me that turning ourselves into a national news story would (1) demonstrate the type of PR we practice, (2) showcase our ability to get media exposure, and (3) attract new business. *USA Today* was the first big media placement for my agency, and it got potential clients to pay attention to the new kids on the PR block.

This anecdote illustrates three basic PR principles that form the core of our agency philosophy and the how-to PR techniques in this book:

- ✔ **You have to be different.** The media and the public are drowning in data but starved for amusement. Conventional publicity strategies get lost in the noise. You have to find a creative way to stand out from the crowd and get noticed — and Strike Back is just one of dozens of examples I show you throughout this book.

- ✔ **Getting publicity is fun, but it's a waste of time and money if it doesn't help you achieve your marketing objective.** If getting on the front page of *The Wall Street Journal* doesn't help you make more money or increase your firm's market share, is it really worth the trouble? In the case of Strike Back, the campaign did achieve a specific objective: getting corporate PR clients to take my PR firm seriously and hire us, despite the fact that we had fewer clients, fewer years of experience, and a fraction of the media contacts of the big PR firms.

- ✔ **You don't have to have media contacts to get big-time publicity.** (Strike Back certainly helped us communicate this principle to our own potential clients!) A creative idea, a clear marketing goal, and effective implementation are what count. You don't have to know Joe TV Star to get on his TV show; you just have to come up with an idea that will interest his producer. So what if you're a small business and you don't have time to schmooze the press? In *Public Relations Kit For Dummies,* you find out how to get all the publicity you need to achieve your marketing objectives — without making public relations your full-time job.

PR Defined: Publicity Plus

Public relations is more than just pitching stories to the media or mailing out press releases. The PR umbrella covers a number of related activities, all of which are concerned with communicating specific messages to specific target audiences. If you're the PR person at ABC Enterprises, you're responsible for managing communications between your company and all of your publics.

The label "public relations" typically encompasses the following:

- ✔ **Research:** You have to thoroughly understand not only your company but also your customers and potential customers. What do you offer that is unique or special? What are customers looking for? And how well do you fill those needs? Market research and an internal company audit are the starting points of successful PR campaigns. For more on the research and audit processes, see Chapter 3

✔ **Strategic planning:** Define each target audience, your marketing objectives for that group, and the messages you must communicate in support of those marketing objectives. Chapter 3 outlines this planning process.

✔ **Publicity:** For most small businesses, the central public relations activity is publicity — getting visibility for your products, the company, and the owners in print and broadcast media. I define publicity as "proactive management and placement of information in the media used to protect and enhance a brand or reputation." Simply put, this means getting ink and airtime. (See Chapters 13 through 16.)

✔ **Community relations:** Recently, I saw a TV news report about local citizens protesting a big retail chain that wanted to build a store in their town, because it would wipe out a popular wooded area with a pond. That chain has a community relations problem in that town, and the PR professional's job is to find a favorable solution that will get the store built while preserving the store's goodwill with the citizens.

✔ **Government relations:** Community relations often involves relations with the local government, and PR people are often called upon to help companies improve their relationships with local, state, federal, and even foreign governments.

✔ **Internal relations:** Employees are the internal audience. With the unemployment rate at an all-time low, good employees are hard to find, and a good public relations program job can help improve loyalty and retain more of them.

✔ **Investor relations:** With the incredible stock market volatility of 2000, we've all seen how emotion and public perception have the power to send stock prices soaring or plummeting. Investor relations is the aspect of PR that communicates the company story to stock analysts and other financial professionals.

✔ **Stakeholder relations:** A stakeholder is anyone or any organization that holds a stake in how well your company performs. A key vendor is a stakeholder; rumors that you are financially shaky may cause them to restrict your credit terms. Other key stakeholders can include top consultants, board members, your bank, suppliers, sales representatives, distributors, and industry gurus.

✔ **Charitable causes:** When a company gives to charity, it wants to help the cause, but it also wants to be recognized for its contribution. PR specialists can help you get maximum publicity and goodwill from the time, effort, and funds you donate.

✔ **Communications training:** In large corporations, PR specialists may spend a lot of time coaching senior executives in dealing with the media and other communications skills. The specialists may also advise the executives on strategy for day-to-day PR as well as PR crises.

What PR Is Not

Public relations is a business tool that often gets confused with marketing and advertising, two related but very distinct activities. I want to clear that up for you.

Marketing: The four Ps

Marketing is typically defined by the "Four Ps" of product, price, place (channels of distribution), and promotion.

- ✔ **Product** refers to the physical product and its packaging. With many products — fruit juice, for instance — the packaging is a key product differentiator: Juice boxes are a separate product category from frozen concentrate. Service can also be an integral part of a product. For example, L.L. Bean has gained widespread fame publicizing its lifetime guarantee on everything it sells.

- ✔ **Price** is what you charge for the product.

- ✔ **Place** refers to channels of distribution — in other words, where the product is sold. Do you sell at a retail store or on a Web site? Do customers buy the product directly from you or through an agent or distributor?

- ✔ **Promotion** consists of advertising, sales promotion, personal selling, and, of course, public relations.

Advertising — you pay; PR is (practically) free

Several characteristics separate public relations from advertising, but one fundamental difference is this: Advertising is paid; public relations is free. When you run an advertisement for your company, you pay for the space; when your press release prompts a newspaper to write an article about your company, you don't pay for that coverage.

Of course, PR is not absolutely free of cost. Your public relations staff member or your outside PR agency has to be paid for services. But compared to the megadollars of advertising campaigns, PR is quite a bargain. Many small- and medium-size businesses that can afford only limited advertising (with limited results) can do much more PR — and get better results — on a fraction of the budget they'd spend on paid advertising.

So the difference in cost is fundamental. But another distinction between PR and advertising gets less attention, though I think it's equally important: Advertising is clearly identified in the media as a paid promotion — readers and viewers know that it is a promotional message paid for by a sponsor. Publicity, by comparison, is not identified as a paid promotion. Even though a story about a product or organization may have resulted from a publicity campaign, the article or report never acknowledges that fact. (For instance, you almost never see an article in a newspaper or a magazine say, "According to a press release sent by the PR department of So-and-So Corporation. . . .")

Four other key differences between PR and advertising are

- ✔ Control
- ✔ Repetition
- ✔ Credibility
- ✔ Attractiveness

Sometimes these distinctions mean an advantage for PR, sometimes not.

Control

When you advertise, you have almost total control over the content, format, timing, and size of your message. You specify how big your ad is and when it runs. You write the copy and design the layout, and your material appears exactly as you created it. With public relations, on the other hand, you have almost no control over the content, format, timing, and size of your message as it appears in the media. You can write whatever you want in your press release, but you can't dictate to the newspaper how it is printed or used, nor can you review or approve any changes made. You provide the press with written materials that they use (or don't use) in any way they see fit. Your press release may appear verbatim in one magazine but may be rewritten almost beyond recognition in another. One industry trade journal may write a cover story based on your material; another may not publish it at all.

Repetition

Advertising is repeatable; PR is not. The same advertisement can be repeated as many times as you wish in a given publication; the same TV commercial can be broadcast night after night. With PR, a media source is going to run a given press release or cover a publicity event only *once*. To get covered again, you have to provide the media with a new story, or at least come up with a different angle or new spin on the old topic.

Thanks for the lousy press coverage!

Clergymen across the United States denounced actress Sarah Bernhardt (1844-1923) as the "whore of Babylon," which, much to their dismay, generated massive attendance at her performances. After a Chicago bishop delivered a particularly critical speech against Bernhardt, which was widely reported in the press, the actress sent him a $200 check along with the following note, as recounted by Clifton Fadiman in *The Little Brown Book of Anecdotes:* "I am accustomed, when I bring an attraction to your town, to spend $400 on advertising. As you have done half the advertising for me, I enclose $200 for your parish."

Credibility

Consumers are skeptical of advertising. They tend not to believe the claims made in advertising, at least that's what many say. Many people believe that if your service or product is as good as you say it is, you don't need to advertise. On the other hand, people tend to take at face value what they hear on radio, see on TV, or read in the paper. They believe that if the newspaper printed it, it must be true. Because publicity is promotion in the guise of editorial, feature, or news material, people do not identify it as promotion and are therefore not skeptical of it; indeed, they believe it.

In many instances, media coverage of your event or story can appear to the public to be media endorsement of your organization or product — for example, a favorable story about your charity on the evening news or a good review of your software package in a computer magazine. What's more, comments or claims that would sound conceited, self-serving, and not credible if you said them about yourself in an ad seem complimentary, flattering, and impressive when the media say them about you.

Attractiveness

Publicity must have an *angle* — that is, a hook or theme that engages an editor's attention — in order for it to have a decent chance of being noticed, read, and used. Therefore, it must appeal to editors and program managers, as well as to the consumers (your sales prospects and the people who read the magazine or listen to the radio show).

An ad has to appeal to only one audience: your sales prospects. You don't care whether the media like or are interested in the ad, because they have already agreed to run it in exchange for a given amount of money.

Publicity Is News

Publicity certainly is free advertising, but it's also legitimate news. By alerting the media to newsworthy events, products, services, and people, you can prompt an editor to cover everything from the opening of a new restaurant to the publication of a new catalog, from the techniques of an acupuncturist to the makings of a new trend.

In the early days of public relations, many PR practitioners held the belief that their job was to get the client's name in the papers as prominently and frequently as they could. George M. Cohan, the famous composer, knew how PR worked. "I don't care what they [the media] call me," he said, "so long as they mention my name." Actress Katharine Hepburn gave that idea a twist, remarking, "I don't care what is written about me so long as it isn't true."

A more recent and, to my mind, relevant definition states, "Public relations is the business of creating public opinion for private advantage." At my PR agency, Jericho Communications, we think of PR as "using the media to achieve a client's marketing objective." By practicing what you find in this book, you can use PR to communicate your message, build your image, motivate desired behavior, and generate greater revenues and profits.

Instead of putting up signs, sending banner ads across people's computer screens, or holding sales rallies, PR practitioners persuade the media to publish and distribute stories, articles, news, and information that promotes our clients' goals — whether it's to attract venture capital to a dot-com start-up or help Domino's Pizza sell more pizzas.

I have sometimes cynically told new clients that we exploit the media on their behalf. But strictly speaking, that isn't true, since it's the media — not the publicist — who is the final judge of what appears in print or on the air.

PR-media partnership

More accurately, public relations is, at its best, a win-win partnership between publicists, the clients whose products they promote, and journalists. Here's how that partnership works:

The journalists have too much to do and not enough time to do it. Every day they must fill pages or airtime with stories that interest, entertain, and inform their readership, viewers, or listeners. The deadlines are too tight, and the editors and reporters are overworked.

The publicists step in and offer assistance by providing what journalists need — ideas, information, interviews, and even ready-made stories — in abundant supply and absolutely free. The media choose from among the press releases, use them as is or reworked, and discard the rest — with no cost or obligation to the publicists who supply the releases. The media can fill their pages and airtime, meet deadlines, keep their audiences happy and entertained, and thereby deliver a large audience to the advertisers.

Fire safety story, for example

When publicists place companies' self-promotional PR stories in the media, the companies, in effect, get free advertising for their products. I've made that point already. Okay, here's an example. A Canadian company wanted publicity for a home-safety device it manufactures — a breathing hood to wear in case of fire. It positioned its press release as a kind of public service announcement (see Figure 1-1). The release describes the product and its advantages, but it also offers fire safety tips that editors can run in their newspapers or magazines.

Figure 1-1:
A press release that works like a public service announcement.

FROM: Brookdale International Systems Inc., Vancouver, B.C.
CONTACT: Ernest Moniz, phone (604) 324-3822

For immediate release

NEW FREE BOOKLET OUTLINES
FIRE SAFETY TIPS FOR FAMILIES
8-point Family Escape Plan Can
Help Save Lives, says Booklet Author

Vancouver, B.C. -- If there's a fire in your home, you and your family have a better chance of getting out safely if you develop an escape plan and practice it on a regular basis.

This advice and other fire safety tips are presented in a new, free booklet, "How to Make Your Family Safer From Fires," published by Brookdale International Systems, manufacturer of the EVAC-U8 Emergency Escape Smoke Hood. The booklet is available free of charge to the general public.

"To have a good fire safety program, you must develop a family escape plan and practice it with your entire family, including small children," says John Swann, president of the firm and author of the booklet. "Go over the escape plan, have fire drills every 6 months, and teach children that they must be prepared to leave the home by themselves if necessary."

The booklet presents an 8-step escape plan families can use and teach to their own children....

The Changing Role of PR in the Marketing Mix Today

The public relations industry is evolving, driven by new market realities. PR is finally taking a step forward, stretching its capabilities and its role in the overall marketing mix that consists of PR, advertising, Internet marketing, direct marketing, and sales promotion.

From the day I started my PR firm in 1985, I have believed that public relations can play a greater role in clients' good fortune than tradition dictates. The reason my agency has delivered so much media exposure to clients is that I'm not afraid to break the "rules" of traditional PR, which is more worried about churning out paper (for example, routine press releases such as "Joe Smith Appointed Product Manager") than contributing to the bottom line. While other marketing genres have shown how to invent successful new ways to do business, many public relations professionals have seemed to care more about following rules. And let's face it: Same-old same-old doesn't get anyone's audience excited.

Where public relations is routine, frankly, I blame PR professionals who are too willing to accept a back seat for the successes of their art. In fairness, I should say that some of them have it tough, receiving very little credit for anything good and all the blame for everything that goes wrong at a company. And that being the case, it's human nature when PR executives grow averse to risk and creativity. Going beyond status quo simply holds nothing for them. The bad part is they often give their outside PR counselors very little room to move, too.

But today, in the fast-paced e-commerce world — where online and offline clients must reach out to grab their target audiences and the investor community — public relations has risen in importance. With this new importance comes more freedom. All of a sudden, the value of creative public relations is apparent. The ability to use what I consider the most credible form of marketing in ways that extend way past the standard is now revered.

So for the first time in a long time, PR practitioners who can do more than just communicate to an audience — people who can create an emotional effect that *motivates* an audience — are free to ply their craft to its fullest potential.

As you can see, I'm passionate about PR. You're using this book and the CD because — just maybe — you are passionate about public relations, too. My goal is to give you all the tools you need to turn that passion into results.

Chapter 2

Who Needs PR Anyway?

In This Chapter

▶ Figuring out when PR may be the missing ingredient

▶ Understanding the compelling reasons to adopt a PR program

▶ Debunking PR myths — a test of your PR IQ

*I*f you have all the business you will ever want and are rich beyond the dreams of avarice, you may not need public relations.

A crisis is an obvious exception. A lot of my work as a PR professional is in response to clients who have an immediate PR crisis to solve, like a tainted shipment of food products or a toy posing an unexpected safety risk to children because of a product defect. So in some cases, even if your sales are skyrocketing and you don't need to promote yourself, you may want to engage in PR activities to avoid negative publicity or correct any bad press that comes your way. (See Chapter 19 for crisis management.)

But if you want to make more money, increase your sales, grow your business, and become even more successful, you probably do need PR.

That's one perspective: your goals, where you are now, and where you want to be. Good PR can turn marginal businesses into profitable ones, and ordinary folks into millionaires.

Another perspective is resources. If you have an advertising budget that approaches infinity (or say, half a billion dollars or more) and you won't miss the money when you spend it, you can probably get your message across without relying on the more subtle medium of PR. That doesn't mean you *shouldn't* use PR as part of your marketing mix, however: Many clients find that a relatively modest investment in PR greatly extends the reach of their total promotional program.

And cost, frankly, is one of the great appeals of PR to both small businesses and large corporations alike. Small businesses with limited budgets simply can't come close to matching the ad budgets of larger competitors. PR can help them level the playing field and get the same or better promotional bang for a lot fewer bucks.

As for the big corporations, if you work for one, you know that getting more money in the marketing budget is always an uphill battle. With PR, you can achieve the objectives senior managers want even if they don't give you the money you think you need to do it.

How to Tell When PR Is the Missing Ingredient

What are the telltale signs that PR is the weak point in your company's marketing communications chain? Ask yourself these questions:

- ✔ Do your competitors seem to get all the publicity in newspapers, magazines, and the trade press? Are you consistently left out of industry round-ups, product listings, and vendor resource guides? Maybe the press omits you because they don't know about you. Maybe it's time to let them know.

- ✔ Do your mailings unleash a stampede of responses? Is your Web site choked with traffic? PR works hand in hand with other kinds of promotions. The better your PR visibility, the more your other marketing communications efforts will pull in responses. Low response rates may not be the result of a bad ad or mailer. That deafening silence could mean that the people reading your ad or receiving your mailing have never heard of you.

- ✔ Do your people in the field find it easy or hard to get deals done? Do they hear "I've never heard of your company" from prospects? Good PR establishes your firm as a player in the prospect's mind before the salesperson calls. If not, your people may meet with increased resistance.

- ✔ Do your vendors list you as one of their customers? If not, maybe they don't think your name is big enough to impress other potential customers. That's a sign you need to strengthen your corporate brand in the marketplace.

Sales graph

Make a graph of your sales by week. If the graph is smooth and your sales are consistent, your marketing is probably steady and continual. But if the sales curve has peaks and valleys, you may need to increase the frequency of marketing communications to smooth out the bumps and eliminate the lows. PR is perhaps the best means of getting your message out on a continual basis and eliminating periodic sales slumps.

Cold-call classic

A classic McGraw-Hill ad shows a prospective customer sitting in a chair, staring straight at the camera and saying, "I don't know you, I don't know your company, I don't know your product. Now — What is it you wanted to sell me?" Better visibility through public relations can warm up cold prospects like this one, making the salesperson's job much easier.

✔ If you're a public company, do major brokerages follow your stock? When you tell your company story to analysts, do they eagerly take notes or stare at you with blank looks? When Wall Street doesn't understand the value in your company, the investor relations side of PR can help fix the problem.

✔ Do audiences see your company the way you are today or the way you want to become tomorrow? Or do they see you as you used to be? PR can help to change your image in the marketplace.

✔ Do headhunters try to woo you away to other companies? Especially in high-tech industries, headhunters raid the hot companies first. You don't want headhunters recruiting your employees (unless it's you and the pay is fantastic!), but you do want to be considered a hot company, don't you?

Think about PR Solutions

If you are nodding "Yes" to any of the questions I've asked you — and if you bought this book to *use,* not just read — some PR activity is probably in your future. Skeptical? Okay, think with me about how public relations responds directly to the real problems I've just listed.

✔ PR can generate traffic, leads, and revenue and directly boost your bottom line. (I show how in Chapters 5 and 6.) And because the cost of PR is relatively low, almost no other form of marketing can generate such a rapid return on your investment.

✔ PR can pre-sell potential customers and make present customers more loyal to your brand. Think about it; don't you feel more confident about your stockbroker when you see him appear as a regular commentator on *Wall Street Week with Louis Rukeyser* or CNN? David Root Jr., who has a financial planning firm in Pittsburgh, says his leads to new customers increased fivefold when he began hosting a weekly half-hour show about personal finance and investing on a local cable station.

✔ PR can target specific audiences. You can spread a message at the grassroots level or design a local, regional, or national outreach, selecting your audience by numerous criteria, as I show later in this chapter.

✔ PR can help you break through the clutter of messages in mass media and grab your audience's attention. Most people don't read most of the ads in their daily newspaper, but almost everyone reads the headlines. If the headlines come from your PR news campaign, you're reaching the audience.

Beyond Stunts: The Real Value of PR

It's fun to see far-out stunts and novelty products like the Pet Rock get truckloads of front-page and primetime coverage. Obviously, PR can work wonders for those who seek publicity for publicity's sake.

Actually, that's the easy part of public relations. The real value of PR is using it to solve a real-life marketing situation for a real product, service, organization, brand, or image. PR can work for any and every industry, from florists to funeral directors, software to soft ice cream. Any organization or individual with a message to deliver or a goal to achieve can benefit from a PR effort. You don't even need a license or special certification to practice PR — this kit shows you how.

You don't have to be promoting a crazy scheme to get publicity. Creative PR, with proper execution, can work wonders for manufacturers, wholesalers, distributors, retailers, resellers, agents, service companies, and professional practices in any industry.

Doctors, lawyers, dentists, chiropractors, therapists, and other professionals can promote their practices with public relations. PR is used with virtually every product category, from construction equipment and industrial goods to food, health and beauty products, health care, travel, tourism, real estate, and investments. In high-tech industries, everyone from hardware manufacturers to software companies, e-commerce Web sites, and service providers has benefited enormously from the power of PR.

You don't need a creative or unusual product to gain publicity; you just need a creative idea that meets two criteria: It's newsworthy, and it communicates the marketing message. I delve into this in detail in Part II of the book, but here's a quick example.

British Knights wanted a way to sell more of its sneakers to kids. As a seasonal promotion, the company sent out press releases announcing an unusual "Summer Exchange" program: Parents who were concerned that their kids were spending too much time indoors watching TV and playing video games, instead of getting wholesome exercise playing outdoors, could mail British Knights their TV remote control and receive in return a brand new pair of British Knight sneakers. (The remote control was mailed back to participants with the sneakers at the end of the summer.)

In another PR campaign, also successful, British Knights sponsored a "World's Smelliest Socks Contest." The top ten winners — individuals who sent in the stinkiest socks — won free British Knights sneakers for three years.

Stinky socks? Joseph J. Kelley, a speechwriter for President Dwight Eisenhower, once said, "There is a kernel of interest in everything God created." How true! Every product or service, no matter how mundane, contains a PR hook or angle if you think creatively. Even sneakers.

Key audiences PR can reach

How far does PR reach? Public relations can connect you with anyone who reads a publication, listens to a radio, watches TV, or rides the Internet — in short, anyone who is exposed to the media, which in the United States means just about everyone.

PR therefore has the broadest reach of perhaps any element of the marketing mix — a mix composed of the four P's: product, price, place (distribution), and promotion, which includes PR and advertising. Web sites and banner ads reach only those people connected to the Internet, which amazingly is fewer than 5 percent of the world's population. Direct mail reaches only people whose names are on mailing lists, and in many countries, mailing lists are not available for rental.

But almost everyone, everywhere, reads a newspaper or magazine, or watches TV. That's why PR is effective at targeting both business and consumer audiences. The best publicity outlets for reaching consumers are radio, television, newspapers, and consumer magazines. For business, use these as well as business magazines, associations, and the Internet. If you want to appeal to a particular industry or profession, target the trade publications they read.

I like to hit a broad target, because you never know exactly what your prospect may be reading. Once, when I was with the CEO of a large corporation, I was amazed to see that when he had a copy of *USA Today,* he went to the Life section first and the Money section last — and often he never got around to reading the Money section. I like to "surround" my prospect by being in all the media he is likely to see; that way, I have a better chance of getting my message to him with greater frequency and repetition.

Employees, of course, are a well-defined audience and reachable at any time. One of the best PR vehicles for employee communication is a company magazine or newsletter. Some large corporations even have in-house TV stations that broadcast the latest company news and information via closed-circuit TV.

Investors and members of the financial community are an important PR audience for publicly traded corporations, and press releases are the way to reach them, says *Business Week.* "Once a relatively mundane communication device, a press release now has the might to dramatically drive the price of a stock," says the respected business magazine. (Underscoring the power of press releases, the Securities and Exchange Commission has even sued companies for posting fake press releases containing recommendations to buy their stock.)

Again, PR's high credibility takes the credit. The financial community and potential buyers are much more apt to believe and act upon a column in *The Wall Street Journal* than yet another image advertisement by a dot-com company. And a survey by the Public Relations Society of America shows that investors rate a story in a financial or business newspaper as second only to a company's own annual report (also a PR vehicle) when it comes to credibility.

More things PR can do for you

PR can get your name into print where prospects and customers can see it. Besides generating immediate leads to new business, the visibility you get from PR yields other benefits. I think the most important benefits are the following:

- ✔ **Reinforcing who you are and what you do.** You may think everyone knows who you are and the type of product or service you offer. In fact, many people may have never heard of you or know exactly what you do or where you're located. Getting your story into the media helps to fill that gap in reaching potential customers.

- ✔ **Letting people know you're active.** Knowing you exist and remembering you when your service is required are two entirely different things. Being visible in the media reminds people and keeps your name in front of them so that when they need the product or service you're selling, they know whom to call. Not being in print is harmful — "out of sight, out of mind" is probably more true in the business world than anywhere else.

- ✔ **Publicizing a specific project or event.** If a tree falls in the middle of the forest and no one is around to hear it, was there really a sound? If you expect people to know what you're up to, you'd better tell them. Don't depend on someone else, and don't be afraid to promote yourself.

- ✔ **Enhancing your company's image and reputation.** Better image is a natural outgrowth of all positive publicity. People begin thinking of your company as a successful organization when they see your name regularly in respected publications. On a personal level, individuals who have been quoted or have written articles are positioned as experts or authorities in their field, and don't we all want to do business with experts?

✔ **Becoming an "of course."** You become an "of course" when a prospect is sitting down to prepare a list of potential vendors or suppliers and says, "Of course I'll have to include (your company)." The prospect is really saying that your company is a major player, and she'd be making a mistake not to at least consider buying from you. One of the key contributors to becoming an "of course" is to constantly remind potential customers of your activities, accomplishments, and capabilities through the printed word. (Selling a quality product or rendering a superior service is another key factor in gaining a reputation as an "of course.")

✔ **Impressing clients, bankers, and investors.** You may not necessarily be impressed with what you see and read about yourself and your company in the media, but you'll be surprised at the effect it has on others. Prospective clients, bankers, investors, and the like often perceive you as a larger, more impressive organization than you may actually be, based on clips and articles about your company (which you or somebody working for you actually wrote).

✔ **Gaining "brownie points" with others on your team.** Few of us work alone, and our successes usually involve the efforts of other team members, such as coworkers, colleagues, subcontractors, managers, bosses, clients, consultants, and other vendors. By publicly acknowledging their contributions, you're not only giving them their just due but building up incalculable goodwill that will come back to you many times over. And it encourages the best people in each field to want to work with you because of your professional attitude.

✔ **Recognizing and rewarding your employees.** Don't forget your own people — those who report directly to you. The same wisdom you use with respect to other team members applies equally, if not more so, to your own employees. Recognition and reward play an important part in employee satisfaction, and public praise goes a long way. (It does not, however, serve as a substitute for more tangible acknowledgments, such as bonuses, pay raises, or comp days.)

Separating PR Myth from Reality

It's ironic: One purpose of PR is to get good press and avoid bad press, but PR itself has had pretty bad press over the years. The public image of PR has been produced in part by corporate flacks who made their living covering up toxic spills and oil leaks; by punk-rock Generation X hucksters hovering around Madonna or Whitney Houston; and by Hollywood operatives keeping drug-addicted movie stars' rehab schedules out of the papers.

PR also is perceived as being "in bed" with the press, meaning the two have a dependent relationship, and there is some truth to this, at least in the origins of PR. In the early days of sportswriting, for example, the sports page was typically seen as a vehicle for promoting teams, and the sportswriter's job was to say nice things about the home guys. Gradually, media and commerce have drawn apart, with sportswriters today saying what's on their minds and not bowing to team owner pressure to be "nice" all the time.

Your first step toward becoming a successful PR practitioner is to separate myth from reality. What really goes on behind the scenes in journalism and PR? How do stories make their way from the mind of the publicist to the front page of the newspaper? What is the relationship between PR and media professionals? I'm going to set up and knock down some of the common misconceptions about public relations.

Myth: Press releases don't work anymore

Reality: Press releases do work, and they are often the most cost-effective and least time-consuming form of PR.

At least once a week, I hear a talk or read an article by a public relations agency executive, industry guru, or consultant proclaiming the death of the press release. "Press releases don't work anymore," they say. "Editors are deluged with press releases, get too many of them. You have to do something different. Fax your material to editors; call them with story ideas; send out fact sheets or fliers — not press releases.

I say, baloney! The fact is, no PR tool is simpler to use or as effective as a basic, well-written, short press release based on a strong hook or angle. Press releases still work. They work well. They're easy to produce. And inexpensive to distribute.

I agree that done *wrong* (as many people do them), press releases can be a waste of time and money — yours and the media's. But done *right* (as explained in Chapter 9), press releases are one of the most hardworking, result-getting marketing tools going: Nothing beats them.

Myth: "Legitimate" media snub PR

Reality: Much of the "news" you read in the newspaper, hear on radio, and see on TV has its origins in PR materials sent to the media by organizations and corporations looking to promote their cause, product, or service.

Press release on a pizza pie

For many years, my agency did public relations for Domino's Pizza. Now when you think about it, pizza is not exactly front-page news. How do you get pizza on the front page?

We realized that, in our office, when we work late, we often order several pizzas, and we knew that other businesses do the same. Could you then judge how busy an organization was by counting how many pizzas it ordered? We asked Domino's in Washington, D.C., to monitor for us the volume of pizza it delivered to the White House, CIA, and Pentagon.

Sure enough, we found that whenever a national crisis was brewing, pizza delivery to these federal offices went up. Could you then monitor the state of the nation by making a graph of White House pizza delivery? Of course!

We sent out a press release talking about the "Pizza-Meter" and proving the link between White House pizza volume and crises in current events. Within days, our client made the front pages and the national TV news; in the same week, the story was featured both on the ABC-TV program *Nightline* and in a skit on NBC's *Saturday Night Live*. And when you think about it, how often is pizza the cover story?

So don't tell me press releases don't work. They do.

Most businesspeople I've talked to tell me, "I know my industry publications will print my press releases, because they want me to advertise with them. But I want to get exposure in *The Wall Street Journal* and the *Harvard Business Review,* and the 'better' publications don't use PR materials. What should I do?"

My reply is that prestigious and well-respected publications such as *The Wall Street Journal, Forbes, Fortune,* and *The New York Times* are interested in and will use good stories, regardless of whether they uncovered the story through intensive investigative reporting or a press release sent to them by a company or group like yours.

Editors are busy and always on the lookout for good material. If your PR materials contain news or information that's of interest or genuine use to their readers, they'll print it. In fact, much of what you read in respected journals, important business magazines, popular consumer magazines, and the nation's largest and most-respected daily newspapers has its origins in public relations materials sent with the hope of promoting an event, cause, product, or service.

Proof? *Columbia Journalism Review* surveyed one issue of *The Wall Street Journal* to find out how many of the stories were generated by press releases. The survey revealed that 111 stories on the inside pages were taken from press releases, either word for word or paraphrased. In only 30 percent of the stories did reporters put in additional facts not contained in the original release.

Virtually any media outlet you're seeking publicity from can be swayed to give you some coverage, provided that your materials are on target and you can offer or create a story of genuine interest to an audience. And doing so is relatively easy because there are only half a dozen or so basic themes or hooks (see Chapter 15) for news and feature stories that will interest editors and program directors.

Myth: Printed PR doesn't work without follow-up

Reality: Follow-up can help increase results, but well-written material will "sell itself" and generate lots of publicity without a single follow-up call or letter.

Follow-up is valuable, does increase results, and can get some editors who missed your material to give it consideration. Hiring a PR agency is a good way to ensure this follow-up if you're too busy to do it yourself. (I talk at length about the "make or buy" decision — doing PR yourself or hiring out — in Chapter 3.)

Follow-up is a big part of what PR agencies do for clients. I call it our "media blitz" tactic: We get on the phone and call and call, and then we call some more. Many of our stories make more media than they would with just a single mailing because we "get in editors' faces" (in an appropriate way) and make our story hard to ignore.

What's not true, however, is the notion that, without follow-up, printed PR materials are not effective and have little or no chance of getting published. In reality, a well-written press release containing interesting information can get wide coverage from a significant number of media outlets without a follow-up phone call to even a single editor.

An example is the Koch Engineering Dry Scrubber press release (see Figure 2-1). Mailed to 50 or 60 technical and trade journals covering pollution, chemical processing, pulp and paper, and related industries, the press release generated more than 18 published stories and 2,500 inquiries to the company . . . without a single follow-up call.

So although follow-up can't hurt and usually helps, it isn't necessary, and the lack of time to follow up press release mailings shouldn't stop you from distributing press releases or from handling your own PR.

NEWS RELEASE
KOCH ENGINEERING COMPANY INC.

Contact: Bob Bly (212) 682-5755
FOR IMMEDIATE RELEASE

DRY FGD SYSTEM OF MIKROPUL AND KOCH AT STRATHMORE
PAPER MEETS CLEAN AIR STANDARDS, CUTS COMPLIANCE AND
OPERATING COSTS

The Dry FGD System now in operation at the Strathmore Paper, Woronoco, Massachusetts, plant of the Hammermill Paper Company has by a wide margin exceeded the rigorous sulfur dioxide (S02) and particulate control requirements of the Massachusetts Department of Environmental Quality; has provided unusual reliability (onstream 98% of the time); and has substantially cut the company's fuel costs.

According to John G. Gallup, president of Strathmore, the system is expected to save the company around 30% of its annual fuel bill, a savings expected to total more than one million dollars per year....

MikroPul supplied and installed the entire system on a turnkey basis with Koch Engineering responsible for the spray dryer. The system was guaranteed to remove 77% of S02 from 3% sulfur coal. In the actual tests over 90% of the S02 was removed....

As demonstrated at Strathmore, dry scrubbers require less maintenance, consume less energy and water, and are less costly to operate than wet systems. Initial investment for installation of a dry system is lower as well. Payback period at Strathmore is estimated to be less than 18 months. This includes the capital cost and costs of operation, reactants, etc.

Figure 2-1:
This release
resulted
in good
coverage.

It's much the same with query letters used to interest editors in running articles by or about you. Many of the successful query letters shown in Chapter 10, for example, generated acceptance and publication of the article without a follow-up letter or call to the editor. If the query letter is written according to the guidelines spelled out in Chapter 10, the letter alone will get editors to respond to you without your having to contact them.

The bottom line: PR works even if your time and resources for editorial contact are limited. Yes, it works even better if you can follow up. Follow-up is helpful but far from essential. Well-written materials state their own case with editors and get printed without your help.

Myth: You need "contacts" to get publicity

Reality: Contacts do help, but you can succeed beautifully without them.

PR professionals like to talk about their media contacts — all the editors, program directors, and other media people they know and what an advantage that is in getting publicity placement. I do it myself!

Does shmoozing — network building — help? Sure. In my early years, I attended every networking function that I could, and every editor and producer knew my name. And when I called, they either took the call or called me back.

Does that mean you have to do the same intensive media networking to succeed with your PR program? Not at all. You can probably do nicely on your own without it, thank you very much.

Although networking got my calls returned, it never once got the media to publish any story of mine that they wouldn't have otherwise used. When we did our Pizza-Meter campaign for Domino's Pizza, I don't think we made a single call: The story was a natural and too good for the media to resist. Same thing with the "Strike Back" idea I talk about in Chapter 1 — the PR campaign that produced my first front cover story in *USA Today*.

One advantage a full-time PR professional has over a person for whom PR is just one of many job functions is the time to spend building media contacts. This investment will pay out over time. For example, an account executive at a PR firm handling a half dozen computer accounts can get to know the important editors at the top half dozen or so computer publications. The investment of time and energy in establishing these relationships is cost effective because it benefits not just one client but a half dozen.

On the other hand, the small-business owner who has total responsibility for all facets of her operation — research, product development, manufacturing, management, finance, marketing, distribution, sales, promotion — can perhaps devote one-twentieth of her time or less to public relations. For the little PR she does (a press release this month, a feature article next month, a press conference the month after, and so on), she simply cannot afford to spend the time getting to know and cultivating editorial contacts in the same manner that the full-time PR professional can.

Myth: Editors want to be wined and dined

Reality: Editors don't have time to be wined and dined.

This is an extension of the myth that close personal contact with media people is necessary to getting media coverage. The intent is to get preferential treatment from editors and reporters by getting to know them personally and establishing a close relationship with them, and also by giving them perks, such as taking them out to lunch in a posh restaurant or giving them tickets to a basketball game.

Although editors are only human and some may respond favorably to such treatment, my experience is that most don't want it and would rather you do not try to monopolize their time with small talk and three-martini lunches. The reason is that, like all of us, editors are busy people. But in addition to being busy, they constantly face tight deadlines. (Few editors in my acquaintance do *not* feel pressed by looming deadlines almost all of the time.)

As a result, most editors prefer to keep PR sources, even good ones, at arm's length. They prefer to receive story ideas and proposals in a letter or press release rather than have the details transmitted in a lengthy conversation. Most editors and producers are print-oriented and so prefer written communication; if they have questions, they'll ask. If a conversation is necessary, they'd rather it be five minutes over the telephone than a two-hour lunch.

So the truth is that it's not necessary to wine and dine editors as you might entertain an important prospect or customer. If you want to socialize, go ahead. Just be aware that doing so is unnecessary.

Myth: Snail mail is awful; overnight delivery services and fax work great

Reality: A simple one- or two-page press release, sent to editors via first-class mail, is just as effective as fax or overnight delivery services, such as Federal Express or Airborne Express — and much, much cheaper.

A number of distribution services and individual PR practitioners contend that using a fax is a better way to distribute news than through the U.S. Postal Service, but that is only partially true. A fax does get your material out much faster than if you print and mail it. However, I see no evidence that editors give faxed materials more consideration than mailed materials.

Similarly, a PR writer I know handled a project for a client who said, "Send all the releases Federal Express — that'll really get the media's attention." (This occurred before faxes and the Internet were common.) The cost was tremendous when compared with regular first-class mail for a one-ounce letter, and we saw no evidence that any editor was duly impressed or took any extra notice of the material because it was sent by Federal Express. Keep in mind that editors get many packages from overnight delivery services, such as FedEx and Airborne Express, and fax messages daily. So sending your press release in such a manner has minimal added impact.

As for electronic submission, some magazines do welcome longer feature material sent on floppy disk or via the Internet, but the standard format is still a printed manuscript, and this is accepted by 99.99 percent of the magazines in the United States. If you can provide a computer file, go ahead. But it is not necessary, nor will it usually increase chances of acceptance.

Myth: You can't buy PR with advertising

Reality: In some publications, you can.

Media and PR people have always been taught that "advertising" and "editorial" are separate. That is, the editorial department of a media organization operates separately, independently, and without the influence of the advertising department. Thus, the fact that you are an advertiser does not increase your chances of getting your press release run in the publication, any more than the fact that you are not an advertiser means the publication *won't* run your release.

But is this really true? Or can you "buy" publicity by promising to run a lot of ads? With some publications, you can. But my experience is that at the higher level, among well-known, nationally respected publications (such as *The Wall Street Journal* and *The New York Times*), you can't buy editorial space by promising to spend money on advertising, nor do the PR materials of advertisers receive even the slightest extra attention from the editorial staff. The exception may be when the advertising department wants the editorial department not to run a negative story about an advertiser, but unless you're involved in toxic dumping or public scandal, don't worry about this.

However, in smaller-circulation publications; in those that are more specialized or regional; and in industry-specific ("vertical") publications versus general business ("horizontal") magazines, the plain truth is that advertisers do sometimes get preferential treatment. I have seen it many, many times and know it to be a fact beyond dispute.

How PR and ads get cozy

My coauthor, Bob Bly, was once the public relations manager of a small company manufacturing chemical process equipment. An advertising salesman of a Canadian magazine wanted Bob's company to buy ads in his journal.

"I told him that while I was happy to see him, it would be unlikely that we would advertise with him, since most of our business was in the United States," says Bob.

The ad rep paused. "Do you have press releases?" he asked. Of course, Bob replied, noting that he had done six or seven recently. "Give me one copy of each release," the salesman said. "Why?" Bob asked. "You'll see," was his reply.

In about two months, he sent Bob a follow-up letter with the latest issue of his magazine. Every one of the press releases had been reprinted, with product photos, in that single issue! His letter suggested that Bob's firm could continue to get such favorable coverage by taking out some ads in the next few issues.

Here was a blatant case of unabashed selling of ad space through favorable editorial coverage; obviously, the advertising department controlled the editorial department at this magazine.

Myth: Every fact reported in the media is checked and verified

Reality: Most PR materials are picked up and run with almost no verification of any kind.

I have found that editors rarely do much interviewing of sources to add to the material in a press release. Part of the reason is downsizing resulting from budgetary cutbacks at media outlets. Newspapers and broadcast stations simply don't have enough people to check every fact. Editors and producers tend to run PR materials pretty much as is; if they edit, it's usually for style, grammar, and space limitations, not to add or verify factual content.

I do PR for many dot-com companies and have mailed dozens of releases. I have found that 90 percent of the phone calls my clients get from editors are to verify the spelling of the Web site URL or the name of the company; rarely do they question the features listed or the accuracy of claims made.

Although editors may be too busy to check the statements in your releases for accuracy, they do not want to appear to be endorsing you, nor do they want to take responsibility for claims you make about your product in your own materials. So if there is doubt as to the accuracy of information, or if your copy states an opinion or makes a claim that is likely to be challenged, the editor may get out of this dilemma the easy way — by simply not printing your material.

Myth: Getting publicity is a matter of luck and timing

Reality: Chance favors the prepared mind, and timing can be controlled.

People who are unsuccessful at public relations (or anything else, for that matter) often view those who are successful with suspicion and cynicism. "Oh, they are lucky," claims the executive at one company who sees a favorable story about his competitor in an important industry journal. "They must have contacted this staff writer with the right story at the right time. When we mailed our release, the magazine wasn't interested in this topic, so they didn't run it. Now, of course, it's a hot topic, and our competitor must have suggested the story to them just when they were planning to cover it."

Do I disagree that timing is important? No. In public relations, marketing, promotion, new product introductions, and selling, timing is critical: You succeed largely because you reach your media contact, target market, or prospect at just the right time.

A strategy that works well for me is to time PR efforts with major events already going on. I noticed that every April 15, TV news stations sent camera crews to the post office to interview last-minute taxpayers as they stood in line filling out and filing income tax returns.

I recommended to my client Domino's Pizza that it send deliverymen offering free pizza to any weary, hungry taxpayers standing in line that evening. Because the cameras were already there, the stunt made national television. Now, many other companies in addition to Domino's use this strategy of "going where the cameras already are."

Controlling Time and Chance

Motivational expert Dr. Rob Gilbert once told me, "The way you control timing is to be there all the time." Here's how that works. Suppose that you own a collection agency and are an expert in collections, and you want to get some press attention for your business. Problem is, you can never tell in what month a particular editor at your city's largest business magazine will want to do a story about the collection problems faced by small businesses and how to solve them. But one thing is certain: If you send this editor a press release on collections strategies and tactics every month, eventually your material will wind up in his lap *in the month he decides to do that story.* And when that happens, whom do you think he will interview, you or your competitor whom he's never heard of?

One more homey example. My wife and I once took our son to a town carnival. At one game of chance, you could win a small stuffed animal by placing a quarter on one of ten numbers and then hoping, when the wheel of chance was spun, that the pointer would end up on your number. It occurred to me that if I wanted to be certain of getting a stuffed animal for Alex, I could do so by spending $2.50 and putting a quarter on each of the ten numbers simultaneously: I'd *have* to hit with one of my ten bets. (In fact, we bet normally and won a stuffed animal on the first spin!)

In PR, the same principle applies: Keep putting yourself "out there" in the media — with query letters, pitch letters, press releases — and you *will* hit the winning number. The prize is publicity for your company or service. It's inevitable.

Does this mean that a one-shot press release or PR promotion won't work? Not at all. Even a single press release or media appearance on TV or radio can generate scads of press coverage and hundreds or even thousands of inquiries and sales. But on the other hand, your first effort may bring little or nothing. When you treat publicity as a one-shot event, you're gambling. When you have a consistent, ongoing program, with efforts going out monthly or on some other regular basis, you'll almost certainly get the result you want sooner or later (sooner if you follow the suggestions in this book).

Chapter 3

X-Raying the PR Process

*T*he key to good public relations creative thought is understanding that it's more than pulling good ideas out of the air. Rather, quality creative public relations concepts come from a deliberate planning process, which I outline in this chapter.

Using Research to Shape the Process

Planning begins with research. At my PR agency, we begin the PR planning process by conducting an audit that covers both internal and external factors. The internal factors include the company environment, marketing objectives, and product features and benefits. The external factors include the audience, the marketplace, the channels of distribution, and the competition.

Some of the methods I use to gather this information include the following:

✔ Interviews with key company executives

✔ Mail or phone surveys with customers and potential customers

✔ Personal interviews with customers and potential customers

✔ Additional interviews with industry analysts, consultants, journalists, and other experts

✔ A review of all current and past PR and marketing materials including article clippings, ad tear sheets, press release archives, product brochures, catalogs, and other promotional documents

✔ A thorough search of Internet and print sources such as articles, case studies, product literature, and other relevant publications

What am I looking for? I want to know where the company and its products are positioned in the marketplace and what people — customers, prospects, and the press — think of them.

I also want to understand what messages are not getting to the consumer that should. In other words, what's the story the company wants to — or needs to — tell to change market perception and increase or preserve market share?

The CD contains a sample audit (file CD0302) that my PR firm did for Big Yellow, an online directory. When you look at the sample audit, notice that I don't bother to "fancy up" the report with a lot of long-winded verbiage. The audit is a working tool and should be treated as such. The more concise, the better.

Defining Your Goals and Objectives

Once the audit is complete, you should have a pretty good idea about the following:

✔ **The key messages you want to communicate:** Often these key messages revolve around the benefits of the product or the advantages over the competition. But not always. Your key message may be that you care about the local community or environment, or that your product is organically grown and has no preservatives or artificial ingredients.

✔ **The marketing objective:** Is the objective to increase sales revenues or market share? One client may ask us to sell as many juicing machines as possible. Another may want to become the dominant Internet portal for small business. What's the end result you want PR to help you achieve?

✔ **The audience:** Who is the audience for your key message? Is it the end user or the channel of distribution (retailer, wholesaler, dealer)? Don't forget geography; determine whether your audience is local, regional, national, or global.

  • If you're targeting a business audience, determine what industry they are in and their job functions, titles, and responsibilities.

  • If you're targeting consumers, picture your ideal audience in terms of age, income, marital status, lifestyle, career, socioeconomic status, hobbies, interests, and spending patterns.

✔ **The response you want to generate:** Just saying "increase sales" isn't specific enough. What do you want your target prospect to do, say, think, or believe after being exposed to your key PR messages?

✔ **The media you want to target:** To reach your target audience, what publications and programs do you want to carry your story? These can include TV shows, radio programs, newspapers, newsletters, magazines, trade journals, and any other media your target prospect is likely to read, see, or hear.

Because I practice what I preach, I regularly use PR to promote my PR agency, Jericho Communications, so we are better known and attract more of the types of clients we can serve best. The PR plan I did for Jericho is reprinted in full on the CD as file CD303.

Putting Together the PR Plan

When you look at the sample PR Plan on the CD-ROM, you will notice it has the following sections. Yours can follow the same basic format.

✔ **Overview:** An executive summary of the marketing challenge you are facing that the PR campaign is designed to help you meet

✔ **Goals:** What you want the PR campaign to achieve for your firm

✔ **Strategies:** The methods by which you will achieve your goals

✔ **Target audiences:** The types of people you want to reach

✔ **Key target media:** The specific publications and programs to which you will direct your PR efforts

✔ **Recommendations:** Which of the PR tactics presented throughout this book you will use, other ideas you have, and the theme, hook, or angle for each

✔ **Next steps:** An action plan — who does what, and when

Budgeting What You Need to Do the Job

PR costs a small fraction of other marketing methods — often less than one one-hundredth of what you'd spend for paid advertising. Yet it's not 100 percent free. Yes, the media do not charge you for featuring you in their publications and programs. But there's still the time involved in planning the campaign and writing the PR materials, plus the cost of printing and distributing those materials and following up with the press. Certain public relations tactics, such as b-rolls and VNRs for television (see Chapter 14 for definitions and details), can actually be expensive!

So it's important to sit down with pencil and paper (or your PC and a spread-sheet) and calculate a reasonable budget before you start spending money. The main expenses will be the staff time of your employees who handle PR responsibilities, fees paid to outside vendors (graphic artists, freelance writers, PR agencies, media lists or directories, clipping services), and out-of-pocket expenses such as printing and postage for mailing press kits.

 There is no magic or special technique for PR budgeting; you do a PR budget like you do a budget for any other project. File CD0305 on the CD-ROM shows a memo format we use at my PR agency to present a proposed budget to a client for approval.

The Four Essential Elements of Winning PR Concepts

Every public relations concept or tactic should be constructed from these four elements: newsmaking, commercial message, media target, and advance target. The following sections explain those elements.

The newsmaking element

Strangely enough, newsmaking is the element that most PR firms are not good at. Concepts don't get media coverage simply because you want them to, and they don't get broad-scale coverage because of "good contacts" in the media. They get coverage because an element makes them newsworthy.

What makes a newsworthy element newsworthy? Well, there are many factors. Some people, such as Bill Gates, make news just because of who they are. But for the majority of PR tactics, a variety of spices to the stew makes it of interest to the media. The number-one spice is emotion. A newsworthy element is effective if it makes people happy, makes them laugh, allows them to channel their anger, or appeals to their personal greed or concerns about home, family, and career.

Newsworthy elements that are most effective in PR are usually *quantitative*. To explain, advertising is the art of the *qualitative* ("this product is great, this product cleans best"). But PR is the art of the quantitative ("studies show that 82 percent of people who use this nasal spray can smell roses better").

A potent PR news element also usually moves from the audience's needs to the product's assets. In advertising, that process is reversed; you usually move from the product's assets out. In other words, in PR, you first discuss the consumer's needs, as in, "we need a better mousetrap because there are a lot of mice," and then you discuss how the product fills those needs. In advertising, you harp on what the product can do, and then you relate it to the consumer's needs.

Finally, the element that makes a campaign newsworthy is usually demonstrative, not stated. Again I compare to advertising: Advertising is the art of statements. You make brazen statements about your product or service, but because those statements are usually very commercial, the media won't run them for free.

The way to get around that is to demonstrate your key message points. For instance, British Knights was launching a new line of canvas basketball sneakers, the key feature of which was that the canvas construction resulted in maximum ventilation. The better-ventilated the sneaker, the fewer the foot odor problems. To demonstrate the main asset of maximum ventilation found in canvas sneakers, my firm developed the search for the world's smelliest sock. The campaign had people send in their socks, and the person with the worst-smelling sock won a lifetime supply of BK canvas sneakers. (I talk about another BK campaign in Chapter 2 — the "summer exchange" program designed to unglue kids from the TV set. You may want to check it out.)

The commercial message element

The thought that any PR is good PR is nonsense — and is the type of belief that can lead to a great waste of money and time. Good PR is PR that gets wide exposure and maintains a clearly communicated commercial message of what you want to sell to your audience. Sometimes you can build a campaign that funnels attention to a clearly stated commercial message, but more often, that commercial message must be demonstrated rather than stated directly, as in advertising.

For instance, if I send out a press release saying, "Jericho Communications Now Handles PR for Dot-Com Companies," nobody cares. I can say we are dot-com experts, but that's a self-promoting boast and people won't believe me.

So instead we did a survey, based on the TV show *Survivor,* and published the survey results showing how dot-com CEOs think differently than brick-and-mortar CEOs about survival issues — such as, what would they bring with them if they were stranded on an island? *The Washington Post* ran a feature story on the campaign, which of course mentioned that our PR firm did the survey. So we became positioned as experts in the way dot-com executives think, but we animated the message in an engaging way instead of stating the message directly.

Media target element

Remember that nothing in PR happens by chance, so if you're targeting an area of the media, you must put an element in your campaign that tempts the attention of that specific area of the media. That advice may sound obvious, but it is not often done. The result is that you end up trying to sell a story to your target media that really doesn't fit their needs.

This is a good time to bring up a very important factor in public relations. In PR, targeting your effort is very cost-effective. If you were doing an advertising campaign, doing a separate ad for each media vehicle would be very costly. Not so in PR. Therefore, to maximize results, create media tactics that seem to be created just for each key media outlet.

For example, an author wanted to promote a book of toll-free consumer hotlines. Different press releases giving sample listings of hotlines focused on excerpts from different chapters: health care, gardening, travel, hobbies, and child care. The press release with the gardening hotlines was sent to gardening magazines and home sections of daily newspapers, while the press release on child care hotlines went to parenting magazines and lifestyle editors. The pickup was substantial, and the reason, I am convinced, is that my firm targeted a general book by topic to appropriate media.

Audience target element

As you target the media, you should also target your audience as a whole, or any key subset of your audience that you're concentrating on. Therefore, your tactic should include an element that lets your audience know that you're speaking to them.

This may seem to be the same task as targeting areas of the media, but it's not. In PR, there is no reason why you can't use the lifestyle media to sell a business product or the sports section to sell beauty products to women. We are all multidimensional people who have many different interests. Therefore, you have no reason not to use all sections of the media to sell your message, as long as an element clearly lets your audience know that you're speaking to them.

For instance, my coauthor, Bob Bly, was publicizing a book he wrote on toll-free hotlines. He did one press release featuring all the toll-free hotlines for sports fans and sent it to the sports editors. Another press release summarized the toll-free lines for leisure and entertainment and was picked up by the lifestyle section editors.

Zeroing in on your media target

Pick up the Sunday *New York Times* and look at each section. You can see how each — sports, arts and leisure, business — targets a difference consumer interest. By targeting your PR materials to the specific slants and interests of the media you are mailing to, you significantly increase the chances of the editors using your material. I call this kind of media targeting "the Sunday *New York Times* approach."

This brings up another important difference between PR and advertising — the difference that makes it so difficult for advertising people to grasp how PR works. In advertising, there is a concept of "waste." Waste in advertising means buying an ad that reaches a lot of people but only a few members of your particular audience. It's waste because you pay a premium to reach this great number of people, but you don't get value because only a few of those people are in your targeted scope.

In PR, waste has little meaning — some, but little. Because you're not paying for each media outlet in which you appear and the size of the media outlet does not affect your expense, you should broaden your range and go after every media outlet, even if only a small percentage of those outlets reach your core customer. Of course, when the tactic is over, you must be able to show that you have reached a large number of core customers, but you can do so by going after *nonlinear media* (those broader and peripheral publications not directly targeted at your core audience) as well as *linear media* (mainly journals, trade publications, and newspapers directly targeted to your core audience).

In fact, by taking your message out of the expected media, it often stands out more and makes you appear bigger than your particular industry. This technique is very effective.

Ten Steps Toward Creative Promotions

The first draft of any document is never the best draft, and that certainly applies to the PR plan. I've discussed the sections of a typical PR plan, and how the "recommendations" section gives the specific tactics you will use and the themes or ideas of these individual promotions. You may have been deliberately vague or general in the first draft of your plan. But now go back and sharpen these recommendations. Doing so involves some hard work and creative thinking — you can't do it in 5 minutes — but it's worth the effort. The more complete and specific your plan is now, the easier your job will be later when it's time to implement the plan.

Here are some steps you can take to make your tactics as creative, sharp, original, and engaging as possible:

- ✔ **Understand that the media is looking for news.** News by definition is anything that is new, different, and creative. Nowhere does that exclamation "Vive la différence" hold more true than in securing the media's interest.

- ✔ **Often, the most successful PR ideas are not totally unique.** Rather, they are old ideas with a new creative slant. For example, one of my clients, a major restaurant franchise, initiated a food drive for the homeless. Its officers believed that such a large-scale undertaking was enough to attract national attention. It wasn't enough, and the franchise received minimal press coverage. Another client instituted a similar promotion. But instead of doing a typical food drive, we called the promotion "Pound for Pound for the Homeless." The difference was this creative twist: The company would donate a pound of food for every pound of chicken sold during a particular month. The media coverage was staggering.

- ✔ **Don't lose sight of who you're creating publicity for.** When writing a press release, be careful not to write it as an advertisement because the media doesn't run advertisements without getting paid for them. If you want your publicity to work, you must design your campaign from the public's point of view, not your own. That is the difference between public relations and advertising.

- ✔ **Use the radio-show test.** If you have an idea for a promotion, ask yourself, "Would this work for a call-in radio show?" Call-in radio shows need stories that are informative and induce the audience to strike up an interaction with the issue at hand. So if your campaign works for them, it will work for all media.

- ✔ **Tie into hot news stories.** Whenever a big news event hits, you can always find coordinated support stories that you can use to get publicity. Years ago, I handled PR for Domino's Pizza. During Operation Desert Storm, we began monitoring Domino's Pizza orders to the White House, CIA, and Pentagon. We noticed that orders went up before any major event or crisis. By announcing this correlation, we were able to get incredible publicity, ranging from stories in *Time* magazine and on *Nightline* to a comedy sketch on *Saturday Night Live*. A similar tactic worked on another occasion. During a presidential election, we offered a free topping on a pizza for anyone who came into a Domino's to register to vote. Not only did we use a hot news story to get coverage, but also we did it in a way that drove up store traffic.

- ✔ **Try making up recipes that are appropriate for certain holidays.** We created a Halloween promotion for Chop Chop Chinese to You, an Atlanta-based Chinese-food franchise, called "scary-titled recipes" for kids' Halloween parties. These recipes were innovative and creative and received tons of press. Whether you use particular events, seasons, or holidays, attaching yourself to a news story offers you a significant advantage. If you do it in a creative way, you're almost guaranteed success.

✔ **Tie into an emotion.** If you can make the media laugh, cry, or even feel anger, your promotion will usually work. When one client wanted to publicize the winning of an independent taste test over its biggest competitors, the emotion we chose was humor. Using the slogan "The good taste for good taste swap," we offered the client's chicken free to anyone who would show their good taste by taking the plastic covers off their furniture and sending them to the client. The campaign worked simply because the media found the whole idea of trading plastic furniture covers for chickens humorous.

✔ **Research your media.** If you want to get into a certain column of the newspaper or on a specific program, watch it or read it every day and notice what type of stories the journalists like to do. Next, fit your news item into that medium. For instance, my coauthor Bob Bly saw that a columnist writing about retirement liked to tell his readers about ways to make extra money in their spare time to supplement their retirement income. Bob sent a pitch letter (see Chapter 10) about a book he had written on freelancing. The columnist liked the idea and featured Bob's book in his next column.

✔ **Take stock of your assets when going after the media.** If you're an e-business, your greatest asset is probably your customer database. If you're a restaurant, your greatest asset may be your food. Now, feeding the hungry is easy to implement, and it is an emotionally effective asset. But so are the emotional ties that people have to food. We had great success when we worked with Domino's because pizza is more than sustenance. To many it represents fun. Therefore, we were able to use it as an inducement for everything from good attendance in school to registering to vote. The point is, never lose sight of how your product can be manipulated to move the public and get the attention of the media.

✔ **Swaps are a popular, effective way to get publicity.** Long before urban areas began sponsoring days during which the populace can turn in guns for cash, we came up with a guns-for-sneakers exchange PR campaign. We also have done successful swap campaigns that included television remote controls for sneakers. The media is very high on swaps these days, but as they become more common, the swap must become more creative and innovative.

Assessing PR Ideas: Will It Work?

As a PR professional, I am at a disadvantage compared to many of the readers of this book. My clients ultimately decide what they will run. I am the adviser, not the decision maker. I may have strong opinions, but it's their money, and they ultimately determine what they let me launch.

If you are a business owner or manager, however, you may not only come up with the PR ideas but also decide which campaign to implement. Here are some questions to help you assess whether a particular idea just sounds good on paper or may actually work in the field:

- ✔ **Does the campaign have emotional strength?** Emotion — a compelling sense of understanding and feeling — is the fuel that drives the influence of PR. It secures media placements, shapes decision making, generates awareness, builds interest, increases response rates, and gets the target audience to believe the messages intended for them.

- ✔ **Does it demonstrate the message?** Creating publicity initiatives, events, or promotions that demonstrate rather than state commercial messages is what makes them newsworthy.

- ✔ **Can the intended audience relate to it?** A winning campaign focuses not just on what you do but also on what your product does for the audience. This customer focus not only guarantees newsworthiness; it also encourages audiences to take notice of the message and change their attitude, opinion, belief, or behavior.

- ✔ **Is it a step above the ordinary?** Public relations tactics are at their finest when they give you a superior position in your industry or marketplace. PR should showcase your natural strengths and assets so that you stand head and shoulders above the competition.

- ✔ **Does it answer the basic questions of who, what, when, and where?** A good PR campaign plan determines what the exact message is, to whom that message has the greatest relevance, and in what aspect of the target's life the message is best communicated. Know precisely why you have a PR program, what you expect from it, and when.

- ✔ **What results do you want?** Determine a budget based on how much you want to achieve. Decide how you will measure your progress: inquiries, market research surveys, focus groups, increased market capitalization, key accounts acquired.

Because all PR concepts are a sum of elements, you can forecast how a concept will succeed by examining the idea not as a whole but by its elements. You can discern which elements will carry the emotion, which will maintain the commercial message, which will create the newsworthiness or interest, and which will point the concept to the exact target media or audience.

By knowing the specific effect that each element will have in directing a concept, you can build a PR campaign that is much more likely to achieve the success you want.

Chapter 4

Hiring Professional PR Help

· ·

· ·

My fellow PR professionals may hate me for saying this, but PR is something that many companies — especially small businesses — can and should do on their own.

I wrote *Public Relations Kit For Dummies* precisely because I know that there is no magic to PR and that do-it-yourself is not only viable but also sensible for many businesses. What Wilford Brimley says about Quaker Oats applies equally to doing your own PR for many readers of this book: "It's the right thing to do." And just as eating Quaker Oats is "the right way to do it" when it comes to nutrition at breakfast, *Public Relations Kit For Dummies* shows all you PR do-it-yourselfers out there "the right way to do it."

The biggest concern that small businesses have about doing their own PR is media contacts. "I don't have time to schmooze the big magazine and newspaper editors," you may be thinking. "A PR firm has the contacts that I don't, so it will be much better able to get my name into the media."

The "contact myth" is a lie perpetuated, in my opinion, by the PR firms in an attempt to make potential clients feel dependent on PR professionals. Some large firms also use it to differentiate themselves from their competitors in selling their services. "We will be able to get you in *The Wall Street Journal*," they claim, "because we have a personal contact with the front-page editor."

The fact is that no personal relationship with the media, no matter how strong, is going to get an editor to use a story that isn't right for her publication or program. As I am fond of telling my clients, "Nobody is getting favors in *The New York Times*."

Sure, media contacts can help; when you know someone personally, it's easier to get through to that person on the phone or have someone return your call. But that's about as far as the value of contacts goes.

The key to getting media coverage is to offer them a story that they can't resist. The two key elements are an understanding of the marketing message and the ability to think creatively in terms of PR campaigns. You already understand your business's market, and I am convinced that, with enough practice, almost anyone can learn to think more creatively. The mechanics of PR — and a lot of sample campaigns to inspire you — are laid out in this book. So you already have everything you need to do your own PR, and you don't need to hire an agency if you don't want to.

The question then arises: If you can do it yourself, why pay someone else to do it for you? Sometimes it's just a matter of the advantages inherent in outsourcing: Your staff is already too busy to do PR, and you don't want to add to your overhead by hiring your own PR department, adding a PR person to your marketing department, or expanding your already overworked in-house PR people. An obvious answer is to outsource PR. In addition to giving you access to outside expertise, hiring a PR professional frees your employees to concentrate on their core business.

Companies also hire outside PR counsel for a fresh point of view and original creative thinking. In-house people may have been working on a product line for so long that they're bored and can't see any excitement in it. To the outside PR professional just brought on board to handle the account, promoting the product is a fun challenge that gets the creative juices flowing.

Another reason that companies hire PR firms is to benefit from the PR firm's impressive list of media contacts. But you already know what I think of that.

Getting Help

Few people in small business have the time to become experts in PR and promotions, even though they may be quite decent at it. So should you hire an advertising agency or public relations firm to handle all this, or can you do it yourself?

Some small businesses use their ad agencies to handle their PR. Others hire PR firms or PR counselors — independent PR advisers, usually one-person shops. Another alternative is to hire a freelance PR writer to create your press materials. In this section, I take a look at each of these options.

Advertising agencies

Advertising agencies provide advertisers with a wide range of communications services: copywriting, art, production, media planning and buying, market research, sales promotion, and public relations.

Many ad agencies promote themselves as "marketing communications" firms and include both advertising and PR in their roster of services. Should you engage separate firms for advertising or PR, or is it better to have them both handled by a single shop?

The argument in favor of hiring a PR firm for PR, and an ad agency for advertising, is simple: They are two different disciplines requiring very different skill sets. Advertising agencies can say practically whatever they want in an ad, because they simply pay the media to carry their message. In PR, we have to convince — sometimes subtly — the media to carry our message for us, because we're asking for a "free ride" — we are not paying for the coverage. It's a different art and not one that all ad agencies practice well.

The argument in favor of having one firm do both advertising and PR is synergy between the campaigns. One danger of having separate agencies for advertising and PR is that they won't communicate well and work in tandem, resulting in ad and PR campaigns that communicate different messages.

But you don't need to take the single-agency approach to solve that problem. Just make sure that your ad agency and PR firm — if you have one of each — talk to each other frequently and are aware of what the other is doing. In my PR firm, we work very closely with our clients' ad agencies, sometimes to the point where our PR campaigns will become the basis of the next ad campaign.

I realize that the very words *advertising agency* are a turnoff to most small-business managers. They conjure up images of Madison Avenue at its worst: three-martini lunches, plush conference rooms, elaborate creative presentations, golf-playing account executives, and other evils that waste clients' time and money.

Yes, it's true that Madison Avenue agencies probably aren't for you. For starters, their "creative time" (for copywriting, artwork, and planning) goes for about $150 an hour and more.

Worse, your company will get lost in the shuffle at a large agency. Say the agency does $200 million a year. Assuming the agency would even talk to you, how much attention will you get if you spend $200,000 or $20,000? (As an interesting aside, industry sources note that major advertising agencies devote three members of their staff to your account full-time for every million dollars you spend.)

This doesn't mean that there isn't an ad agency out there that's right for you. The advertising business has more than its fair share of entrepreneurs — small agencies ranging from one- or two-person shops to those with perhaps a dozen or so employees. Many of these small advertising agencies do work that rivals the creative excellence of Madison Avenue — and costs far less. A six-person agency in New York, for example, bills creative time at $95 an hour, while a one-person shop in Akron charges $65 an hour. In addition, small agencies often distinguish themselves from their giant competitors by specializing in a particular area such as medical, financial, dental, corporate, retail, fashion, or industrial advertising. A small specialty agency can be ideal for a small business.

Public relations agencies

Public relations agencies are the professionals to turn to when you want to get coverage in the media. Now, sending out a press release or calling up a local editor are two things anyone can do — you don't need to be a specialist to practice public relations. So why hire a PR agency? One reason, as noted, is that PR firms are PR specialists.

At Jericho Communications, the PR firm of which I am cofounder, our staff are experts at writing, planning, timing, and executing publicity campaigns. A big reason is that doing PR is their full-time job and their only business. We give it priority, we treat it as a critical task, and we spend all our time doing PR and nothing else. Although novices tend to be unstructured and haphazard in their PR efforts, professionals can plan and execute a campaign that supports marketing strategy.

Many public relations firms charge their clients a monthly retainer for their services; a typical monthly retainer can be $3,000 to $15,000 a month or more, depending on the scope of the work. Larger and mid-size PR firms usually require a retainer of at least $10,000 to $15,000 a month or more. Smaller PR firms are more flexible, with minimum monthly retainers in the $3,000 to $5,000 range. You can even find solo practitioners — one- or two-person PR firms, often working out of someone's home — who will take you on for $2,000 to $3,000 a month.

Should you use a PR firm?

Do you need the highly professional and somewhat costly services of a PR agency? Or can you do things less expensively and better yourself? Here's a list of do's and don'ts to help you decide:

- ✔ Do use an agency if effective PR is crucial to your success and if you feel that you can afford the going rates.

- ✔ Do consider using an agency if you spend $3,000 or more a month on PR. That's probably the minimum amount it will take to interest even the smallest agency in handling your account.

✔ Don't hire an agency because you're trying to cut costs. Getting outside help is almost always more expensive than doing it yourself.

✔ Don't hire an agency solely because "you don't have time to do it yourself." Yes, the agency will free your time for other tasks. But when you hire an agency, you're hiring creativity coupled with PR expertise — and not just another pair of hands.

✔ Do hire an agency if your company is marketing oriented.

✔ Do hire an agency if you intend to use its services to full advantage.

✔ Do hire an agency for fresh thinking, outside objectivity, and a more creative approach to PR.

✔ Do hire an agency if you need help planning promotions, introducing new products, and selecting target markets.

✔ Do hire an agency to do things "first class."

✔ Don't hire an agency if you're certain that only you know the best way to promote your business and that outsiders can never make useful suggestions in this area.

If you decide to hire an agency, you need to know how to select the one that's right for your business.

Selecting a PR firm

Here are eight useful tips for selecting the PR firm that can best serve your company:

✔ **Prefer a PR agency with expertise in your area.** All else being equal, accountants, brokers, and bankers should select a PR agency that specializes in financial accounts. A manufacturer of globe valves for petroleum refineries should choose an agency with industrial expertise. A designer of men's swimwear would do best to seek counsel from a PR agency with other fashion accounts. By choosing an agency that already has some experience in your industry, you save yourself the costly and time-consuming process of educating its staff from scratch.

Make sure that the agency does not have any of your competitors as clients. A conflict would surely arise. Another warning: Take my caveat "all else being equal" seriously. A more important factor than expertise in your area is whether the PR firm is good at getting PR for its clients. All else is usually *not* equal, and I'd rather have a great PR firm that didn't have experience in my industry than a mediocre one, with weak results, that did.

✔ **Do not hire an agency with more capabilities than you need.** Do you really need an agency with overseas branch offices, television production capabilities, a market research department, and clout with the White House? All of an agency's clients pay to support its complete operations — so, to save money without sacrificing service or quality, select an agency that offers only those communications services you need, which will likely be account management, PR writing, and media relations.

✔ **Make sure that the agency is the right size for you.** A $20,000 account represents only 0.01 percent of a $200 million agency's income and consequently receives only 0.1 percent of its management attention and 0.1 percent of its creative effort. Make sure that your agency is small enough to consider your account profitable and worth its best efforts, yet large enough to have the resources to get the job done.

✔ **Ask to see the agency's work.** Examine a prospective agency's portfolio of press clippings and client case studies. Do you like what you see? Is it the kind and caliber of work you want done?

Avoid agencies that "talk the talk" but haven't "walked the walk." Lots of PR firms say they can get you in the media you want. But have they constantly delivered on this promise for their existing clients? More importantly, do they just get a bunch of press clipping for their clients, filling up portfolio books? Or do they execute targeted campaigns that have actually helped build major brands and achieve a significant improvement in the client's bottom line?

✔ **Get the names of some current and past clients and talk with those clients.** Find out what the PR agency did for them and whether the results were worth many times the fees paid in terms of increased business results.

Also ask the PR agency for the names of two or three clients who fired them. That's right, ex-clients who left them. Find out why the PR firm was fired. If it was for lack of results, that's bad. If it's because the PR firm's ideas were too daring and the client was afraid to try them, maybe you're more daring and won't be so afraid.

In reviewing my career, I have found that the number-one reason I lost an account is that I gave the client my opinion and it disagreed with his own opinion. If you're simply looking for someone to parrot your own ideas, don't waste your money on an outside PR firm or consultant. A large part of what you pay an outside service for is a fresh point of view and ideas different from what you would come up with on your own.

I tell my own employees, "It's okay to have an opinion different than mine; it is *not* okay to have no opinion." As a client, you should give your PR advisers the same instructions I give my employees.

✔ **Make sure that the agency is sympathetic with the needs of small business.** Especially if you're a small business on a limited budget, explain to prospective agencies that your goal is to create PR campaigns that increase sales — and not to win PR industry awards. Tell them that your money is limited. Tell them that you want a PR campaign to generate traffic or boost sales, not to get your picture in the paper just to please your mother.

✔ **Check the personal chemistry.** PR is a people business. My PR agency's most precious assets all leave the building in the elevator every night: my employees. If you don't like the people who will be working on your account, or if you sense they don't like you, look for another PR firm; it's not a good fit.

✔ **Be clear about fees.** Check out the price. What is the average monthly retainer the PR firm's clients pay? The minimum monthly retainer? How much do they propose to charge you? And what do you get in return? Have them spell out what they will do and the level or degree of activity you can expect for your investment.

My agency has hourly rates established for me, my partner, and every other employee. We keep track of everyone's time and bill it against the retainer. So if Joe bills at $100 an hour and does 10 hours of work this month for Client X, $1,000 of that client's $12,000 monthly retainer has been spent on Joe's services.

How many PR agencies should you interview when making your selection process? I recommend you meet with at least three different agencies, so that you can see the different perspectives from which they approach PR in general and your business problems in particular. You may find it helpful to spell out what you're looking for in a PR firm and what you want it to do for you in a Request for Proposal (RFP).

Review the proposals that the PR firms submit. A good proposal should give you, the client, insight into how the agencies think, the strategies they use, their costs, and their time line for implementing your campaign. Although their fee is paid monthly, you usually need at least six months of working with a PR firm before you can accurately evaluate results.

After reviewing the proposals the PR firms submit, ask the ones you like to come in and do a presentation. That means a presentation of their capabilities and what they can do for you, not actual creative work on your account. You shouldn't ask for that until you've made your decision and hired one of the agencies.

Graphic design studios

Most small businesses rely on print promotions — posters, signs, pamphlets, ads, point-of-purchase displays, coupons, media kits, and brochures — to reach their customers and prospects. Graphic design firms can often meet this need with great quality at a reasonable fee.

Graphic design studios do not, as a rule, offer media, marketing, writing, and PR services. They are simply the experts in designing and producing print material.

Some small-business managers have a good grasp of sales and marketing, know their business well, write lucid copy, and understand the basic promotional tools. They just need help turning their ideas into polished print material, and a graphic design studio can provide that help.

The rates for graphic design services vary according to where your business is located. In Manhattan, a city that may have more working graphic artists than anywhere in the United States, the design rate ranges from $100 to $150 an hour.

Freelancers

Many creative types of people — especially writers, artists, photographers, and publicists — are skilled in areas of promotion and work as freelancers, serving both advertisers and advertising agencies. Freelancers are capable of delivering the same high-quality work as advertising and PR agencies at a fraction of the cost. Using freelancers can be the least expensive way of getting professional help to create your promotions.

Before hiring a freelancer, check his resume, portfolio, and client list. Find out his rates and get a written estimate in advance. Most important, make sure that you like (or at least can tolerate) the freelancer as a person. With advertising agencies, an account executive separates you from the writer or artist. With freelance help, you deal with the creator of your promotion directly. To have a successful collaboration with the freelancer, you must be able to work well together.

Some freelance PR writers may say they can also do PR placement, but be wary of this claim. Part of the reason I can follow up so effectively is that if I send a press release to a thousand editors at a thousand publications, my staff personally calls every one of them — some several times — to follow up and get more placements. Now, if each call takes ten minutes, a thousand calls would take one person seven consecutive days if he worked 24 hours a day without a break. A lone freelancer with limited time and no staff cannot duplicate this level of effort from a home office.

Working with Professional Help

You've looked at your checkbook, looked with dismay at your current promotion campaign, and made a major decision: You want your promotions to be first class, and you've decided to get professional help — an advertising agency, a PR firm, a graphic design studio, or a freelancer. Here, then, are some helpful hints for getting the best work out of your outside supplier with the least amount of trouble:

- ✔ **Brief your agency.** The more your PR firm or advertising agency knows about your product, your company, and your markets, the better. Tell your agency what makes your product unique. Explain its advantages over the competition's products. Explain your marketing strategy. Provide background material in the form of current ads and press releases, brochures, articles on your industry, and market-research reports. The best clients prepare comprehensive agency briefings in writing.

- ✔ **If you use separate agencies for advertising and PR, brief them both at the same input meeting.** Doing so further helps ensure integration between your advertising and PR campaigns. It also saves you from having to present the same background briefing twice.

- ✔ **Do not compete with your agency in the creative area.** You certainly can disapprove of the brochure copy or the press kit that your agency turns in. Make helpful criticisms and turn it back for a revision. But don't tell outside talent how to do the job. If you can write better than the writer and take better pictures than the photographer, fire them and do the work yourself.

- ✔ **Don't strain your promotions through many layers of approval.** You, and possibly your business partner, should approve or disapprove the work that the outside agency submits. But don't look for approval from your purchasing agent, your accountant, your cashier, and your mother-in-law. Too many levels of approval muddy clear writing and water down the impact of the message. Worse, they dampen the creative spirit of your writers or artists so that the next thing they do will be mediocre enough to get your company's instant approval.

- ✔ **Be reasonable about paying.** Making a good profit in PR or advertising is difficult, and many agencies and freelancers have gone out of business waiting for late payments from their clients. Be fair to your agencies and freelancers and pay them promptly.

By all means, watch expenses carefully, and don't pay for something you never asked for in the first place. On the other hand, too much haggling over money can cause your outside professionals to put forth less effort on your account. You will get a competent promotion, but not a great one.

Where to find help

You want to hire a PR firm, ad agency, or free-lancer, but you don't know where to turn. The following mini-directory of creative talent should be of some assistance:

✔ *The Agency Red Book,* published by the National Register Publishing Company, Inc., 5201 Old Orchard Road, Skokie, IL 60077. This directory lists 4,400 advertising agencies in the United States and overseas. For each agency, the Red Book reports agency income, number of employees, key accounts, and the addresses and phone numbers of its offices. It also includes a useful index listing agencies by state. The Red Book is available in most libraries.

✔ *O'Dwyer Directory of Public Relations Firms,* 271 Madison Avenue, New York, NY 10016. Lists 1,200 PR firms. Available in most libraries.

✔ *The Creative Black Book,* published by Friendly Publications, Inc., 401 Park Avenue South, New York, NY 10016. Lists thousands of photographers, illustrators, graphic designers, printers, TV producers, ad agencies, and other creative resources.

Available by mail order through the publisher and in some major bookstores.

✔ *Adweek Creative Services Directories,* published by Adweek, 820 Second Avenue, New York, NY 10017. Similar in scope to the *Black Book,* the *Adweek Creative Services Directories* list photographers, artists, illustrators, designers, printers, and other creative resources. The *Adweek Directories* are published in five regional editions (East, Southeast, Midwest, Southwest, and West) and can be purchased from the publisher.

✔ *Public Relations Journal,* a monthly magazine published by the Public Relations Society of America, 845 Third Avenue, New York, NY 10022. Many PR agents offer their services each month in the classified ads section of this journal.

Also check your local Yellow Pages for listings under "Advertising Agencies," "Public Relations Agencies," "Graphic Design Studios," "Illustrators," "Writers," "Copywriters," "Artists," and "Photographers." More resources are available on the CD-ROM at the back of this book.

Part II

Brainstorming and Thinking Creatively

The 5th Wave · By Rich Tennant

A pie factory is no place to ask for PR ideas that are more in-your-face.

In this part . . .

PR depends on creative ideas, and Part II equips you to hatch those ideas by the truckload. The first step is to set up your own PR program (Chapter 5). In Chapter 6, you get a process for formulating creative ideas, and Chapter 7 gives you some creative PR tactics you can apply to your own campaigns.

Chapter 5

Setting Up Your PR Department and Program

. . . .

In This Chapter

▶ Creating your PR department

▶ Defining your authority

▶ Putting your resources in place

▶ Planning your PR program

▶ Targeting your PR efforts

. . . .

*T*o win the Super Bowl, you don't just show up that day, play, and hope for the best. Long before you get there, you put together a team and a plan. You also review your strategy, practice your moves, buy the equipment you need, and train your players.

Winning in PR is similar — early preparation leads to lasting success. This chapter covers the steps to follow whether you're planning to do your own PR campaigns in-house or manage the activities of an outside PR specialist or agency you hire (as covered in Chapter 4).

Picking the PR Team

One person in your organization should be responsible for PR, serving as a liaison between your company and your PR specialist or agency, as well as coordinating communication between your firm and the press.

If you're a self-employed professional or a small home-based business, the PR coordinator or manager will probably be you. You probably can delegate a lot of the administrative work to an assistant, and if she is bright, maybe she can take on some strategic and creative responsibility as well.

Large corporations usually have a separate PR department or at least one or more managers who have PR as a full-time job responsibility. They go under a variety of names, including PR manager, corporate communications director, and media relations manager.

In mid-size firms, the sales manager, marketing manager, or advertising manager may handle PR as part of the company's overall marketing communications mix, which may also include trade shows, advertising, a Web site, and direct marketing.

Whoever you select, that person — whether PR is a full-time responsibility or just one of many responsibilities — is in charge of PR and is accountable for getting programs done on budget, on time, and in synch with communications objectives.

Defining the Scope of Your Authority

Unless the PR manager is also the owner of the business, he may have the responsibility for PR but probably does not have the final authority. That is, the PR manager reports to someone else who has approval authority over all major PR activities, including copy for press releases, decisions about event planning or special promotions, and what to say to the press.

Because effective PR depends on being able to give the media a fast, accurate, honest response when reporters have questions, the PR manager cannot operate effectively if everything said in PR — in print, in person, and on the phone — has to go to a half dozen people to get approval. By the time the response is approved, the story has grown cold and the media is alienated.

To make PR efforts effective, the PR manager needs to be able to make decisions quickly. That means a simplified chain of command. For approval on major PR documents, the PR manager should have to circulate copy to no more than two or three people — the product manager, a technical expert for accuracy, and perhaps the CEO or marketing director. For media contact, the appropriate spokespeople within the company, such as the CEO or product manager, should be committed to giving priority to media response and to understanding that the press can't wait.

Integrating PR with the Rest of Your Business

In an organization large enough to have a PR manager or department, the danger is that these PR specialists may operate in a vacuum and become removed and remote from the day-to-day business. Ironically then, those assigned the task of communicating company messages and information to various outside audiences (the media, the public, shareholders, the community) risk becoming the least informed.

Half the job of a full-time PR professional is disseminating information to the media; the other half is understanding what the company is really doing.

Don't sit at your desk all day. Get out and walk around the factory, the warehouse, the shipping department, and the product managers' offices. Ask people what's important, what's interesting, and what messages they want to communicate to the outside world. Your job is then to understand these stories and package them in a way that's appealing to the media and their audiences.

Every PR manager, full-time or part-time, should do the following to keep up-to-date with a company's activities:

- ✔ Read industry trade journals.
- ✔ Attend major trade shows at which your company is exhibiting.
- ✔ Frequently visit your own Web site and read new postings.
- ✔ Frequently visit competitor's Web sites and see what they're up to.
- ✔ Read all new sales literature your company publishes.
- ✔ Respond to competitors' ads in magazines and request their sales literature.
- ✔ Talk with sales reps to see what customers are saying about your products versus the competition.
- ✔ Go with sales reps on actual sales calls to prospects.

Before you start a flurry of PR activities, have a PR plan in place that clearly defines audiences, objectives, and key messages you want to communicate. The PR planning process is covered in detail in Chapter 3.

Setting Up the PR Command and Control Center

To be an effective and efficient PR professional, you need to create a "PR Command and Control Center" — a place in your business where you can, from a single location, develop and implement all your PR campaigns.

Fortunately, such a space needn't be elaborate or expensive; all you really need is a desk, a phone, a computer with Internet access, a fax machine, a good photocopier, a postage meter, and some reference directories. Here are some suggestions to help you transform your own desk into a tiptop PR command and control center in short order:

✔ **Invest in a set of media directories.** The major media directories, listed on the CD included with this book, are books or CDs that contain complete contact information for thousands of media outlets — newspapers, syndicates, television and cable stations, radio stations, magazines, and new media to whom you can send your press releases. These guides give you much valuable, time-saving information such as media outlet descriptions, reporter contact information, tips on pitching your story, reporter beats, and circulation numbers.

  • As you can see on the CD ROM, some media guides are national and some are local. If your business is strictly regional, a local media directory may be all you need.

  • If you do any sort of regular PR campaign, I would advise you to own one or more of these directories, such as Bacon's or Gebbie's All-In-One. If you are truly only going to do a one-shot press release once or twice a year, you can often find some of these books in the reference section of your local library.

✔ **Develop a good media list — a list of media contacts to call when you want to get a story in print or on the air.** Ideally, your media list is a work in progress that is comprised of contacts from a current media directory in addition to personal contacts. A thorough media list contains not only contact and outlet information but also information on deadlines, preferred means of contact, and other useful notes. A media list is an invaluable tool when you're sending any announcements or responding to queries.

  • Keep your lists updated. Reporters commonly switch beats or even outlets, so keeping in touch with your contacts is important so you know whom to call or where to send your releases.

  • As the years go by, your media contacts will change jobs. Keep your media contact list up to date, and follow these contacts as they move from job to job. Failing to do so means you have lost a valuable contact you have spent time and effort in building.

- As people make career moves, they often climb the corporate ladder. As a result, the young journalists I knew when they and I were in our 20s are now in their 40s. Many are media big shots, and by keeping in touch, I now have personal access to high-level producers and editors at media outlets I did not have before. Remember, one easy way to get to the top of the oak tree is to plant an acorn and sit on it.

- For more information on building a media list and working it to your advantage, refer to Chapter 12.

✔ **Use a monitoring service.** A monitoring service, also known as a clipping service, helps you track your media placements. Monitoring services provide two benefits: They track the stories you place and the news you don't as well. For example, if you sent a release to *The Wall Street Journal,* and the service finds nothing about you in the *Journal,* you know your release didn't get used. In addition, reporters don't have time to clip and mail you the stories they write about you when they are published. So without a monitoring service, you may not even know that a story has come out.

Monitoring services are a great safety net when reporters can't give you a publication date on a story they're writing about your company or when a television station picks up an announcement as soon as you release it. Several free but very limited services, such as my.yahoo.com and northernlight.com, do a better job monitoring an industry than a specific company. Fee-based services such as Factiva are online and have a comprehensive list of publications and radio and television stations that they monitor through company- or keyword-specific searches. Also fee-based are traditional clipping services such as Luce or Burrelle's, which send you photocopies of newspaper or magazine clippings but have a longer delivery time. Broadcast monitoring services such as Video Monitoring Services or Media Link monitor both radio and television programs for clients. (Refer to the CD for a complete list of monitoring services. Contact them for current rates.)

✔ **Become acquainted with the media outlets.** The media directories are a great starting place and an ongoing resource for getting to know the media. But the best way to fully understand what a newspaper or television or radio station covers or to find out about a specific reporter's beat is simply to read the newspapers in the morning, turn on your radio on your way home from work, and catch the evening news on television. Doing so helps you to better frame your stories and to avoid PR blunders — such as pitching a reporter on a story that he covered only two days ago. Building relationships with reporters is key.

✔ **Collect and maintain editorial calendars for key media.** Magazines and special sections of some national daily newspapers have yearly editorial calendars that note upcoming topics or issues they will be covering. To obtain a calendar, log on to the publication's Web site or call its advertising sales department.

✔ **Assemble a complete list of vendors.** You will deal with many different vendors on different projects. From printers for press kits to release distribution services (services that distribute your press release to the media for you via mail, fax, or e-mail), many vendors can enhance your activities. Some vendors excel at making color media kits, while others are known for broadcast faxing out a press release. You can find a list of vendors and their descriptions on the CD in this book. Other helpful sources for finding vendors include your local Yellow Pages and networking with other businesspeople in your city or town.

✔ **Do your homework.** Research your competitors, your company's history, and trends, while keeping abreast daily on breaking news and new developments. What's the best way to do this? Get as many company materials as possible. Go to the library and search a database of past news stories in your industry (some clipping services come with this option) and read as much as you can every day to keep abreast of breaking news and trends.

✔ **Develop a standard kit of core press materials.** As I discuss in Chapter 9, a good press kit consists of the following elements:

  • **Company fact sheet:** This one- to two-page document gives a brief description of the company, its primary activities, products and services, and any other relevant facts, such as sales/revenues, number of employees, and names of key management personnel.

  • **Biographies:** Prepare short biographies of your company's key management, usually the CEO, chairman, president, and other key executives, such as the CFO or senior vice presidents. The bios should discuss their current position and responsibilities in addition to a brief professional history.

  • **Key releases:** Depending on your objectives and your audience, key releases can be anything from quarterly results to product or service announcements.

✔ **Sharpen your writing skills.** PR professionals write everything from press releases, media alerts, and letters pitching ideas, to speeches, strategy plans, and client correspondence. You may want to consider taking a PR writing or journalism course at a local college to learn how to write for your different audiences. You should always have at your fingertips these three writing resources — a dictionary, a thesaurus, and an AP (Associated Press) Stylebook to guide you on matters of grammar and style. And remember, professionalism is critical in your relationships with both clients and media, so always carefully proof your materials. Or better yet, ask someone else to look over the material for mistakes. Sometimes you can easily fail to see errors in documents that you have written. For more tips on how to write better, refer to Chapter 25.

✔ **Network.** Try to continually meet other PR professionals and journalists to help you develop and maintain relationships. Here are some ways to do this:

- Join industry trade groups like the PRSA (Public Relations Society of America) or the NIRI (National Investor Relations Institute), both listed in the CD in the back of the book. They offer seminars that provide access to some of the most well-respected PR professionals and key media people. They also offer invaluable training and informational seminars on a wide range of areas, crisis management, for example.

- Invite reporters out to lunch, not to pitch a story to them, but rather to give a general background on your company and to find out more about what stories they're interested in covering.

As an alternative to formal networking, a business owner or manager who has part-time responsibility for public relations can build up a list of media contacts slowly, over time. You do this by creating and maintaining a list or database of any media contact or outlet that runs a story or short item about you based on PR materials you sent. Your media contact list consists of the names, titles, publications or stations, addresses, phone numbers, e-mail addresses, and fax numbers of editors, writers, reporters, program directors, hosts, and other media people who have previously given coverage to your PR efforts. Putting together your personal media contact list is outlined in Chapter 12.

Every time you get media coverage, send a thank-you note to the reporter or editor who used your material. Your note should thank the person for taking the time to write about you, while also giving brief mention of one or two other story ideas that may be right for the publication and that you could help with by providing more information. The letter should be short and primarily focus on a sincere thank you; the mention of new ideas should be a soft-sell and take only one or two lines.

Don't offend the media! Members of the media are extremely sensitive about the symbiotic relationship between the press and PR people. Be extremely cautious not to suggest in any thank-you letter that the journalist is doing you a favor or helping to promote your product.

Also, enter the media person's name, publication, and other contact information (address, phone, and so on) into a card file, your Rolodex, or a computer database. Whenever you get coverage from a media source that hasn't written about you before, add that name to your database.

In a short time, you will have a contact database of media people who have covered you or used your PR materials in some way and therefore have some familiarity with you and your company.

Just as in direct mail, sending letters to your "house" list of existing customers will almost always produce a greater response than mailing the same letter to a rented list of "cold" names. Sending PR materials to your house list of media contacts will result in greater use of your materials than mailing the same press releases to a list of editors or program directors taken from one of the media directories listed in the appendix.

Does this mean that you should send your PR materials only to your house media contact list and not to other sources? No. Any release you distribute should go to your house list as well as to all other appropriate publicity outlets listed in whatever media directories you're using.

The purpose of maintaining a media contact database is to ensure that these people get all your materials and are not accidentally left out. Make sure that your media contacts get all your PR mailings because these people are most likely to give you coverage.

To sum up: For the small and part-time PR practitioner, it is not cost-effective to "court" the press for purposes of making personal connections to increase the odds of media placement. The better strategy is simply to keep track of and maintain constant contact with every media source who *does* cover you, based on the assumption that any editor or program director who has featured you once is likely to want to do so again if you present a story or angle of interest.

Targeting Your PR Efforts

You can target your market in any of several ways (or a combination of ways). The nine major ways are: industry, company size, location, job function or title, product application, distribution channels, affinity groups, specific users, and buying habits. Once you select your target market, you must then seek out, identify, and collect information on the publicity outlets reaching your various market segments.

Industry

You can target by industry, specifying industry segments by name or by SIC (Standard Industrial Code). The Standard Industrial Classification system uses a series of eight-digit codes to organize U.S. businesses into 15,000 categories and subcategories. The definitive reference work to SIC is Dun & Bradstreet's SIC 2 + 2 Standard Industrial Classification Manual, listed on the CD-ROM.

Here is an example of targeting by industry for a company that sells plastic diaphragm pumps. The PR manager creates two different press releases describing the same product. Why two different releases? Because the users in different markets are interested in different performance features. Buyers in the chemical industry are interested primarily in corrosion resistance; buyers in the pharmaceutical industry are more concerned with purity and cleanliness. Press releases sent to the editors at top trade journals covering these markets stress these different themes. The advantage of doing this? Editors respond better because the press materials they receive talk about what is of interest to their readers.

Many of the available directories of publicity outlets are organized by industry segment or cross-referenced by industry segment or at least allow you to specify industry-specific publications when ordering mailing lists. The volume of Bacon's Publicity Checker covering business magazines is especially helpful when you're looking for the publications covering a particular industry segment. For details, contact Bacon's PR Service, listed in the appendix.

Size of company

Your market can be segmented according to the size of the company. I see American business divided into three basic markets: small business, middle-size companies, and large corporations. How you define "small," "medium," and "large" for your marketing and PR purposes is really up to you. But here's how I think of it:

- ✔ **Small companies** are generally privately owned and usually family-run businesses, with anywhere from 1 or 2 employees up to 30, 40, or maybe 50 employees. For a manufacturer, this means sales under $10 million; for a service firm, sales under $2 million.

  The small company is usually run by an owner who keeps a tight rein over all aspects of the business. Entrepreneurs are skeptical, pressed for time, not terribly interested in technical details, bottom-line oriented, and cost conscious.

  Home-based businesses are a distinct submarket within the small business market. Many computer, fax, copier, telephone, furniture, and office supply companies are aggressively targeting this market segment because of the rising popularity of working at home. The disadvantage in targeting this market, however, is that home-based businesspeople are usually frugal and on a limited budget, and they rarely offer opportunities for repeat business or volume sales. They tend to buy only one of everything, and that only after much deliberation. And they also tend to require a lot of after-sale support and service.

✔ **Medium-size companies** may have from several dozen to several hundred or more employees, with sales usually above $10 million if a manufacturer (or above $2 to $3 million if a service provider) but less than $100 million. Your prospect here is probably not the owner, but he may very well report to the owner. Some prospects have a lot of autonomy and authority; others have to check with the boss to spend $50 on office supplies. This market segment is difficult to put neatly into a single category, because it is so big: There's a lot of difference, for example, between a firm with $10 million in sales versus a firm with $150 million in sales.

✔ **Large corporations** typically include the Fortune 500 firms and those of similar size: big companies with thousands of employees and annual sales in the hundreds of millions of dollars.

Typically, managers in these firms are part of a chain of authority and must consult with others in their company to make a purchase decision of any consequence. Prospects at big corporations frequently are as concerned with making an "acceptable" buying decision (one that pleases the immediate supervisor or top management committee) as they are with bottom-line results. Many hesitate to take risks.

What publicity outlets reach businesspeople? These would include the following:

✔ General business magazines

✔ Local and regional business magazines

✔ Chamber of commerce magazines and newsletters

✔ Industry-specific trade journals

✔ Industry-specific newsletters

✔ Business sections of major daily newspapers

Readership overlaps among these publications, so you can't strictly target publicity outlets by the size of the business in your PR mailings. For example, *Business Week* is written for corporate executives, but I'm sure that many small-business owners read it, too.

The best you can do when targeting PR by the size of a company is to give a little extra attention and focus to those publicity outlets known to concentrate on your market segment. For example, I'd probably devote a separate effort to getting my material into *Inc.* if targeting small to medium-size businesses; for reaching top executives in large corporations, I might concentrate on *Across the Board, Forbes,* and *Fortune.*

You can get a good feel for the audience of any business publication simply by flipping through a recent issue. Or you can read the descriptive listings of these publications in *Writer's Market,* available at your local library or from F&W Publications, 1507 Dana Ave., Cincinnati, OH 45207, 513-531-2222.

Although *Writer's Market* is published primarily for freelance writers as a guide to where they can sell their work, businesspeople seeking publicity also find it useful: The listings are more detailed than in the standard publicity outlet directories, especially concerning the readership of each publication and the types of articles sought by their editors.

Location

Some marketers target PR geographically; others do not. Most of my clients in the food business, for example, sell to customers across the country, and geography does not affect their marketing efforts. Regional or local chains, on the other hand, might market only in their immediate and surrounding states because they can offer delivery that is both fast and economical only to prospects who are nearby.

Many companies selling professional, consulting, and technical services to businesses are often similarly restricted to serving markets within the immediate geographic area of their headquarters or branch offices. Companies that sell to businesses from retail outlets — resellers of computer systems, for example — also serve a market within driving distance of the shop or store, as do firms that offer on-site repair services.

Even some companies that sell products may do target marketing based on location. One company, a vitamin chain, finds that marketing efforts do better in some states than others, and it deletes the poorer states when targeting PR efforts.

In today's global marketplace, many U.S. firms are looking to expand into overseas markets. Most certainly, a separate international campaign will be developed; larger, more sophisticated marketers may even have separate campaigns aimed at different regions (Europe versus Asia) or even countries.

To target by location, you can select from *Bacon's Publicity Checker* and many of the other media directories listed in the appendix those newspapers, business magazines, and consumer magazines with circulations limited to a specific town, region, or state.

In addition, a few directories list all major media in a specific city or area. These include *Metro California Media* and *New York Publicity Outlets.*

Job function or title of prospect within the company

Another means of targeting prospects is by job title. By concentrating your marketing efforts on those people who are responsible for buying, recommending, or specifying your type of product or service, you eliminate the waste of marketing to people not involved with your product or its purchase.

Although PR mailing lists are not categorized by job title, certain publications are aimed at people with specific job titles. *CEO,* for example, is written for chief executive officers; *Purchasing,* for purchasing agents. If I want to reach female consumers, I arrange for the CEO of my client to give a speech at a women's group, such as female entrepreneurs. To reach teens, we might offer a free print or Internet newsletter written specifically for high schoolers. Consult the publicity directories listed in the appendix to research publications that are job-title-specific.

Application or use of your product

You can target your marketing efforts based on how the prospect uses your product. Good examples are the pocket planners, daily calendars, time management systems, and other pocket schedulers and diaries sold to businesses.

Some companies sell them to be used personally by the buyer. Their catalogs and mailings go into elaborate detail about how the time management systems work, how they save you time, make your life more efficient, and so on.

Other companies market these items as gifts to be bought by businesses and given to customers, prospects, and colleagues. When selling these same items as a gift, rather than for personal use, copy is much shorter and doesn't detail how the systems work. Instead, it stresses the high value, elegant look, leather cover, personal imprint, and other aspects that make the books and diaries an appealing gift item.

Press releases should be slanted similarly, depending on how you want your product to be positioned in the marketplace. Example: One client sells a software package used by systems analysts to develop applications, but saw that they needed software to help them generate reports in different for mats. Because the client's product could handle this function well, a separate marketing and PR campaign positioned the product as a first-rate "report generator."

Take a look at the Sunday *New York Times* and how the different sections reach different readers with different interests. Your releases should be similarly targeted, so that people who use a particular product (for example, computers) for a particular application (for example, a home-based business) are attracted by your message.

Channels of distribution

You can target different promotions aimed at getting response from different people in the distribution channel — end users or customers, distributors, agents, resellers, wholesalers, agents, reps, OEMs (original equipment manufacturers), VARs (value-added resellers), stores, and catalogs.

Campaigns aimed at end users or customers naturally stress the benefits of using the product, while promotions aimed at the distribution channel tend to stress how much money or profit the distributor can make by carrying the item in his line and selling it aggressively.

Marketers sometimes use the term *push* to describe marketing to the distribution channel and *pull* to describe marketing to the end user or customer. This is because promotion to dealers is aimed at pushing the product on them and getting them to push it onto their customers, while marketing to customers creates demand that pulls the product through the distribution chain from manufacturer to distributor to end user.

PR aimed at pushing the product through the distribution channel by promoting it to the trade should be sent to trade publications, while PR aimed at pulling the product or service through the distribution channel should be sent to magazines read by consumers and other end users.

For example, to promote a book such as this one to the trade, press releases may be sent to *Publishers Weekly, Library Journal,* and other magazines read by those in the book trade. To promote this book to potential buyers such as business owners, managers, executives, and marketing professionals, press releases may be sent to such publications as *PR Journal, Advertising Age, Business Marketing, Inc.,* and *Business Week.*

Is it better to concentrate your PR efforts toward end users or the distribution channel? It depends on the market and the timing. If customers tend to buy the product directly from the manufacturer and distribution channels account for only a small percentage of sales, then naturally you concentrate your PR efforts on the end user.

In other markets, distribution channels are pretty important. Take books, for example. If bookstores don't buy a particular book from a particular publisher and put it on the shelves, it has very little chance of selling. And with 50,000 new books published each year, most get little or no shelf space in bookstores. So selling the distribution channel is essential.

A similar situation exists in supermarkets. With too many products competing for limited shelf space, many packaged goods manufacturers actually pay the supermarket a fee to stock and display their products.

The same situation affects many PC software packages. Thousands of software packages are on the market, yet most computer stores have room on the shelves for only a few dozen titles. If they don't carry yours, you either have low sales or must direct sales through other channels, such as catalogs, space ads, or direct mail.

How do you overcome this resistance? At first you may think that heavy marketing to the distribution chain is the answer. But suppose that you do this, and the bookstores carry your book. Readers may see it and snap it up. But perhaps they've never heard of it, so they walk right by it. With no demand from the end user, the title will be pulled quickly.

Often, creating a heavy customer demand is effective in getting the distribution channel to buy your product: After all, if your book gets rave reviews and dozens of people ask for it every hour, the bookstore will naturally want to carry it and order many copies from you.

For products where the distribution channel is important, then, you will probably target both the customer and the distribution chain. In most cases, the bulk of your effort will go toward end-user marketing; a much smaller portion will go toward dealer and distributor promotion. Exceptions? Of course.

If you study the publicity outlets as described in the media directories listed in the appendix, you will see that many industries have different magazines aimed at various segments in the distribution channel. In the computer field, *VAR* magazine is aimed at value-added resellers who customize, repackage, and resell software for specific applications, while *Dr. Dobb's Journal* is written for people who design and write software.

Affinity groups

An "affinity group" is a group of prospects with similar interests. These might include classical music buffs, computer gurus, bodybuilders, health and fitness enthusiasts, and other people who vigorously and enthusiastically pursue specialized hobbies, interests, or activities.

When you market a product that appeals to their common interest, you can get much higher results than with mass marketing of the same product to the general population because the people in the affinity group have a demonstrated interest in your product category or in the benefits your product provides.

A good example might be computer enthusiasts who use Prodigy, Dialog, CompuServe, electronic bulletin boards, and other online computer services. If you did a promotion for a bulletin board or other online electronic information or communications service and targeted the general population of computer users, you may be unsuccessful — not because your service or promotion is bad, but because the average computer user isn't "into" online communication, doesn't actively use a modem, and is intimidated by the whole thing. On the other hand, if you could target your promotion to existing users of such services, selling them an additional service — yours — would be much easier because you'd have to sell the service only, not the whole concept of online communication or buying a modem.

This is a good example of marketing made more efficient through targeting. It's always easier to "preach to the converted" — it makes more sense to advertise your steaks to beef lovers rather than trying to convince vegetarians that meat is good for them. Targeting to an affinity group assures that your audience is already converted before you start preaching to them.

PR lends itself very well to affinity-group marketing, because in today's publishing industry, the general-interest magazine has given way to the special-interest magazine. Most successful magazines today cover a niche: They report on a specific topic for an audience composed of people with a strong interest in the topic. Examples include bodybuilding magazines, karate magazines, gun magazines, pet magazines, computer hobbyist magazines, car magazines, gourmet magazines, and home magazines. By selecting these publications from the media directories listed in the appendix, you can easily build a list of publicity outlets that reach your affinity group audience.

Users of specific devices, products, machines, systems, or technologies

Targeting members of this category is a simple, sensible strategy. Its premise: If you're selling fax paper, you'll do a lot better selling to people who own fax machines than to those who don't.

A good example is in the computer field: If you have software that runs only on a Macintosh, you can go to a source of publicity outlets such as *Bacon's Publicity Checker* or *Media Map* and select publications written specifically for Macintosh users. This increases the odds for success and eliminates waste; the editor of a magazine for IBM PC users isn't going to run a story on your Macintosh software (no matter how great the program) because readers can't run the software because they don't have the right machine.

Buying habits

Although this is not a major method of targeting the market, there is some evidence that you can increase marketing results by tailoring your marketing efforts to fit the buying habits or patterns of the target prospects.

In consumer direct marketing, for example, results show that mailings using a sweepstakes do best when mailed to lists of people who have previously responded to sweepstakes mailings. Apparently, these people enjoy sweepstakes and will go through the trouble of entering, more so than the general population that contains a number of people who do not have patience for sweepstakes and do not respond to mailings.

So, if your company is running a big contest or sweepstakes as a promotion, make sure that, in addition to announcing the promotion to all the regular media, you hit publications such as *Contest News* and any others highlighting sweepstakes and contests.

Or, if most of the orders for your product or service are placed with credit cards, you might contact the person at American Express responsible for producing the newsletter mailed with its monthly bill, and see whether you can get a mention in one of its service articles or resource lists.

Recently, companies have begun targeting customers by the buying habit of online purchasing. PR campaigns are targeted to Internet surfers based on their (often) younger age and technical proficiency.

Chapter 6

Formulating Ideas

. . . .

. . . .

After spending my entire professional life in public relations, I am convinced that PR — unlike, say, brain surgery or local area network design — does not require special education, knowledge, or background for success. Anyone can do it. In fact, to succeed in PR, here's all you need:

> ✔ **A knowledge of the basics** — the formats, techniques, and methods typically used to communicate with the media. There's nothing mysterious or difficult about them, and they're all in this book.

> ✔ **The ability to think creatively** — to come up with ideas that are clever, compelling, and relevant to the marketing message.

I hire a lot of creative people at our agency, and yet some of my readers may not feel that they are strong in this area. I am often asked, "Can creativity be taught, or is it something you either have or you don't?"

The answer is: Although some people are more naturally inclined toward promotion and creative marketing, anyone who tries can come up with good PR ideas for his business on his own.

Creating Profitable PR Ideas

Just as public schools are remiss in not teaching how to study, degree programs in marketing and business are remiss in not teaching how to think creatively. If I were to create such a course, I would teach idea generation as a series of simple and repeatable steps.

Step 1: Identify the problem

The first step in solving a problem is to know what the problem is. But many people forge ahead without knowing what it is they're trying to accomplish. Don't apply a solution before you have taken the time to define the problem.

When Trillium Health Products hired my agency, the problem was that the company needed to sell more juicers. IKEA has given us many varied assignments, from getting a local community to be receptive to the construction of a new store in their area to launching a new line of furniture. You should be able to state the marketing objective in a single sentence — for example, "Convince people that they should read books on e-book readers and download them off the Internet instead of reading paper books bought in bookstores." If you can't articulate the problem, how can you articulate a solution?

Step 2: Assemble pertinent facts

In crime stories, detectives spend most of their time looking for clues. They can't solve a case with clever thinking alone; they must have the facts. You, too, must have the facts before you can solve a problem or make an informed decision.

Professionals in every field know the importance of gathering specific facts. A scientist planning an experiment checks the abstracts to see what similar experiments have been performed. An author writing a book collects everything she can on the subject: newspaper clippings, photos, official records, transcripts of interviews, diaries, magazine articles, and so on. A consultant may spend weeks or months digging around a company before coming up with a solution to a major problem. When I took on a cigar club as a client, I began smoking expensive cigars and socializing in the cigar culture to get a deeper understanding of that world.

Keep an organized file of the background material you collect on a project. Review the file before you begin to formulate your solution. If you're a competent typist, use word processing software to rewrite your research notes and materials. This step increases your familiarity with the background information and can give you a fresh perspective on the problem. Also, when you type notes, you condense a mound of material into a few neat pages that show all the facts at a glance.

Step 3: Gather general knowledge

In business, specific facts have to do with the project at hand. They include the budget, the schedule, the resources available, and the customer's specifications, plus knowledge of the products, components, and techniques to be used in completing the project. General knowledge has to do with the expertise you've developed in your life and includes your storehouse of information concerning events, people, media, culture, science, technology, management, and the world at large.

You can accelerate your own education by becoming a student in the many areas that relate to your job. Subscribe to the journals that relate to your field. Scan them all, and clip and save articles that contain information that may be useful to you. Organize your clipping files for easy access to articles by subject.

Read books in your field and start a reference library. Take some night school courses. Attend seminars, conferences, and trade shows. Make friends with people in your field and exchange information, stories, ideas, case histories, and technical tips. Most of the successful professionals I know are compulsive information collectors. You should be, too.

Step 4: Look for combinations

Someone once complained to me, "There's nothing new in the world. It's all been done before." Maybe. But an idea doesn't have to be something completely new. Many ideas are simply new combinations of existing elements. By looking for combinations, for new relationships between old ideas, you can come up with a fresh approach.

The clock radio, for example, was invented by someone who combined two existing technologies: the clock and the radio. The Earl of Sandwich, who invented the sandwich, did so because he wanted to hold his meat in his hands and eat while gambling.

Look for synergistic combinations when you examine the facts. What clever promotion can you think of that ties in with your marketing objective and demonstrates your message in a creative way? For Empire Kosher Chickens, we wanted to dramatize how carefully each chicken is inspected. Our promotion was to offer a free chicken to anyone whose income tax form was being "inspected" (audited) by the IRS. The press ate it up (excuse the pun).

Step 5: Sleep on it

Putting the problem aside for a time can help you renew your idea-producing powers just when you think that your creative well has run dry. But don't resort to this method after only five minutes of puzzled thought. First, you have to gather all the information you can. Next, you need to go over the information again and again as you try to come up with that one big idea. You'll come to a point where you get bleary, punch-drunk, hashing the same ideas over and over. This is the time to take a break, put the problem aside, sleep on it, and let your unconscious mind take over.

A solution may strike you as you sleep, shower, shave, or walk in the park. Even if that doesn't happen, when you return to the problem, you will find that you can attack it with renewed vigor and a fresh perspective. I use this technique in writing: I put aside what I've written and read it fresh the next day. Many times, the things I thought were brilliant when I wrote them can be much improved at second glance.

Step 6: Use a checklist

You can use checklists to stimulate creative thinking and as a starting point for new ideas. Many manufacturers, consultants, technical magazines, and trade associations publish checklists that you can use in your own work. But the best checklists are those you create yourself, because they're tailored to the problems that come up in your daily routine.

For example, Jill is a technical salesperson who is well versed in the technical features of her product, but she has trouble when it comes to closing a sale. She could overcome this weakness by making a checklist of typical customer objections and how to answer them. (She can cull the list of objections from sales calls made over the course of several weeks. She can garner possible tactics for overcoming these objections from fellow salespeople, from books on selling, and from her own trial-and-error efforts.) Then, when faced with a tough customer, she doesn't have to reinvent the wheel but is prepared for all the standard objections because of her familiarity with the checklist.

However, no checklist can contain an idea for every situation that arises. Remember, you use a checklist as a tool for creative thinking, not as a crutch.

Step 7: Get feedback

Sherlock Holmes was a brilliant detective. But even he needed to bounce ideas off Dr. Watson at times. As a professional publicist, I think I know how to plan an effective PR campaign. But when I show a draft to my partner, he can always spot at least half a dozen ways to make it better.

Some people — maybe you — prefer to work alone. But if you don't work as part of a team, getting someone else's opinion of your work can help you focus your thinking and produce ideas you hadn't thought of.

Take the feedback for what it's worth. If you feel that you're right and that the criticisms are off base, ignore them. But more often than not, the feedback provides useful information that can help you come up with the best, most profitable ideas.

Of course, if you ask others to take a look at a piece, you should be willing to do the same for them when they solicit your opinion. You'll find that reviewing the work of others is fun; critiquing someone else's work is easier than creating your own. And you'll be gratified by the improvements you think of — things that are obvious to you but would never have occurred to the other person.

Step 8: Team up

Some people think more creatively when they work in groups. But how large should the group be? My opinion is that two is the ideal team. Any more and you're in danger of ending up with a committee that spins its wheels and accomplishes nothing. The person you team up with should have skills and thought processes that balance and complement your own. For example, in advertising, copywriters (the word people) team up with art directors (the picture people).

In entrepreneurial firms, the idea person who started the company often hires a professional manager from a Fortune 500 company as the new venture grows. The entrepreneur knows how to make things happen, but the manager knows how to run a profitable, efficient corporation.

As an engineer, you may invent a better microchip. But if you want to make a fortune selling it, you should team up with someone who has a strong sales and marketing background.

Thoughts on creative thinking

Here are a few of my favorite quotations about creative thinking:

✓ "The best way to have a good idea is to have lots of ideas." — Linus Pauling

✓ "The best ideas come from jokes. Make your thinking as funny as possible." — David Ogilvy

✓ "When in doubt, make a fool of yourself. There is a microscopically thin line between being brilliantly creative and acting like the most gigantic idiot on earth." — Cynthia Heimel

✓ "If you want to make something happen, you have to be outrageous. You have to go beyond what is acceptable. Unwillingness to do that is the biggest risk of all." — Mike Vance

Finding Other Ways to Come Up with Good Ideas

Thomas Edison said that genius is 1 percent inspiration and 99 percent perspiration. But sometimes you need more inspiration to get your creative juices flowing. Here are a few ideas that have worked for me and people I know:

- ✔ Go to a toy store and look around. Can you create a game to publicize your message?

- ✔ Keep a "swipe file" — a file of promotions that you especially like or that at least caught your eye. Use them for inspiration when planning your own PR.

- ✔ Ask employees for suggestions. Reward the winning idea with a $100 gift certificate.

- ✔ Browse the library or bookstore. Or hang out at a museum. Inspiration often strikes in places where you're surrounded by ideas.

- ✔ Look outside your industry. What is a common, successful promotion in one industry may be creatively copied and applied to your industry, in which it is unheard of and therefore novel.

- ✔ Read literature on creative thinking. I recommend *A Whack on the Side of the Head,* by Roger von Oech, and anything on creativity by Michael LeBouf.

- ✔ Keep a pad and pen with you at all times to record thoughts as they occur to you. We have ideas all the time, but we lose them when we don't write them down.

- ✔ Whenever you write down a creative idea, drop it into a paper file or enter it into your computer. Keep a central idea file that you can dip into when you need a new creative promotion.

Giving New Ideas a Chance

Many businesspeople, especially managerial types, develop their critical faculties more finely than their creative faculties. If creative engineers and inventors had listened to these people, we would not have personal computers, cars, airplanes, lightbulbs, or electricity.

The creative process works in two stages: The first is the idea-producing stage, when ideas flow freely. The second is the critical or "editing" stage, where you hold each idea up to the cold light of day and see whether it's practical. Many people make the mistake of mixing these stages. During the idea-producing stage, they are too eager to criticize an idea as soon as it's presented. As a result, they shoot down ideas and make snap judgments when they should be encouraging the production of those ideas. Many good ideas are killed this way.

A common idea killer is, "We did that already and it didn't work." Yes, but with the rapid pace of change, it's a different marketplace than when you last tried the idea. Maybe the idea can be dusted off and altered a bit to make it work now.

Even more dangerous (and perhaps absurd) is the often-voiced objection, "We don't do things around here like that." My answer: Perhaps it's time to try something new. In over two decades of working as a PR professional, I have learned one indisputable fact about public relations: When you do the same old thing, you are likely to get the same old results. The only way to get new results is with a new idea.

Chapter 7

Using PR Tactics

*I*n the old cartoon *Felix the Cat,* Felix was able to win the day by reaching into his "bag of tricks." All PR practitioners have a similar bag of tricks — favorite PR tactics that they have used with success and often resort to when creating campaigns. This chapter presents a miscellany of some of the best tricks in my own bag.

Find a Tie-in to the News

Look for creative ways to tie your product in with current news or trends. At the time Earth's Best introduced a new line of organic baby food, the safety of eating genetically engineered foods was making headlines. We grabbed our share of these headlines for our client, Earth's Best, when we sent out a press release (reprinted in Chapter 15) announcing that its baby foods would not contain any genetically engineered ingredients.

Although organic foods had been around for a long time and were of interest in themselves, promoting the new baby foods as "100% pure" and "made without GMOs (genetically modified organisms)" was a new twist that allowed us to grab some of the media attention already focused on the controversial issue of genetic engineers.

The power of a news tie-in is that it eliminates the need to create a news story from scratch and then attempt to get the media to cover it. Piggybacking on an existing news story with a relevant promotional tie-in — one that is both credible and favorable to your product — is much more cost-effective.

I call this principle "Going Where the Cameras Already Are." The idea: Get included in a story the press is already covering, and getting yourself covered is that much easier. The example I often use — because it makes the point — is our free pizza from Domino's Pizza for last-minute taxpayers. By sending free pizza to the post office on April 15 at midnight, we didn't have to call the TV camera crews and try to convince them to film the event — they were already there filming last-minute taxpayers standing in line trying to make the filing deadline. When our pizza delivery team showed up, how could the TV crews do anything but turn the cameras on our client's product, which was right in front of them?

Create a Tie-in to a TV Show or Movie

You know that the hot motion picture — usually the one that was number one at the box office over the weekend — gets an incredible amount of public attention for a short period, usually a few weeks. The highest-rated new TV show of the season gets a similarly disproportionate share of buzz for a somewhat longer period — up to several months.

By creating a campaign that ties your product to these popular big- and little-screen attractions, you can siphon off some of their buzz and apply it to your own story for greatly expanded media coverage. For example, when the movie *Coneheads* was hot, we created a promotion for a chain of sandwich shops in which any customer coming in to a store and claiming to have seen an alien would get a free sandwich.

More recently, when Regis Philbin's *Who Wants to Be a Millionaire* became a hit, we did a promotion for a client that linked *Millionaire* to fitness — by offering to make you fit and strong enough to beat up a millionaire.

Spotlight the Product

You can use many products as props or devices to add visual and tactile interest to PR and promotional campaigns. One publisher who advertised his magazine as the "hot" publication in its field sent a handsome tin containing a pound of chili powder to potential advertisers.

Once, my agency staff taped press releases for a client — a pizza chain — to pizza boxes containing hot pies and delivered them to local broadcast media 20 minutes before the evening news. The broadcast personalities not only talked about the promotion on the news but also actually ate the pizza on camera!

Stage a Contest

Contests can work, but I always prefer to do them a little offbeat. I also believe that the contest should relate to the product.

Figure 7-1 is the release we did as a promotion for Jose Cuervo. It's a takeoff on the old "message in a bottle" theme. The contest was that if you found the bottle, you won a lifetime supply of tequila. The tongue-in-cheek style was appropriate both to the nature of the promotion and to the fun-oriented image of the product.

Before running any promotional contest, run all the copy and materials by your attorney. Contests and sweepstakes are regulated by laws, and noncompliance can give you PR you wish you never had.

Work for a Worthy Cause

If you're going to help others, do so creatively. Merely giving sums of money to charity, even if large, gets you little PR bang for the buck. Creative giving that helps a group or cause in a novel or offbeat way can provide much benefit for the recipient while promoting your brand or corporate image.

Rhinotek, a manufacturer of ink cartridges for laser printers and fax machines, based its brand on the rhinoceros. Dealers get a brochure telling how, of every product purchased, a percentage is donated to help preserve the rhino as a species. Rhinos are featured on product packaging and promotional giveaways, such as rhino mouse pads.

For food companies, the most obvious helping hand they can lend is to feed hungry people. Unfortunately, food drives are commonplace, and therefore the media don't always see them as particularly newsworthy stories.

Tie In to a Holiday

Relating your campaign either to a holiday (Valentine's Day, Halloween, Christmas, Thanksgiving) or to an event (National Secretary's Week, Elvis Presley's birthday) works because it adds an element of timeliness that your campaign would not otherwise have.

PLEASE HELP US FIND OUR BELOVED BLOW-UP BOTTLE

Jose Cuervo Offers Lifetime Supply* of Tequila as a Reward for Safe Return of Promotional Bottle

Last seen wearing a red and gold Jose Cuervo label at the CozyMel's Bar and Restaurant in Westbury, Long Island on the night of May 5, 2000. Various witnesses reported last seeing the bottle at 1:30 AM (EST) on the morning of May 6, 2000.

At the time of the disappearance, the bottle was only four days old. It weighs approximately 300 pounds when deflated and stands 3 stories tall. Often full of hot air and known for occasional "outbursts," the bottle had been partying all night in celebration of Cinco de Mayo and reportedly disappeared between 1:30 AM and 1:50 AM on the night in question....

"Although only four days old, we were very attached to the bottle," explained Velvet Mickens, Director of Marketing, Tequila Portfolio at UDV-NE, Jose Cuervo's parent company, as she held back tears. "It may be big, and even a bit clunky... but it has a lot of heart." Other employees at Jose Cuervo have been holding a candle vigil at their corporate offices in Stamford, CT, since the incident.

All information given will be confidential and we will be not be pressing charges. The person that comes forward with information or the bottle itself will receive a lifetime supply of tequila.*

For additional information contact: Lara Hauptman at 212/645-6900.

The lifetime supply of tequila is equivalent to 1 bottle every four months for 25 years.

Figure 7-1:
Message in a bottle release for Jose Cuervo.

The aphrodisiac survey campaign (reprinted later in this chapter) tying in with Valentine's Day for AllHerb.com, an herb and nutritional supplement e-commerce Web site, is a good example of a holiday tie-in. We also did a tie-in for AllHerb.com with Cancer Awareness Month called "Stop Smoking, mon, for Pokemon."

Conduct a Survey

By definition, the news media are interested in news above everything else. And it's not always easy for PR people to come up with something that is news — or even new.

Surveys are my secret weapon in PR; they're one of the easiest ways to provide the news media with the news they crave. The reason is simple: There is very little new information in the world. But a survey, by definition, always creates new information. If you survey 1,000 business executives and 87 percent answer yes to your survey question "Do you feel stress on the job?" then you have created a fact — "87 percent of 1,000 executives surveyed by XYZ company say that they feel stress on the job" — that you and no one else owns.

For a trade association of pet manufacturers, we did a survey showing that pet owners were more successful than non-pet owners at keeping their New Year's resolutions — promoting the value of owning a pet. Another survey for the same association promoted pet ownership by showing that 73 percent of companies surveyed said that having pets in the office increases productivity.

For Calyx & Corolla, a direct marketer of flowers, a survey indicated that corporate CEOs like flowers, and sending flowers to your CEO may help you land a raise.

We also did a survey for a client who sells nutritional supplements over the Internet. Again, we tied in with a holiday. The holiday was Valentine's Day, so we used the theme of romance. How to relate nutritional supplements to romance? By linking foods (which are nutrients) to their roles as aphrodisiacs. Figure 7-2 shows the press release for this campaign.

Stage an Event

Surveys are one sure way to create news. Another effective tactic for making news worth covering is to stage an event.

The National Hockey League (NHL) hired my PR firm to create excitement around the playoffs. To accomplish this objective, we worked on an event called the "Cup Crazy" traveling festival. The event was like a traveling carnival show. It included a range of hockey-related and other games, such as an inline hockey tournament, slap shot contests, and ticket raffles. The event, which was capped off by the appearance of the Stanley Cup in each playoff city, was covered in *Sports Illustrated, USA Today,* and *Newsweek* and on *Hard Copy* and *Extra.* More than half a million people attended the event during the playoff.

For more information on using events as PR promotions, see Chapter 17.

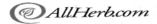 **AllHerb.com**

Contact: Marisa Milo
Jericho Communications
212-645-6900 x126

THIS VALENTINE S DAY, DON T SAY IT WITH FLOWERS, DIAMONDS, OR WORDS FROM THE HEART SAY IT WITH GARLIC???!!

Do oysters really get you in the mood? Or does chocolate actually make you romantic?? People have always questioned whether or not aphrodisiacs really work. Well, finally someone has actually put aphrodisiacs to the test. According to the study conducted by AllHerb.com, an online herbal resource, **the number one foods that couples who spoon frequently ate during the week they were surveyed were made with garlic, followed by dishes prepared with shiitake mushrooms, chocolate, and lemon.**

The survey, which queried 314 couples nationwide for a week to determine what aphrodisiacs make you feel sexy, romantic and cuddly – had couples fill out a form documenting how many times they had sex, orgasms, felt romantic, and did different "nuzzling" activities comparable to what they ate that evening. The study also discovered that couples who cooked regularly with certain ingredients found themselves to be "in the mood" more often: **the top five spices that couples who had sex the most often during the week cooked with were: cayenne pepper, followed by rosemary, garlic, onion, and basil.**

"Food is a source of many natural ingredients that can do anything from curing a headache to stimulating your hormones," explained Ken Hakuta, CEO of AllHerb.com. "Many of the foods we eat everyday affect us in ways we're not even aware of, and with Valentine's Day approaching, we wanted to take a look to find natural ingredients that act as aphrodisiacs"….

Figure 7-2:
Valentine's
Day
aphrodisiacs
press
release.

Make Them Laugh

Don't overlook humor as a source of PR inspiration and ideas. If you can play off something familiar in a fun and different way, you can get people smiling. Many editors and producers look for light material and filler to run between harder news stories, and you can gain a lot of media coverage by providing material for this feature.

As an example, several comedians joked in their routines about removing the "Do Not Remove Under Penalty of Law" tags from furniture. To announce a bedroom furnishing sale for IKEA Home Furnishings, we created a campaign in which we offered a discount to anyone who removed and brought us the "Do Not Remove" tags from their pillows. As an added creative element, the tags became entry tickets to a sweepstakes, the grand prize for which was a trip to Alcatraz. The campaign received extensive media exposure nationwide.

Keep in mind that humor is often an effective way to make a serious point. In a campaign for Empire Kosher Chicken, for example, the objective was to communicate how carefully the company inspects its chickens. In the campaign, people who sent in proof that they were being audited by the IRS got a free chicken. We said that if you get audited by the IRS — an excruciating process for most consumers — you have some idea of how Empire's chickens feel after they are inspected! The campaign got wide media play, and even *The Wall Street Journal* ran a feature on it.

Wage a Trade-in Campaign

As Chapter 15 outlines more fully, trade-ins — while clearly a gimmick — can catch the media's attention if you do them in a clever way.

For British Knight Sneakers, for example, the objective was to promote its shoes to the youth market. We created a special promotion to encourage kids to play outdoors rather than watch television. If the parents sent in a TV remote control (which we actually returned, so they lost nothing), the child would get a pair of free sneakers. In another campaign for British Knight, we had consumers trade in smelly socks for new sneakers.

To promote Domino's Pizza as comfort food, we offered a free pizza to anyone who turned in a pink slip (termination notice) or layoff notice from work or a rejection letter from a college. The tie-in with pizza? The creation of "Eat Your Rejection Letter" month. Pizza sales soared the day after Johnny Carson started his monologue with this story on *The Tonight Show.*

Create a Character

Who doesn't know and love Mr. Whipple, Aunt Jemima, Sam Breakstone, Colonel Sanders, Ronald McDonald, or the Dunkin' Donuts "Time to Make the Donuts" guy? Creating characters has proven successful in advertising for decades. Now we're finding that it can work in PR, too.

Empire Kosher Chicken once asked us to stimulate sales during the winter months. We created a character named Bubby and dubbed her "America's Jewish Grandmother." Bubby offered people a chance to treat their colds by trading in their modern cold medicine for a free soup recipe and a free kosher chicken. Thousands of people wrote in to Empire Chicken to take advantage of this offer, putting the chickens (and the attitude of an Empire Chicken being nourishing and even medicinal) in the households of many first-time users.

Part III
Laying the Groundwork

The 5th Wave   By Rich Tennant

HISTORIC PR BLUNDERS

"The Queen says if the people have no bread, let them eat cake that's baked here at the castle and distributed free of charge. That's a little wordy. We need to sound bite it. Let's hear ideas..."

In this part . . .

A large part of PR is creating the variety of documents that deliver your story to your various audiences, including the media, the public, customers, and employees. One of the most versatile of these documents is the company newsletter, and Chapter 8 shows how to produce a newsletter and use it to promote yourself. Chapter 9 shows how to write and format the most commonly used weapon in the PR arsenal, the humble but powerful press release. In Chapter 10, I give you complete instructions for writing and placing articles that promote your business, as well as getting the press to write articles about you or quote you in their pages. But PR isn't all paper; sometimes you've got to get on the phone or even dress up and go out of the office to sell your story to the media. Chapter 11 deals with delivering your message to the press in person.

Chapter 8

Creating a Company Newsletter

· ·

· ·

*W*hen Charles Dickens completed a new chapter of a book (in the 19th century, the chapters were sometimes printed as separate booklets and sold as a series), people crowded around the docks and held their arms out as boxes of booklets were lowered from the ship.

In today's society, however, most books are published with much less fanfare, and most people are drowning in all sorts of information, ranging from books to online content to newsletters. For example, more than 50,000 new books are written and published each year. Therefore, with so much written material competing for your audience's attention, every communication naturally has less impact on your audience than it would have had years ago when there was less competition, and it's more difficult than ever to break through the clutter and gain attention. This information overload means that your PR message is vying for attention against magazines, newspapers, Web sites, television shows, movies, software, and video games. A targeted PR placement, while effective, is still a one-shot communication, so your article or PR placement gets noticed less than it may have in Dickens's time and has less impact.

However, there is one marketing communications tool that you can use to assure regular, repeat, consistent exposure to your company name, message, and information: the promotional newsletter, also called the company newsletter or house organ.

For some companies, a single publication serves as both their internal (employee) magazine as well as their external (customer) publication. However, in this chapter, when we say "promotional newsletter," "company newsletter," or "house organ," we mean a corporate publication sent to customers and prospects to promote the firm and its products.

These newsletters, magazines, tabloids, or other regular publications are published primarily as marketing tools. They range from simple sheets published in-house to elaborate, four-color company magazines with photography and professional writing rivaling the quality of newsstand magazines.

Even a regular, frequent *program* of public relations, as described throughout this book, cannot guarantee consistent exposure of the target audience to your key messages. There are several reasons for this: not every effort is certain to yield equal results, you cannot control the exact timing and placement of PR pickups, and the media outlets are widely dispersed and read by different people, so not every prospect will see every pickup.

In today's age of specialized information, newsletters are popular. Sources estimate that more than 10,000 newsletters are published in the United States. About a fifth of them are subscription newsletters, sold for profit by entrepreneurs for whom the newsletter is their primary source of income.

Staying in Touch with Your Audience

The main purpose of a promotional newsletter is to establish your image and build your credibility with a select audience (the people who receive the newsletter) over an extended period of time.

Instinctively, most marketers recognize that they should be in touch with their customers and prospects far more often than they actually are. You know, for instance, that you may not think about, see, or talk to certain people in your life for long periods of time simply because you're busy and not thinking of them.

Your customers and prospects are busy, too. And although you may be agonizing over why Joe hasn't placed an order from you recently or called your firm to handle a project, Joe isn't even thinking about you because he has so much else on his mind.

You know that you should be doing something to keep your name in front of Joe and remind him of your existence. But how? You may want to call or send a letter, but you think doing so is too pushy. And besides, you don't have a real *reason* to call, and you don't want to seem begging for business.

The newsletter solves this problem. It regularly places your name and activities in front of your customers and prospects, reminding them of your existence, products, and services on a regular basis. And you need no excuse to make this contact, because the prospect *expects* to receive a newsletter on a regular basis. The newsletter increases the frequency of message repetition and supplements other forms of communication such as catalogs, print ads, and sales letters.

Deciding on Size and Frequency

How long should your newsletter be? How often should it be published?

In my opinion, four to eight pages is the ideal length for a promotional newsletter. More than that is too much reading, and two pages seems insubstantial — more like a flier or circular (which is perceived as junk mail) than a newsletter (which is perceived as a useful publication).

As for frequency, four times a year — once every three months — is ideal. Publish fewer issues, and people aren't aware you're sending them a newsletter per se; they perceive that they're just getting a piece of mail from time to time. Four times per year is enough to establish credibility and awareness. Publishing six times or more per year is unnecessary, because some months you may prefer to make contact with your prospects by using other media, such as the telephone or direct mail or catalogs.

What's more, my experience indicates that most companies don't have enough news to fill six or more issues each year. If your schedule is too frequent, you may find yourself putting unnecessary fluff and filler in the newsletter just to get something in the mail. Your readers will be turned off by the poor content and lack of quality, eventually hurting rather than helping you.

Creating a Mailing List

Basically, your company newsletter should go to anyone with whom you want to establish a regular relationship. These people can include the following:

- Current customers
- Past customers
- Current prospects
- Past prospects
- Expired accounts (past subscribers, "expires," and so on)
- Employees
- Vendors
- Colleagues
- Consultants, gurus, and other prominent members of your industry
- Referral sources (influential people who can refer business to you)
- Trade publication editors, business columnists, and other members of the press who might use material in your newsletter in their own writings

All your current customers should receive your newsletter. The newsletter is an important vehicle for keeping in touch on a regular and predictable basis. It confers automatic high visibility and does so in the best possible way: by reflecting you as a knowledgeable and competent professional. This not only builds your image but also helps to ensure that current customers will remain responsive to your recommendations.

Also send the newsletter to customers who use your services or products in a very limited manner and to those whom you have not visited with recently. You may not think of them as current customers, but, of course, they are. What's more, the newsletter offers the kind of visibility that prompts many marginal customers to expand their use of your products and services instead of drifting away from you.

Here are some ways to build your subscriber list:

✔ Include all current and past prospects and customers on the list. But don't use names that are too old. For example, include past prospects and customers that are no more than two or three years old.

✔ Add all the names of the people your company's salespeople call on regularly. Salespeople have their own favorite prospects who may not be in the corporate database. Ask your salespeople to give you these names. You essentially want to convert the dozens of individual Rolodex files kept by various salespeople and sales reps into a single, integrated subscriber list for your newsletter.

✔ Add the people on your media list.

✔ Automatically add all new inquiries and new customers to your subscription list. Include every response and every sales lead generated by your ads, direct mail, and other lead-generation programs.

✔ For trade shows, create a subscription application form and offer a free one-year subscription to anyone who stops by your booth and completes the form.

✔ Don't forget to include the names of your immediate supervisors, your product and brand managers, your sales and marketing managers, your CEO, and any other key personnel whose support you need to run an effective PR effort. Company managers enjoy getting the newsletter and often offer ideas for articles and stories you can use.

Using the Company Newsletter as a Marketing Tool

You can do several things to promote your newsletter (and to use the newsletter offer as a promotion).

Consider offering the newsletter as an extra incentive to people who respond to your direct mail. You can do something as simple as adding a line to the business reply cards that you include with your mailings with a box that says, "Check here if you would like a free one-year subscription to our quarterly newsletter." You can also emphasize the newsletter offer in the P.S. of your sales letter.

You can offer the newsletter as an extra incentive for responding to your company's print advertising campaign, especially if you use print ads to generate sales leads. You can generate inquiries from ads by including a coupon the reader can fill out and return to request a free catalog or product brochure. You can get more coupons returned by adding another check-off box to the response coupon that says, "Check here for a free one-year subscription to our newsletter." While a brochure or catalog sounds purely promotional, people perceive newsletters as valuable information. So offering a subscription to your company newsletter will get more people to respond to your ads.

 At speeches, seminars, and presentations, your company representatives can use the newsletter offer to get listeners involved in conversations with them, which in turn can help turn listeners who are qualified prospects into sales leads. Ask your company's presenters to say something like this at the end of their talks: "Our quarterly newsletter will give you more information on this topic. Just give me your business card, and I'll see to it that you get a free one-year subscription." This way, the presenter collects many more business cards for follow-up than she might otherwise receive.

 Here's another marketing technique: Rent a list of names and send them two or three free issues of your newsletter. With the third or fourth issue, send a cover letter that says, "We hope you find our newsletter informative and helpful, and we would be happy to continue sending it at no cost. To continue your free subscription, just complete and mail the enclosed reply card." Then continue sending the newsletter only to those who return the reply card, eliminating the cost of continually renting names.

Finally, try sending out a press release offering a free sample copy of the newsletter to people in your industry.

Designing Your Company Newsletter

You want your newsletter to stand apart and be easily recognized by those who receive it. But newsletters don't have to be elaborate to get readers' attention. The design, however, should be attractive, easy to read, and consistent from issue to issue in order to build recognition and awareness. After a time, many recipients will come to welcome your newsletter, even seek it out from among the pile of mail in their in-basket. But you'll get that result only if the newsletter has a distinctive, recognizable, and consistent design.

Although many paid subscription newsletters are simply pages of typewritten text, a more graphically pleasing design that uses some color and artwork will enhance your image and make your newsletter stand out from the rest. Desktop publishing software programs such as PageMaker and QuarkXPress make today's newsletter production easier and faster.

You'll need to make several decisions as you begin the design process. Do you want a two- or three-column layout? Do you want rules (lines) between the stories? Do you plan to use white or colored paper stock? Are you going to use one or two colors of ink? What font (type style) is appropriate for your audience? What size will your headings be? Another important design element that you need to develop is the nameplate highlighting the name of the publication. In some cases, you may want to use the services of a graphic designer or artist to help you with some of these design issues.

You need to determine the look, content, and feel of your newsletter long before you even publish the first issue. In addition to the basic format, you also need to decide approximate length of copy, the type of graphic elements (photos, line drawings, graphs, and so on) needed, the technical depth of the content, and the types of articles to be featured.

For instance, you may decide that each issue will contain two feature articles, one biographical profile, a regular question-and-answer column on technical issues, one product-related story, three or four short news tidbits, and a box with short previews of the next issue. Your newsletter may be different, of course, but the point is, you'll eventually find a formula that works and stick with it from issue to issue.

Readers like this consistency of format because they know what to look for in each issue. For example, when people open the Sunday newspaper, some readers turn to the sports section first; others go to the comics; still others read "Dear Abby" first. In the same way, some readers may check your technical tips column first, while others will read the profile. Make these features look and read the same in each issue (even position them in the same spot) so that readers gain a comfortable familiarity with your publication.

Putting your newsletter together

After you have a newsletter design, putting each issue together is not terribly difficult.

Don't reinvent the newsletter wheel

The material in your promotional newsletter doesn't have to be original, nor must it be created solely for the newsletter. In fact, a company newsletter is an ideal medium for recycling other promotional and publicity material created by your company, such as speeches, articles, press releases, annual reports, presentations, and so on. Try to get maximum use out of material you've already created while minimizing the time and expense of writing and producing the newsletter.

The first step is to make a list of any possible story ideas. (See the sidebar "Newsletter story ideas," later in this chapter.) Then narrow down the list to only the ones to be featured in the next issue. If you're unsure about how much room you'll have, it's better to select one or two extra ideas than too few. You can always use the extra material in a future edition.

Create a file folder for each article and collect the information that will serve as background material for the person writing the story. This background material typically includes sales brochures (for product stories), press releases (which are edited into short news stories), and reprints of published trade journal articles on a particular topic (which are often combined and compiled into a new article on a similar topic).

The next step is to write each story based on this material. Many businesses hire freelance writers to write and edit their company newsletters. Others do it themselves. A few hire their PR or ad agency to do it. Using freelancers is usually more cost-effective. Besides, although most freelancers relish such assignments, most ad agencies don't like doing company newsletters because they find them unprofitable.

Some articles may require more information than is contained in the background material. In this case, supply the writer with the names and phone numbers of people within your company whom he can interview to gather the additional information. Notify these people in advance that a freelance writer will be calling to interview them for the newsletter. If they object, find substitutes.

Once you get the copy, the next step is to edit it, send it through for review, and make any final changes. The shorter the review cycle, the better. An article on a new product, for instance, should go to the product manager, an engineer, and maybe the company president for comment. But don't give it to ten people for review; too many cooks spoil the broth.

Then give the final copy to your graphic artist or printer, who will create a layout. Carefully proofread and review this before it is printed. Many companies today use desktop publishing systems in-house or hire outside desktop publishing services for newsletter layout and creation.

Once the copy is approved, make any final changes and send the revised layout to the printer. Find out whether your printer prefers to work with hard copy originals or computer files and what resolution is required.

If your subscriber list is small, say, only a few hundred names, you can have your computer generate gummed mailing labels and affix them on the newsletters in-house. After you have a thousand or more subscribers, you may want to use a letter shop, fulfillment house, or similar mailing service to handle the mailing and distribution on a regular basis. Get an estimate from an outside service. Then compare this estimate against the time it takes to do it yourself in-house. This comparison will give you an idea of whether it makes sense to outsource newsletter circulation.

Checking out a sample newsletter

My own company newsletter has been pretty successful in getting our PR firm lots of new clients. To see a sample issue, look at file CD0801 on the CD in this book.

Newsletter story ideas

Stuck for ideas for your newsletter? Use this checklist for inspiration:

Product stories: New products; improvements to existing products; new models; new accessories; new options; and new applications.

News: Joint ventures; mergers and acquisitions; new divisions formed; new departments; industry news; and analyses of events and trends.

Tips: Tips on product selection, installation, maintenance, repair, and troubleshooting.

How-to articles: Similar to tips, but with more detailed instructions. Examples: How to use the product; how to design a system; how to select the right type or model.

Previews and reports: Articles about special events such as trade shows, conferences, sales meetings, seminars, presentations, and press conferences.

Case histories: Product applications, customer success stories, or examples of outstanding service or support. These can be in-depth or brief.

People: Company promotions, new hires, transfers, awards, anniversaries, employee profiles, human interest stories (unusual jobs, hobbies, and so on).

Milestones: Events such as "1,000th unit shipped," "sales reach $1 million mark," "division celebrates 10th anniversary," and so on.

Sales news: New customers; bids accepted; contracts renewed; satisfied customer reports.

Research and development: New products; new technologies; new patents; technology awards; inventions; innovations; and breakthroughs.

Publications: New brochures available; new ad campaigns; technical papers presented; reprints available; new or updated manuals; announcements of other recently published literature or audiovisual materials.

Explanatory articles: How a product works; industry overviews; background information on applications and technologies.

Customer stories: Interviews with customers; photos; customer news and profiles; guest articles by customers about their industries, applications, and positive experiences with the vendor's product or service.

Financial news: Quarterly and annual report highlights; presentations to financial analysts; earnings and dividend news; reported sales and profits.

Photos with captions: People, facilities, products, events.

Columns: President's letter; letters to the editor; guest columns; regular features such as "Q&A" or "Tech Talk."

Excerpts, reprints, or condensed versions: Press releases; executive speeches; journal articles; technical papers; company seminars; and so on.

Quality control stories: Quality circles; employee suggestion programs; new quality assurance methods; success rates; case histories.

Productivity stories: New programs; methods and systems to cut waste and boost efficiency.

Manufacturing stories: SPC/SQC (statistical process control/statistical quality control) stories; CIM (computer integrated manufacturing) stories; new techniques; new equipment; raw materials; production line successes; detailed explanations of manufacturing processes.

Community affairs: Fund-raisers; special events; support for the arts; scholarship programs; social responsibility programs; environmental programs; employee and corporate participation in local, regional, and national events.

Data processing stories: New computer hardware and software systems; improved data processing and its benefits to customers; new data procession applications; explanations of how systems serve customers.

Overseas activities: Reports on the company's international activities; profiles of facilities, subsidiaries, branches, people, and markets.

Service: Background on company service facilities; case histories of outstanding service activities; new services for customers; customer support hotlines.

History: Articles about the history of the company, industry, product, or community.

Human resources: Company benefit programs; announcement of new benefits and training and how they improve service to customers; explanations of company policies.

Interviews: Q&A with company key employees, engineers, service personnel, and so on; with customers; with suppliers (to illustrate the quality of materials going into your company's products).

Forums: Top managers answer customer complaints and concerns; service managers discuss customer needs; customers share their favorable experiences with company products and services.

Gimmicks: Contents; quizzes; trivia; puzzles; games; cartoons; recipes; computer programs.

Chapter 9

Putting Your Message on Paper: The Press Release

*W*hat you say and how you say it can greatly influence the media and your audiences. Revolutions have been started with nothing more than a quill and parchment. Even today, a few postings on the Internet can cause a stock's price to plummet or even take a nosedive in the entire market. Similarly, you can sometimes do more to build awareness with a single simple press release than a million-dollar ad campaign.

If you can write English, you can write PR materials — as long as you follow a few simple rules of style and the accepted formats, examples of which abound throughout this book. In this chapter, you find out how to write press releases, media kits, and other printed PR materials. If you want to know how to write for the Web, see Chapter 16.

How to Write a Press Release That Gets Picked Up by Media

The typical press release is a one- or two-page, typed document of news or information about a company and its activities. The *Dictionary of Advertising Terms* (Crain Communications, Inc.) defines a press release as "a document of informational material on a recent or current event, as within a business organization, distributed to broadcast stations, newspapers, and magazines for public relations purposes."

A press release is a mini-article that you prepare and send to the media for their use. The parts of a press release include the following:

- ✔ **Contact information:** Company name, name of individual the editor should contact for more information, and the phone number of that person.

- ✔ **Release date:** A specific date the information can be released. If timing is not critical, just type the words "For Immediate Release."

- ✔ **Headline:** Designed to get the editor's attention and get him to start reading.

- ✔ **Body:** What you want the media to know about your product or service.

- ✔ **Response information:** How the reader can get in touch with you for more information on your product or service.

PR firms sometimes include a *tip sheet* with the press release. A tip sheet, typed on a separate sheet of paper, highlights extra information that may catch an editor's eye.

Because the press release is not an exclusive, you can send the same press release to hundreds of publications and stations. (Wondering what an "exclusive" is? Head over to Chapter 10.) I've had a single press release picked up by dozens of publications and generate thousands of inquiries. No marketing method is more cost-effective than the humble press release for getting your message out to a wide audience.

Preparing a press release is simple and straightforward. Just type your copy double-spaced on regular letter-size (8½-x-11-inch) sheets of paper.

Press releases can be duplicated at a local quick-print shop, or you can run off copies on your office copier if the quality of reproduction is good. You can print the press releases on plain paper, business stationery, or special PR letterhead with the words "NEWS RELEASE" or "PRESS RELEASE" printed across the top; however, special paper isn't necessary, and plain paper is fine.

At the top

Follow the format of the samples presented in this chapter. At the top of the first page, put "FROM:" or "SOURCE:" followed by the name and address of your company. Underneath this, type "CONTACT:" followed by your name and telephone number.

If you use a public relations agency, it will list its own name and address (under "FROM:" or "CONTACT:") followed by the name and address of the client (which is you).

Below the contact address, type "For immediate release." This tells editors that your story is timely, but it doesn't date the release. That way, you can keep a supply on hand and send them out to editors as the opportunity arises. If the release is tied to an event that takes place on a specific date, type "For release: Monday, August 22, 2002" (substituting the actual date) rather than "For immediate release." You also put a date on the release if it contains breaking news or other timely or dated information. Underneath this comes the headline and then the story. (See the section called "The headline act and the lead role" in this chapter for information on writing headlines.)

The headline act and the lead role

The *headline* and the *lead* (first paragraph) of your press release need to grab an editor's attention. After all, you may be competing with hundreds of other press releases that cross an editor's desk. You certainly don't want yours ending up in the "circular file"!

The best press release headlines summarize the unique nature of the story and gain the editor's eye without being blatantly promotional. Inject news into the headline whenever possible. Type the headline in boldface; it can be as short as one line or as long as three lines.

Leave some extra space between the headline and the first paragraph of the story. The first paragraph can begin with a dateline, such as "New York, NY, October 2000 —" with the first sentence of the first paragraph coming immediately after that dash. The city and state given in the dateline are usually the city and state where your company is headquartered.

Press releases use one of two basic types of leads:

✔ **News leads:** The news lead is the prototypical "who, what, when, where, why, and how" opening of a straight news story as taught in Journalism 101. The advantage of using the news lead is that, even if the editor chops the rest of your story and prints only the first paragraph — as is frequently done — the gist of your story still gets across. The sample press release for Plato Software (see Chapter 15) is an example of a straight news lead:

"Kingston, NY — PLATO Software recently released an upgraded version of its modifiable business and accounting software package, P&L-Pro Version 6.0.

"What makes P&L-Pro unique is that it's the only affordably priced accounting software that can be modified by the user with no programming required, claims Richard Rosen, president, PLATO Software."

To see more examples of news leads, pick up any major daily newspaper and study the first paragraphs of the stories running on page 1.

✔ **Feature leads:** The feature lead is written in an entertaining, attention-getting fashion similar to the opening of a magazine feature article. The purpose is to grab the editor's attention by being clever, startling, or dramatic, so that more editors read and use your release.

Figure 9-1 shows a good example of a feature lead. To see more examples of feature leads, pick up any issue of *Glamour* or *Cosmopolitan* magazine and read the first paragraph of each of the major articles listed on the content page.

Body building

After the lead comes the *body,* or text, of the story. If you are coming to the end of the page and it looks as if the paragraph will have to continue onto the next page, move the entire paragraph to that page. Don't divide paragraphs between two pages.

Why not? Some editors may want literally to cut up your release into paragraphs with scissors, then tape it together in a different order. (This is how some editors edit.) For the same reason, releases are always printed on one side of a sheet of paper, never on two sides.

You may say at this point, "But I don't want the editor to edit my story. I want it to run as is!" This is an understandable attitude, but it is self-defeating. In public relations, the editor is in clear control and is the "customer" for your stories, and you must meet the editor's needs and standards first if you are to have any chance of reaching your final audience — readers.

If editors want to edit, make it easy for them, not difficult. If they want a new angle on your story, don't protest — help them find it. The more you cooperate with editors and give them what they need, the more publicity you will get.

The last paragraph of your press release contains the response information, including name, address, and telephone number. For example, "To get Smith Widget Company's new 32-page Widget catalog, contact: Smith Widget Company, Anytown, USA, XXX XXX-XXXX."

Including response information for the consumer is critical. If you don't write it into the release, the editor may leave it out of the story, dramatically decreasing inquiries generated as a result of the media placement.

To let editors know that they've reached the end of your story, simply type "END" or "XXX" or "-30-".

For Immediate Release

CONTACT: Kathy Bell
Jericho Communications
212/645-6900 x117

Worried About Paying For Your Child's College Education? You Could Start A Trust Fund, Get A Part-Time Job ...Or Shop For Car Insurance

"Insure Our Future" Provides A Way To Start Your Child's College Fund

Mayfield Village, OH, January 24, 2000 -- For many parents, the thought of funding their child's college education occurs as early as the time of birth, sometimes even the moment of conception. If you think you can't possibly save enough to fund your children's college education, think again. The money could be right in front of you -- in the form of your auto insurance premium.

Progressive Insurance has announced a program, "Insure Our Future," designed to help consumers better understand the savings available to them if they only shopped around for their auto insurance. The fact is, rates vary widely. The potential savings are enough to significantly contribute to a child's education. **Details of the program can be found on progressive.com.**

Progressive's research shows that the average difference between the highest and lowest auto insurance premium available to the same consumer from different companies is $522 every six months...Most consumers don't understand that they may be leaving money on the table by not shopping around for auto insurance.

If a person shopped for auto insurance and realized savings equal to the average variance every six months and put this 'found money' ($522) into an interest-bearing account (averaging 6 percent interest compounded annually), in 18 years, the savings on auto insurance would accrue to more than $34,000 (without considering taxes). This could be a big step toward paying for the college education for the more than 15 million American children under the age of three.

Figure 9-1:
Press release with feature-style lead.

Putting News in Your News Releases

Editors get hundreds of press releases weekly, all typed in the correct format, and they throw out 99 percent of them. A professionally prepared release is important — the editor probably won't read one that is handwritten on a scrap of grocery bag — but *content* is what makes your release the one in a hundred that actually gets read and used.

The following factors can help your release stand out from the crowd and actually make it into the publication or program:

- ✔ **Make sure that the subject of your release is important to the publication's readers.** If you were the editor and you had dozens of releases but could publish only a few, would you select your own release? Are the information and story in your release really important — not to your business, but to the publication's readers? If not, forget it and look for a new angle.

- ✔ **Make sure that your release is really news and not just an advertisement in disguise.** Editors aren't in the business of publishing advertising. Almost all will immediately discard publicity that is really advertising in disguise. Of course, most publicity has some advertising value or purpose, but write your publicity to give news or helpful information only.

- ✔ **Write your release so that the publication's readers benefit from it.** Your publicity will get published more often if it contains important news that will benefit the publication's readers. This could be new technology the readers will be interested in, helpful information, or a new trend that is emerging.

- ✔ **Keep it short and to the point.** Editorial space is very limited, and busy editors don't have the time to sort through irrelevant copy and cut it down to the main points. Write clear and crisp sentences using only the important, relevant information. Tighten the writing. Keep paragraphs and sentences concise. Avoid jargon and repetition. Use strong verbs. Create lively, but accurate, text.

- ✔ **Include what the editor wants in your press release.** That is, does it have facts to back up your statements? Include who, what, when, where, how, and why details.

- ✔ **Use subheads in longer stories, at least one per page.** A *subhead* is a smaller head that divides documents into sections, as do the smaller subheads throughout this book. Subheads in a press release help the editor grasp the entire story at a glance.

- ✔ **Consider adding a tip sheet for details that would otherwise clutter your release.** *Example:* A new restaurant, when sending out a press release announcing its grand opening, included a separate tip sheet listing five specialty dishes along with the ingredients and recipes.

✔ **Make the release stand on its own.** Don't include a cover letter. If you feel a cover letter is needed to explain why are you sending the release or why an editor should be interested in using it, then your press release isn't strong enough. Go back and rewrite until it is irresistible to editors.

✔ **Get all the facts and establish perspective before starting to write.** Adding and rewriting later costs time and money.

✔ **Keep the news up front, not behind the interpretation or buried in paragraphs of analysis.**

✔ **Cut out puffery; stick to newsworthy information.**

✔ **Put opinion and interpretation in an executive's quotation.** Example: "Within a decade, file transfer between different computer platforms will be seamless and device-independent," says Bill Blathers, CEO, MicroExchange Software.

Operating under pressure to be objective and neutral in reporting, editors won't run subjective opinion statements unless they can attribute such statements to a source. To solve this problem and get editors to run all your material, put controversial statements and claims in quotations and attribute them to an executive from your organization.

For example, if you write in a press release, "AML is currently the only logistics company specializing in the shipment of medical products and materials," the editor may say, "To print this statement, I have to check every business directory in the country to make sure that indeed there is no other firm offering such a shipping service." If she didn't, and in fact there were other firms providing the medical shipping service, she'd be printing inaccurate information. Because the editor cannot conclusively prove through research that AML indeed has no competitors, her most likely move would be not to print the statement.

But when we phrase the same information as an attributed statement, for example, "As far as we know, AML is the only logistics company currently specializing in the shipment of medical products and materials," says Norman Freeman, company president, the editor will readily print it, because she is on safe ground. By printing it as an attributed quotation, she is not claiming that AML is in fact offering a one-of-a-kind service. She is merely reporting that the company president claims his service is one-of-a-kind — and the fact that Mr. Freeman has made such a claim is beyond dispute, because it's right there in his press release.

✔ **Use straightforward headlines.** Forget the cute headline that forces an editor to dig through a paragraph or two to discover the who, what, when, where, and why. The headline should summarize the release so that an editor quickly understands your point.

✔ **Leave plenty of white space (blank space).** Doing so is especially important at the top of page 1 because editors like room to edit. Double space and leave wide margins. Never use the back of a page.

✔ **Write for a specific editorial department: news, lifestyles, real estate, financial, new products.** Similarly, provide separate story slants (in separate releases) for different categories of magazines. To publicize a directory of free information, for example, press releases could highlight the free information resources of interest to different editors. A press release featuring free information on gardening, real estate, and do-it-yourself tips could be aimed at home magazines. A different release featuring free information on starting your own business could target business editors.

✔ **Create separate, shorter releases for radio and, at minimum, color slides and scripts for television.**

✔ **End releases with a boilerplate paragraph that explains the organization or division.** Many press releases include, before the closing paragraph containing the response information, a standard description of the company and its products. This information is helpful for editors who are unfamiliar with you or want to give their readers a little more description of who you are and what you do.

✔ **Consider editing the news release copy for product bulletins, internal publications, and other uses.**

✔ **Write to gain respect for your organization and your next release.** Be accurate and honest. Present clear and useful organization. Deliver value to the reader. Avoid hype and blatant self-promotion.

✔ **Streamline the clearance process so that only two or three executives approve each release.** Doing so saves time and minimizes the chance to muddy the text.

Getting copy approved faster

Send press releases and other PR copy requiring review within your company only to those executives who absolutely must sign off before the release is distributed. Attach a note explaining that their comments are needed and specify the date by which they must respond. As for others on the routing list, attach a note explaining that they are being copied for their information only and no reply is required.

Never lie to the media, ever

Should you put falsehoods, exaggerations, or puffery in your press materials simply because you can get away with it? No. Your materials should be accurate and newsworthy, giving real information, not advertising puffery.

The reason? Aside from the fact that it's bad business to lie to your prospects, customers, and the public, lying to editors is worse. If you trick them into printing something inaccurate, and a reader points it out to them, they'll be displeased with you, and they won't use you as an information source again, because they don't trust you. So you will get no further publicity as long as those editors are working at those publications.

Chapter 10

Writing and Placing Feature Articles

*P*lacing feature articles with appropriate trade, consumer, or business publications is one of the most powerful and effective of all marketing techniques.

Unlike a news article, which gives a straightforward report of recent events, a feature article is a longer piece that explores its subject more in-depth. Feature articles often present a detailed case study, explanation of technology, or guidance on how to do something, whether it's how to write a business plan or pick a telephone carrier.

Many people naturally assume the feature articles they read are written by freelance writers or reporters employed by the newspaper or magazine. Wrong! Every day, thousands of articles appear that have been written by nonwriters — PR professionals, self-employed professionals, business executives, and technical specialists — as a means to promote themselves, their business, or their products or services.

How does it work? A company seeking publicity and exposure submits an article in hopes that a publication will spotlight or feature the company, its ideas, or products or services. A "planted," or "placed," feature story is an article written and submitted to a publication by a corporation, entrepreneur, or business professional — either directly by the business or on its behalf by its PR firm or consultant.

Mum's the word

Although as a businessperson you are writing an article for self-serving promotional objectives, and editors know it, keep it to yourself. Editors are interested in serving their readers, not you. Keep the self-promotion in your article to a minimum — for instance, don't mention your company name 50 times — and give the editor an article that will be of real value to her readers. That serves your purpose, too, because the more useful the article, the more readers will contact the author for additional information — which can often lead to purchase of your products.

In this chapter, we explore two time-tested methods of getting feature articles written about your company or service: proposing and writing the article yourself, and sending a "pitch" letter to editors to encourage them to write their own article about you.

You can get one, two, or more pages devoted to your product or service without paying for the space. (A paid advertisement of that length could run $3,000 to $20,000 or more.) Your message has far more credibility as "editorial" material than as a sponsored advertisement. The publication of the article results in prestige for the author and recognition for the company. And reprints make excellent, low-cost sales literature.

Just one article in a magazine can generate hundreds of leads and thousands of dollars in sales for a company. And with more than 6,000 magazines and trade journals from which to choose, you can safely bet that at least one is interested in a story from your company.

Getting an article published in a trade journal or local business magazine isn't difficult — if you know how. Trade-journal editors are quick to reject inferior material or "puff" pieces, but they are hungry for good, solid news and information to offer their readers. And, unlike newspaper reporters who are investigative and frequently antagonistic and adversarial toward businesses, trade-journal reporters are a friendlier audience and are more willing to work with you to get information to their readers.

Avoid Beginners' Mistakes

Common mistakes that novices make when writing and placing articles include the following:

✔ **Not querying the publication** first to find out whether it has an interest in running an article on the topic you propose.

✔ **Mailing to "Dear Editor"** instead of finding out the name of the editor and addressing your communications directly to him.

✔ **Offering the editor a bribe** to run the article ("We'll buy a big ad if you run our article") or making a threat ("We won't buy ad space unless you run our article").

✔ **Handing in a sloppy, incomplete article** and saying, "I'm not a writer; here's the information; you fix the grammar and make it read right." (The editor does not have time to do your work and expects articles that are well-written and edited.)

✔ **Not being able to submit your article as a computer file** in Word, WordPerfect, text, or another common format.

✔ **Missing the deadline after you got the go-ahead** to write an article for submission. Even worse is missing the deadline and not notifying the editor that the manuscript will be late.

✔ **Not reading the magazine and being totally unfamiliar** with its reader-ship, style, content, and editorial requirements.

Coming Up with Ideas for Articles

Your chances of getting your article published increase dramatically when you offer editors an article of the type they regularly publish. For instance, don't send an article of recipes to a magazine that doesn't run recipes.

A handful of standard article types account for 90 percent of the articles published today. These include the following:

✔ **Case history:** Product success stories. They focus on a company that had a problem and how they used a particular product, service, or method to solve the problem.

✔ **How-to:** Instructional advice ("How to size lighting for industrial facilities").

✔ **New products:** Explains how a new technology works ("New mounted chip technology doubles processing speed").

✔ **Developments and trends:** Analysis to help business readers plan their strategy ("Plastics industry moves to global supply chain business model").

The *case history* or *application story* is one of the most popular types of articles that trade and business magazines publish. This type of story tells how a specific company solved a problem or addressed a need, and usually highlights the product or service the company used to solve its problem. The PR depart-ment of the company whose product or service was used to solve the prob-lem sends a "query letter" (see the section "Writing a Query Letter," later in this chapter) suggesting case histories to editors. Getting case histories published is an effective marketing tool because it shows readers how to apply your product and demonstrates its proven success.

Aside from case histories, most planted feature articles are of the how-to variety, aimed at executives, managers, professionals, or technicians in a given field. Editors are also interested in stories on new products, developments, or trends in their industry.

One way to come up with article ideas is to make a list of the ads you would run (and the magazines in which you would run them) if you had an unlimited ad budget, write articles based on topics related to those ads, and place them in those magazines.

For example, if you wanted to advertise your new wood-chip stacking system in *Pulp & Paper* magazine but didn't have the budget for it, consider writing an article titled, "A New Way to Stack and Inventory Wood Chips More Efficiently" for that magazine. Writing and placing articles in magazines and for secondary markets in which print advertising is unprofitable or beyond your budget is cost-effective.

Many trade journals will send a sample issue and set of editorial guidelines to prospective authors upon request. These guidelines can provide valuable clues as to style, format, and appropriate topics. The guidelines often tell you how to contact the magazine, give hints on writing an article, describe the manuscript review process, and discuss any payment or reprint arrangements.

Tie in with special issues

Companies can increase their chances for coverage by requesting a magazine's editorial calendar and scanning the list of "special issues" to see whether there is a possible tie-in between their products and services and any articles to be featured in these issues. Call the magazine's advertising department, say that you're a potential advertiser, request a free media kit, and ask for an editorial calendar of special issues along with a sample issue. These items will be sent without charge to potential advertisers.

"If people respond to our editorial calendar with ideas for specific issues, great!" says Rick Dunn, editor of *Plant Engineering.* "Or if they can provide background for a story we want to do, they'll have an edge in getting into the magazine."

You may even want to suggest feature story ideas for the next year's calendar. The trick is to do that tactfully. "Don't come across as pushy or demanding," warns Dunn. "Stay away from saying things like 'This is important to your readers' or 'You should run this story.' If someone knows our business better than we do, we'll hire him or we'll go back to school."

However, if you spot a new trend in, say, packaging food in recyclable cardboard containers rather than plastic, and you can provide statistics and information to back up your claim that this trend is important, contact the editors at the appropriate packaging magazine. She will probably appreciate your interest and effort.

The quickest way to turn off editors is to offer an idea that has nothing to do with their magazines. Every magazine is a little different in some way from other magazines. To increase your chances of getting a placement, you must study tone, style, content, and the quality of a journal's writing and graphics.

Offer an editor the type of article that his magazine seems to prefer, and your odds of placing the story increase. If a magazine contains all short articles of one or two pages, don't send a 6,000-word thesis. If it doesn't run case histories, don't propose one.

Study issues of magazines to see which topics they cover. The key to success is not to send an idea for an article on something never covered, but to offer an article that presents a new slant or angle on one of a magazine's frequent topics.

Selecting the Right Magazine

The best magazines to target are the ones you are now getting. This is because you read them, are familiar with their editorial slant and style, and are aware of what articles related to your topic they have run recently. You may not receive or be familiar with many magazines in your industry, however. A good resource you can turn to is *Bacon's* or *Writer's Market* (both listed on the "Media Directories" section of the CD-ROM at the back of the book). Contact each and ask for a sample issue and editorial guidelines. When the sample issue comes, study it and become familiar with the publication.

Here's another way to target magazines for article placement. You probably have a wish list of five to ten publications in which you would love to advertise — if you had the budget. Advertising is an expensive way to get exposure in these magazines, but you can hit all of them affordably through feature article placement. The result: You can get pages of coverage without paying for them!

Writer's Market, although not traditionally used for PR purposes, is in fact especially good for getting a sense of a magazine — its slant, topics, appropriate editors to pitch stories to, and editorial requirements. *Writer's Market* lists more than 4,000 consumer, general, business, and trade publications that accept articles from outside sources. Listings give detailed descriptions of what editors are looking for, along with names, addresses, phone numbers, and other contact information.

Many directories of magazines, editors, and their editorial requirements are designed for PR purposes. These are listed on the CD-ROM that appears at the back of this book.

Timing is important. For a monthly magazine, an article to appear in a special issue should probably be proposed to the editor three to six months in advance of the publication date.

Avoid puffery

Impartiality is a must with many editors. They're not there to praise your company's products.

"We're certainly not prejudiced against articles from PR firms," says Mark Rosenzweig, editor of *Chemical Engineering*. "We just generally have to make more revisions to eliminate their tendency toward one-sidedness. We want all the disadvantages spelled out, as well as the advantages." Adds Rick Dunn: "If an article is about storage methods, we want to see all 15 methods discussed, not just the ones used by the writer's company or client."

Approach editors one at a time — offer an "exclusive"

Many potential home buyers avoid a "cookie cutter" home, and editors are no different when it comes to printing articles. After all, what value does a story add to a publication if its competitor has the same one? Emphasize *exclusivity* by never submitting the same idea or story to more than one competing magazine at a time. Approach another editor only if the first publication rejects your idea. Most editors want exclusive material, especially for feature articles.

If a story is particularly timely or newsworthy and has run in a magazine not directly competing with the one you're approaching, however, you may be able to get around this problem by working with the editor to rewrite the piece. But be up front about it or you'll risk losing the editor's confidence and goodwill.

"I'd like everything to be exclusive," says Russo. "That increases its value to us and can sway us toward acceptance if it's a borderline story."

"Exclusivity is a quality consideration for a feature article," adds Dunn. "Editors don't want their readers to pick up their magazine and see something they've already read elsewhere."

Make the initial contact

Should you call or write the editor? Most editors don't object to either method of pitching an idea, but they usually prefer one or the other. It's simply a matter of personal choice and time constraints.

If you don't know how a particular editor feels on the subject, call and ask. An appropriate opening might be: "This is Joe Jones from XYZ Corporation, and I have a story idea you might be interested in. Do you have time to spend a few minutes over the phone discussing it, or would you prefer that I send you an outline?"

Editors who prefer to get it in writing will tell you so. Editors who prefer a quick description over the phone appreciate your respect for their time, whether they listen to your pitch on the spot or ask you to phone back later.

But even those editors who listen to your idea over the phone also want something in writing. If your idea is on the right track, the editor may request a detailed outline describing the proposed article. Also, some editors may not be able to make an editorial decision until they see the query letter.

At *Modern Materials Handling,* assistant editor Barbara Spencer suggests that writers send in a letter of introduction, followed by a phone call a week or two later. "We look for someone who knows his field and products, and the letter helps us gauge that expertise," she says. "But call the magazine first and find out which editor handles the type of article you have in mind."

All letters should be addressed to a specific editor by name. A letter that begins "Dear Editor" may not reach the right one and also indicates you were too lazy to find out that person's name.

Writing a Query Letter

The best way to communicate an article idea in writing is to send a *query letter.* A query letter is a miniproposal in which you propose to the editor that you write an article on a particular topic for his magazine (and that it be published).

A query letter is, in essence, a sales letter. The "prospect" is the editor. The "product" you want to sell is the article you want to write for the magazine.

Here are a few basic facts about query letters:

  ✔ **Editors look for professionalism in query letters.** This means no typos and no misspellings. You address the letter to a specific editor by name. And you spell her name right.

✔ **Editors look for good writing.** If you can, write the first paragraph or two of your query so it can be used, as is, as the lead for your article. This shows the editor that you know how to begin a piece and get the reader's attention.

✔ **Editors hate lazy writers — those who want to see their byline in a publication but refuse to do research or get their facts straight.** Put a lot of hard "nuts and bolts" information in your letter — facts, figures, statistics — to show that you know your subject. Most query letters (and articles) are too light on content.

✔ **Credentials impress editors.** State why they should trust you to write the article. If you're an expert in the subject, say so. If not, describe your sources. Tell which experts you will interview, which studies you will cite, and which references you will consult. Highlight the breakthrough research your company has done to become a leader in its field.

✔ **Editors hate to take risks.** The more fully developed your idea, the better. If you spell out everything — your topic, your approach, an outline, and your sources — editors know what they will get when they give you the go-ahead to write the piece. The more complete your query, the better your chance for a sale.

✔ **Editors have high standards for article acceptance, no matter who writes the articles.** Don't think you can get away with a poorly written query because "the editor realizes you're not a freelance writer and are just 'trying to get some PR.'" The editor's readers don't expect PR-placed articles to be inferior, less objective, or less interesting than the other material in the magazine, and neither does the editor.

✔ **Never state in your query letter,** *"And best of all, you don't have to pay me for this article, because I'm doing it to publicize my firm."* Even though editors know this, it's a breach of etiquette for you to come out and say it. (Why this is, I have no idea.)

✔ **If you want to increase your chances of acceptance, offer the article to the editor on an exclusive basis.** An *exclusive* means that you won't offer the article to any other publication and she is getting first look at the query. If she accepts, you're assuring her that you're not doing the same or similar articles for any other publication. If she turns you down, you're free, of course, to offer it to the next magazine on your list.

Following are some typical query letters you can refer to for style and format.

In Figure 10-1, note that the article proposal is in two parts: a letter selling the basic idea and an outline listing the details. The author used this format simply because it fit the material; the outline can be separate from the "sales pitch," if you wish, but usually is not.

Ms. Jane Doe, Associate Editor
Chemical Engineering
1234 Main Street
Anytown, USA 12345

Dear Ms. Doe:

When a chemical engineer can't write a coherent report, the true value of his investigation or study may be distorted or unrecognized. His productivity vanishes. And his chances for career advancement diminish.

As an associate editor of *Chemical Engineering,* you know that many chemical engineers could use some help in improving their technical skills. I'd like to provide that help by writing an article that gives your readers "Ten Tips for Better Business Writing." An outline of the article is attached. This 2,000-word piece would provide 10 helpful hints—each less than 200 words—to help chemical engineering write better letters, reports, proposals, and articles.

Tip number 3, for example, instructs writers to be more concise. Too many engineers would write about an "accumulation of particulate matter about the peripheral interior surface of the vessel" when they're describing solids buildup. And how many managers would use the phrase "until such time as" when they simply mean "until"?

My book, *Technical Writing, Structure, Standards, and Style,* will be published by the McGraw-Hill Book Company in November. While the book speaks to a wide range of technical disciplines, my article will draw its examples from the chemical engineering literature….

I'd like to write "Ten Tips for Better Technical Writing" for your "You and Your Job" section. How does this sound? An SASE is enclosed for your reply.

Sincerely,
Bob Bly

Figure 10-1:
This query and outline got an immediate go-ahead to write the article, which was accepted and published.

The first paragraph of the query letter in Figure 10-1 became the lead paragraph of the published article. This is no accident. A catchy lead in the query — one that could logically be used to begin the article — helps grab editors' attention and convince them that you have something interesting.

Figure 10-2 shows a query letter pitching a case history application story. An application story shows the reader how a particular product or system was used in the workplace or home to solve a specific problem. This letter and two follow-up calls gained acceptance from the publication's editor.

SASE, please

The term SASE in the heading stands for "self-addressed stamped envelope" — meaning the envelope is addressed to you, and you have already provided the postage. To communicate with you, the editor can scribble a note on you query letter, pop it in the SASE you have provided, and drop it in the mail. This eliminates the need for the editor to type an envelope and search for a postage stamp. Including a SASE is generally a good idea when writing to editors because doing so makes it easy for them to respond to your letter. Make your SASE look professional — type your name and return address on it or affix a mailing label; don't hand-write the envelope.

Joe Smith, Editor
Engineering Trade Journal
Anytown, USA 12345

Dear Mr. Smith:

Attached is a promotional brochure describing our client XYZ INDUSTRIES' High-Flow Lifting System.

I have sent this to you as initial reference concerning High-Flow use in an industrial situation. The application involves the specialized handling and absolute precision positioning and insertion of TV picture tubes into a console lined with a quick-drying adhesive, thus permitting NO removal or replacement. This custom-designed unit presently operating at an RCA plant in Pennsylvania.

Because of the unique safety, economic features, and functions of the High-Flow System, I believe you might want to treat the above a feature article.

I will call within a few days to ascertain your interest. Please know we will cooperate with you or your staff to develop any editorial detail including up to submission of a complete manuscript.

I look forward to talking with you.

Sincerely,
[signature]

Figure 10-2:
Sample
query letter
for a
product
story.

Also, note that the query letters shown are detailed, not superficial. You may object, "But that's a lot of work to do with no show of interest or commitment from an editor." Yes, it is. But that's what it takes to get published, and there's no way around it.

Figure 10-3 shows a query letter that was successful in getting an editor to request an article on a new product. (A PR firm wrote and sent this letter to place a story about a new product developed by the firm's client.)

Must you query?

Many businesspeople ask me, "Why bother with a query? It seems to slow things down and creates an extra step and more work. Why not just write and send the full article?"

In my opinion, you should always query. Ninety-five percent of editors prefer a query and will not look at a full manuscript they did not request.

Why do editors prefer queries to completed manuscripts? Two reasons. First, time. It takes less time to read a one-page query and make a decision than to read the entire article. Second, the query is a proposal. If the editor wants a different article than is proposed, he can go to the writer and request it. The editor perceives that authors are more willing to change direction in the query stage than they would be if they have already submitted a completed article. So queries give the editor a greater degree of editorial control, enabling them to tailor articles to their readership.

In *The Query Letter Book* (Communication Unlimited), Gordon Burgett, author of more than 1,000 magazine articles, says the reason to query is that it raises odds of acceptance. Burgett says the chances of getting an unsolicited manuscript into print are slim to none, but when you send a manuscript that an editor has asked to see after reading your query letter, the odds of publication increase to 50 percent or higher.

Submitting unsolicited manuscript is an iffy proposition — except for very short news pieces and case histories. Most editors don't want to see an unsolicited manuscript; only a few are willing to review and publish them.

Most editors prefer you to ask about story ideas before you write the article. A query saves them the time it takes to read a lengthy manuscript to determine whether the subject is right for the magazine. Querying also saves you, the publicist, the time and trouble of researching and writing an article that may never get accepted anywhere.

Even if you have already written the article, it's better to condense and summarize it in a query, and send the query first — acting as if you have not yet written the article. You should send the story only when the editor reads the query and says, "Let me see the article."

February 27, 19XX
RE: Article on synthetic cork

Dear Mr. Hiaring:

This is to propose an editorial feature on the subject of a new synthetic cork as it relates to traditional wood bark cork for wine bottles.

Despite the numerous disadvantage of natural corks, consumer associate them with quality wines, both correctly and incorrectly. Correctly because wineries have only resorted to screw cap closures for lower-priced wines, thereby establishing a correlation for the consumer. Incorrectly because wood bark wine cork is responsible for wine taint and leakage, resulting in off-flavor in a minimum of every three bottles per hundred on average.

Rising unit cost and processing costs of wood bark cork have compounded the wineries' problems.

The synthetic cork products are entirely uniform, are manufactured by Lermer Packaging in Southern California, and are the first wine closures to satisfy the needs of the winery and the demands of the consumer virtually without compromise. The enclosed comparison chart outlines all important characteristics of both closures….

We sincerely feel that Cellukork is such a major trade development, it is likely to revolutionize one important aspect of a most traditional industry. As such, we believe that an editorial article on the subject will be of great interest to the vast majority of winery publication readers worldwide.

We would be gratified to have this news appear in your respected publication on an exclusive basis. We would of course be flexible about the article's preparation by providing complete copy and photographs, photographs only, or reference materials to assist your staff.

Because the news and acceptance of Cellukork is spreading more quickly than anticipated, I would greatly appreciate your reply by March 20.

Thank you in advance for your consideration

Sincerely,
[signature]

Figure 10-3:
Another
query letter
for a
product
story.

What about illustrations?

Depending on the publication, you may or may not need to offer photos or drawings to get your article published. Most newspapers and magazines require only text for the article and will design graphics in-house to go with it.

Other magazines do not require, but certainly prefer to get, good photos or illustrations to run with articles. The availability of such material can sometimes be the deciding factor in choosing one story over another. Even though the larger journals have illustrators on staff to produce high-quality finished drawings, they often work from materials supplied by the article contributor.

You can get a good idea of how important visuals are to a particular magazine by scanning a couple issues. Consider the following:

- ✔ Is there no, little, moderate, or heavy use of photos and drawings to accompany articles?

- ✔ If photos are used, are they black-and-white or color?

- ✔ How many visuals appear per magazine page?

Prepare and supply the quantity and quality of visual material the editor desires. Otherwise, your article may have a lesser chance of publication.

Professional photographs, while nice, aren't necessary for most trade journals. Straightforward, good-quality 35-mm color slides are good enough for most trade editors. Some magazines also take black-and-white glossies or color prints. An editor will be happy to tell you what's acceptable.

Today, digital cameras can capture images that are of high enough quality for many publications. You can submit digital images on disk or even e-mail them to the editor.

Follow up your query

One of three things will happen after you mail your query letter:

- ✔ **The editor accepts your article *on spec* (on speculation).** This means the editor is interested and wants to see the completed manuscript but is not making a firm commitment to publish. This response is the most positive one you are likely to get, and unless the article you write is terrible, there is better than a 50 percent chance it will get published.

- ✔ **The editor rejects your query.** The next step is to send the query to the next editor and magazine on your list.

✔ **You don't receive a response either way.** This alternative is the most likely one to happen because

- The editor may not have gotten around to your query.

- She may have read it but has not yet made a decision.

- She didn't receive it, or she lost it.

Your follow-up should be a polite note or phone call asking editors (a) whether they received the article proposal, (b) whether they had a chance to look at it yet, and (c) whether they're interested.

If you send a letter, you can enclose a reply card, as shown in Figure 10-4, that editors can use to check off their response. The reply card should be stamped and self-addressed. It includes a space for you to write the article title, so when it comes back from the editor, you know what article he is responding to.

Figure 10-4:
Optional
reply card to
include with
query letter.

*Article:*_____

*Author:*_____

____YES, we're interested. Please submit manuscript (on spec, of course).

____NOT for us. Sorry.

____MAYBE. We haven't made a decision but will let you know shortly.

____DIDN'T receive your query. Send another copy.

Many professional writers use such reply cards for making it easy for editors to respond. Others don't supply a reply card but enclose a self-addressed stamped envelope (SASE) so that editors can jot replies on their letter and mail it back in the envelope.

If you don't get a reply to your query after four weeks, send a follow-up letter asking whether editors received the original query (copy of which should be enclosed), and whether they are interested. A quick phone call can also be used to prod the editor's memory.

Call again if you don't get a reply to your query after four weeks. You can also send a follow-up letter asking whether editors received the original query (a copy of which should be enclosed) and whether they are interested.

If you don't receive a reply to the follow-up letter, make another phone call. If you don't get through after three or four calls, move on and submit the proposal to the next magazine on your list.

You may be thinking, "If it takes four to six weeks to get an answer from each publication, it may take many months to get my story into print." The answer is to have multiple press releases and query letters in the mail simultaneously. Doing so ensures a steady stream of media pickups and makes the results of any individual query much less critical in terms of your overall PR success.

Build a personal editorial Rolodex. Whenever editors respond to a press release or query or they call to interview someone in your company, put them on your media list to ensure they receive all future news you issue.

Get the Editor's Go-Ahead

An editor is interested. Hurrah! You've passed the first step in getting your article published. Now the real work begins.

After your idea is accepted, you need to know the requirements for story length and deadlines. If the editor doesn't volunteer this information, ask. The answers may prevent misunderstanding later on.

As a rule, be generous with length. Include everything you think is relevant, and don't skimp on example. Editors would rather delete material than request more. But avoid exceeding the promised length by more than 20 percent. Example: If you promised 2,000 words, it's better to send 2,400 words than 1,600 words. Removing 400 words is easier than creating 400 new words to bring it up to length.

Although a few magazines are flexible on length, most editors give authors specific *word lengths* (or *word counts*) to shoot for. To measure word count, you can manually count the words or, if you use Microsoft Word, click "Tools" and then "Word Count." The software will display an exact word count.

Ask how long your article should be. To translate word lengths to typed pages, every 500 words is equivalent to two, double-spaced, typewritten manuscript pages. In its final printed form, a "solid" page of magazine copy (no headlines, photos, or white space) is an average of 800 to 1,000 words for a magazine with a standard 7-by-10-inch page size. The first page, which has to leave room for a headline and byline, is approximately 700 words. By comparison, a double-spaced manuscript page from your PC is approximately 200 words. Therefore, three manuscript pages equal one published page in the magazine.

Table 10-1 can help you translate word length and magazine page length to typed manuscript pages.

Table 10-1	Guide to Article Length	
Number of Words	*Number of Magazine Pages*	*Number of Manuscript Pages*
800–1,000	1	3–4
1,500	2	6
2,000	2–2½	8
2,500	3	10
3,000	3½–4	12

Deadlines also can vary considerably among journals. Some don't like to impose any deadlines at all, especially if they work far enough in advance that they are not pressed for material. But if the article is intended for publication in a special issue, the editor will probably want the finished manuscript at least two months before the publication date. This deadline allows time for revisions, assembling photos or illustrations, and production.

Don't put an editor's patience to the test. Missing a deadline may result in automatic rejection and waste the effort you spent making the placement and writing the article. Hand in every article on the deadline date, or sooner. If you cannot, advise well in advance and request a reasonable extension. Editors dislike late copy, but they hate surprises.

The Best Target for Articles: A Place Where They Know You

The editor most likely to be receptive to your queries is one you have written for successfully in the past. When you sell one article to an editor, it makes sense to fire off a second letter immediately if you have another good idea that might be right for him. Figure 10-5 shows a sample of such a follow-up query.

In a P.S. to the follow-up query (Figure 10-5), Bob gave a thumbnail sketch of his professional background. What was the point of that postscript when the editor had already done business with him? Remember, she had accepted only one previous article and didn't know Bob all that well, so he felt it would be beneficial to remind her of why he was exceptionally well qualified to write this article for her. It couldn't have hurt, because he got the assignment.

Ms. Kimberly A. Welsh, Editor
Circulation Management
859 Willamette Street
Eugene, Oregon 97401-2910

Dear Kimberly:

Thanks for publishing the article on mailing lists so quickly. I hope you get good reader response to it. I'm writing because I have another idea that might be right for *Circulation Management.*

How about an article -- "Do Premiums Work?"

Background: As you know, response rates are down all over. In attempt to combat this, publishers are offering more and more expensive premiums to attack first-time subscribers. *Sports Illustrated*, for example, is offering a videocassette on great sports flubs. *Time* recently offered a camera. And then there's *Newsweek's* successful free telephone offer.

Questions: Is there some point at which a premium ceases to be an added inducement and actually becomes a "bribe," overshadowing the primary offer and becoming the key reason why people respond to a mailing? If so, how does that affect the quality the subscriber-base circulation is delivering to the publication's advertisers?

This would be the basis of my article, which would attempt to answer these specific questions:

Do premiums still work? Are they still profitable? Or is their effectiveness declining as more and more publications jump into premium offer?....

To get the answers to these questions, I will interview circulation directors, advertising managers, direct-response agencies, DM consultant, and freelancers responsible for creating and testing premium-based packages. I see this as a feature article running 3,000 + words.

Kimberly, may I proceed with this article as outlined?
Thanks for your consideration. An SASE is enclosed.

Regards,

Bob Bly

Figure 10-5:
A follow-up
query.

The Other Approach: Writing a Pitch Letter

An alternate method of getting feature story placement is to get stories written *about* you and your product rather than place stories written *by* you.

How do you get the press to write about you? Sending press releases, as described in Chapter 9, is one method. If an editor receives a release to an article he is planning, he may contact you to interview people in your company even if the material in the release isn't exactly what he needs.

Another way to get articles written about you — or at least get your company mentioned in articles — is to send a pitch letter. Unlike the query letter, which proposes that you write a specific article, the *pitch letter* simply offers your company as an expert source for interviewing purposes. Figure 10-6 shows a pitch letter that my PR firm did for one of our clients — the home furnishings company IKEA.

Figure 10-7 shows another sample pitch letter. This time, the lead contains a news angle, based on an industry trend.

Sending pitch letters is effective because editors and reporters are constantly on the lookout for accessible sources of expert information they can call to get a quote or fill in a missing fact for a story when on deadline.

Always follow up the pitch letter. The first follow-up is to confirm receipt and to make clear the availability of the expert to be interviewed on these issues. Then, whenever a big news story breaks that your expert could appropriately speak about or shed some light on, call the journalist again. Remind him of your expert and the link between his expertise and the story the journalist is probably following. If the expert can contribute to a particular aspect of the story or provide new information, say so.

One tactic that pays off is to include a Rolodex card with your query letter that reporters or editors can file under the appropriate category. That way, when a reporter is working on a story on CDs, she turns to her card file, finds Edward Dempsey's name, calls him for a quote, and quotes him in her story. Edward Dempsey, then, and not his competition, becomes known as the industry leader because he is constantly quoted in the press.

I'm sure you've noticed that within your own industry, the same spokespeople are quoted again and again. Well, it's not by accident. Diligent public relations efforts — not fate — ensure that one person or company is publicized while others wallow in obscurity.

Dear Editor:

Anxiety, indecision, intimidation and agony are common feelings that surface whenever you begin the process of decorating your home. Do you tackle a big room in the house — the kitchen — or start with something smaller like reorganizing the closets? What simple home accessories can you use to brighten up the look of your living room? What type of storage do you have to keep your space from looking cluttered?

IKEA has quick and simple decoration solutions to all of these questions that are frequently asked when taking on the daunting task of decorating your home.

Enclosed, please find examples of before and after visuals with easy and affordable tips on how to reorganize a closet as well as redo a kitchen. Also included is an anxiety fact sheet and an IKEA 2000 Catalog.

An IKEA spokesperson is available to demonstrate simple and quick makeover steps for the kitchen, living room, bathroom, closets, and any other room in the home. We will literally create these rooms on your set with "before" and "after" displays that are simple, fun, creative and affordable — and most importantly — will not cause anxiety and fear about decorating a room.

I will follow up with you later this week. In the meantime, if you have any questions or need more information, please feel free to contact me at 212-645-6900 x128.

Regards,

Jeanette Chin

Figure 10-6:
Pitch letter
for IKEA.

Dear Robert:

Compact disc (CD) sales are booming. In fact, some music industry executives are projecting disc sales will surpass album sales by the end of the year:

The first "compact disc only" retail store, Compact Disc Warehouse, in Huntington Beach, California, opened in November, 20XX. It grossed nearly $1 million in sales in just 18 months operating out of a 1,200 square foot store.

Now Compact Disc Warehouse, Inc. is launching the first CD franchise offering to meet the national demand for the hottest home entertainer product in the music industry today.

Edward Dempsey, president of CD Warehouse, is an expert on why CDs are changing an industry that has been dominated by record albums for decades and how the retail world is gearing up to meet the CD demand.

If you would like to arrange an interview, please call our offices.

Sincerely,

Mitch Robinson, Account Executive
S&S Public Relations, Inc.

Figure 10-7:
Another
pitch letter,
based on an
industry
trend.

Chapter 11

Delivering Your Message in Person

*B*ased on Chapters 8, 9, and 10, you may have the impression that PR is only about writing. Not so! Writing is a big part of how you communicate your PR message, but don't discount the spoken word. The more effectively you speak with the press, local government agencies, regulatory boards, and other audiences, the better your chances of getting the results you want. What you should say to the media — and where and when you should say it — is the topic of this chapter.

Meeting the Press

The number-one rule in dealing with the media is *be available*. When a reporter is doing a story, needs information for a deadline, and calls with a question, take the call. If you're doing something else, drop it. A journalist on deadline for today's broadcast or tomorrow's edition can't wait for you and won't accommodate your schedule. If you're immediately available, you have a good chance of being quoted or covered in the story. If not, the reporter's going to move on to the next source. That's true whether you're the mailroom clerk or the CEO.

When a company president tells me that he's too busy to talk to a media outlet he's been trying to get into without success (and calls him at last because of a tie-in with a current story), I tell him, "You don't understand. You are only important to this publication or program *right now*. Tomorrow, they won't even return your call." Journalism is a *now* business. You either play by their rules or lose before you start.

Whatever your story, *it is not as important to the media as it is to you.* Media people are under deadline, and if you aren't available right now, they'll do the story without you — or skip the story and do another.

Suppose the press is not banging down your door for an interview or a quote, but you still have a message that you want to get out to your market. The three most popular venues for reaching the press in person are analyst meetings, media tours, and expert interviews.

Analyst meetings

Most companies are familiar with the power that major industry analysts wield in the marketplace. However, many companies are reluctant or don't know how to approach influential firms such as the Gartner Group, International Data Corporation, and Datapro Corporation, to name just a few. And they don't understand how to tell a story that grabs the attention of a research analyst at a brokerage firm and gets him or her to write an exciting report for investors on the stock.

A company seeking market share or planning an IPO must submit to the scrutiny of at least a few industry analysts. But a poorly planned visit to an industry analyst can be damaging. Analysts ask tough questions about every facet of a company's business — technical and financial — so it's paramount that the company be prepared.

Show them your orange juice

Unless an analyst can understand the business value of your technology, she is unlikely to recommend your stock. One CEO of a company that makes color measurement devices was repeatedly asked, "What's so important about color? Why does it matter?" He dramatized the point by pouring three glasses of orange juice from three juice containers: Two were normal orange, but one was an off-color orangish-brown. "Would you drink this juice?" he asked, indicating the off-color glass. The message: Consumers judge products on colors, so colors must be right. Analysts got the point, and the demonstration made it memorable.

Although analysts write lengthy reports, and investors do sometimes read them, a lot of stocks are sold by brokers who describe the company to their clients over the phone in about 30 seconds. Therefore, you need to create a sound-byte description of your firm. For example, a company that designs search engine software used by major Internet portals described itself as the "toll takers of the Internet," because every time somebody accessed the Internet through a popular search engine running on their software, they got a royalty.

Media tours

A media tour involves sending a company or product spokesperson on the road to talk about or demonstrate a product to local media in different cities. For example, my PR agency has a literary division, and we frequently arrange book tours for the major authors we handle. We arrange for the author to do book-signings at bookstores in major cities across the country. Up to eight weeks in advance before the author is scheduled to arrive, we fax media alerts (see Chapter 14) to local TV and radio stations letting them know the author is available for interviews.

We have successfully applied the book-tour concept to our nonpublishing clients. One of our clients, Bob Lamspon, invented the Kitchen Coach, a CD-ROM-based system that teaches people to cook. He demonstrated the device to food writers and appliance editors in press tours and deskside briefings, receiving a ton of publicity as a result.

How can you use the book-tour technique to publicize your business? Substitute "product" for "book" and "author" for "company owner" or "product expert." Set up demonstrations, seminars, or other events in cities in key target markets. Alert the media via advanced notices. Call to follow up before your appearance to remind them that you're coming and tell them why your topic will be of interest to their audience.

Press conferences

For a press conference, you invite print and broadcast journalists from various media outlets to a central location to announce an important story. The story should be major news; reporters and on-air personalities don't want to be dragged away for a trivial announcement.

Deskside briefings

In deskside briefings, you (or your expert or spokesperson) visit journalists individually at their offices for conversation or interviews. Instead of the journalist going to a press conference, you take the press conference to the journalist. And you do it one-on-one instead of in a group.

Every day, reporters seek expert commentary on all kinds of breaking stories, many of them about technology. How often do you see articles in which your company's product or service has a direct or peripheral relationship to the subject being written about? Every one of those instances represents an opportunity for your company to have a spokesperson give a professional opinion that reflects positively on the entire organization.

In Chapter 10, I discuss strategies to get the press to call on you as an expert instead of your competition. I call this the "go-to guy" strategy because the goal is to become the person the media goes to for interviews on your particular topic. A well-written pitch letter (see Chapter 9) can help you get the press to ask for your opinion.

Print journalists are easier to speak with because they often interview you over the phone. Radio producers may want you to be a guest on their show, which you can often do on the telephone while sitting in your office. (Rarely does a radio show require you to come to the studio.) A TV interview, of course, requires you to go to the studio and appear on television, the rules for which I cover later in this chapter. Chapter 13 covers the ins and outs of radio interviews.

Handling Media Interviews Like a Pro

I've spent a good part of the last two decades training businesspeople how to speak with the media. What follows is a written guideline of the course I give my clients:

> ✔ **Start with a goal.** Approach all media interviews with a game plan and key messages in mind. Planning ahead — being prepared — is the key to a successful interview. In preparing for a media interview, first develop communications objectives — the key points or messages that you should convey to the audience. Select one or two core messages to convey during the interview. One way to measure the effectiveness of your PR campaign is to count how many of your key message points make it into the articles and broadcasts in which you receive coverage.

✔ **Take control of the interview.** *Control* is a key word in planning for a successful interview. Don't sit back and hope that the interviewer will ask the right questions — take control. Work your key message points into the interview early. Answer questions, but always steer the conversation back to what you want to get across. Don't wait, or it will be over before you know it, and you'll kick yourself for not getting to what you wanted to cover.

✔ **Preview the media outlet.** Educate yourself in advance about the print or broadcast outlet that will be conducting the interview. For *print* interviews, read the paper or magazine to get a feel for its editorial position and reader demographics. For *broadcast* interviews, preview the program before the interview and have a brief conversation with the show's producer or host. Will the interview be taped or live? How long with the interview last?

Be cautious when asking questions of media people. Some will answer them happily, but others may resent having the interview subject turn the tables and interview *them!* If you sense resistance or annoyance, stop asking questions and let it go.

✔ **Anticipate questions and prepare answers in advance.** The next step in interview preparation is anticipating the interviewer's questions and planning how to answer them. Compile a list of questions that are likely to surface during the interview and prepare the answers.

I recommend preparing a list of relevant questions you want to answer and giving this list, sometimes called a *tip sheet,* to radio and TV producers prior to the broadcast or taping. Show hosts usually do not have the time to read your press kit or do much preparation, so a tip sheet saves them effort and is a much-appreciated shortcut. Your benefit is that you make sure the questions you want to answer are asked. For a sample tip sheet, refer to Chapter 12.

Prior to the interview, ask the reporter what topics are going to be covered. Find out what other sources the reporter has contacted and what those sources may have divulged.

✔ **Be a credible spokesperson.** Always stick to your knitting — your area of expertise. Talk about things you've experienced firsthand, things you believe in. Give facts that prove what you're saying. It's essential to support a statement, especially a controversial one, with proof. In advance of the interview, gather all relevant facts so that you have them ready to use when appropriate. But don't overwhelm the listeners with information. Be clear and concise. Avoid reams of statistics, dates, or numbers that might confuse the audience. Summarize your proof in one or two pithy statements.

How you handle questions that you don't understand or can't answer for lack of information also affects your believability. If you don't understand, ask for clarification before responding. If you don't know the answer, offer to get information. Then do so at once and get back to the person who asked. Admitting that you don't know the answer is not a mistake, but failing to follow up is.

✔ **Learn the reporter's name.** Using the interviewer's first name positions you as a warm, caring, courteous individual. In contrast, addressing the interviewer by his surname may suggest coldness or stiffness. By maintaining this formality, you create an artificial barrier in the minds of the audience, which is not what you want.

✔ **Be conversational.** Keep the tone conversational and informal, especially during a broadcast interview. Use short words and simple sentences to create an air of informality, and avoid industry jargon. Strive to make the interview a conversation with the reporter rather than a scripted performance. By doing so, you increase your believability and make a more favorable impression on the audience.

Have you been framed?

I don't mean to imply that the media has framed you with a false accusation in the press. Rather, I'm referring to the concept of *framing* — presenting information in a manner that helps the listener relate to it.

An effective technique for communicating with any audience is to frame your story within the listener's experience. Framing helps you organize your thoughts and present them clearly, and also helps the audience absorb key messages quickly and easily. Frames help reporters and editors structure the story — without having to analyze or interpret the information provided.

Depending on your audience and your message, you can use framing in several ways. The *frame of definition,* for example, helps you introduce a new product, service, or concept by answering these four key questions:

✔ What is it?

✔ How does it work?

✔ Who benefits?

✔ Why should anybody care?

By addressing these four questions, you give the reporter and the audience a concise, well-structured presentation. You also ensure that the story communicates the key points you want to convey.

Another useful frame is the *Frame of Perspective.* The answers to these questions quickly communicate your organization's mission and goals to those unfamiliar with you:

✔ Where were we?

✔ Where are we?

✔ Where are we going?

✔ Why are we going there?

Don't confuse the reporter!

Not all journalists are experts in the topics they cover. Some trade publishers hire technologists and train them to be reporters, but many others prefer to hire professional journalists and train them to understand the industry. The latter often aren't as familiar with the industry jargon as practitioners in the field, so speak in plain English. If you use jargon when talking to reporters, at least half won't have a clue as to what you're saying — and may be too embarrassed to ask. Instead, they'll skip the technical parts, and the audience may not pick up your message.

The *Frame of Scope* is appropriate when your product, service, or organization deals with a cause, illness, condition, or need, whether it's protecting the environment or improving worker safety. The media is probably passingly familiar with the problem but unaware of its scope. In your press conference, you should answer the following questions whether they're asked or not:

✔ What is the problem?

✔ How bad is it?

✔ Who has been affected?

✔ What measures are being taken to prevent reoccurrence?

You use the *Frame of Clarification* to correct misconceptions. State the misconception, identify it as such, and then give the correction, as follows:

(Myth):   It's been suggested that XYZ is what happened.

(Fact):   In fact, what really happened is ABC.

Turning bad press into favorable coverage: The 15-10-15 formula

What if you've been getting negative coverage and you fear that the media is planning more of the same? You need to do some planning of your own to seize opportunities to convey the messages you want to get across (for example, that your company is friendly to the environment or your pretzel is made without chemicals). With advance planning, you can use negative questions as bridges to communication objectives. You accomplish this transition — from negative to positive — by responding directly to the interviewer's questions and then continuing the answer by developing a positive statement or the key message that you want to emphasize the most.

When planning such responses, it's helpful to use the 15-10-15 formula to ensure conciseness. Time the direct response to about 15 seconds, the transition statement to 5 or 10 seconds, and the positive conclusion to about 15 seconds. That way, the response will not exceed the 40- or 45-second period that is usually most effective in a news interview.

Simple transition statements include the following:

- ✔ You should also know . . .
- ✔ One other related topic that we should discuss . . .
- ✔ Before I forget, I want to tell your viewers . . .
- ✔ What's important to remember, however . . .
- ✔ What I really want to talk to you about is . . .
- ✔ And don't forget . . .
- ✔ Let me also add . . .

When the list of questions and responses is as complete as possible, rehearse the answers — out loud — until you're confident with them.

When Mike Wallace calls: Handling hostile interviewers

Some interviewers like to heighten the entertainment value of their programs or interviews by baiting their guests or trying to get them emotionally involved. The types of interviewers described in this section are the exception and not the rule. Usually, interviewers are very accommodating and are interested in what their guests have to say. However, it's important to be prepared for all types of interviewers.

No "off the record"!

Never say anything to a reporter that you wouldn't be comfortable seeing in print, hearing on the radio, or seeing on TV. Reporters will not always honor an "off the record" request. If you say it — even if you *say* it's off the record — it's on the record. The media's job is to report and gather news, not promote your product or business. If you give them something juicy, they'll use it whether you like it or not.

✔ **The Interrupter:** The Interrupter constantly interrupts your thoughts with controlled questions or comments that throw you off the main point. When dealing with an interrupter, you can do one of two things:

- Stop, listen to the question, suggest that you'll address that topic in a moment, and then continue your thought with, "As I was saying . . ."

- Ignore the interruption, complete your thought, and then address the interviewer, "Now, Sally, you asked me something else. What was it again?"

✔ **The Machine Gunner:** The Machine Gunner fires several questions in rapid succession. Suggest to the interviewer that he is posing several questions and ask, "Which one would you prefer that I address first?"

✔ **The Paraphraser:** The Paraphraser is an antagonistic interviewer who incorrectly (and unfairly) restates everything you say. Respond by restating your position: "I guess I didn't make myself very clear. What I said was . . ."

✔ **The Personalizer:** The Personalizer tries to separate personal views from professional ones in order to solicit a more controversial response. Don't get trapped into contradicting yourself or expressing inconsistent ideas.

✔ **The Dart Thrower:** Probably the most dangerous type of hostile interviewer, the Dart Thrower attempts to convict you, your company, or your industry by innuendo. Never answer a Dart Thrower's question without first addressing the innuendo. If you don't respond, you've tacitly admitted the truth of the implication.

✔ **The Repeater:** The Repeater's technique is to ask the same question over and over with slight modifications each time. Concentrate on what is being asked. When the same question resurfaces in a different form, point out to the reporter that you've already answered that question.

✔ **The News Relater:** This interviewer makes a special point of scanning the day's headlines and looking for stories that may relate to your company's interests. The day's news then forms the basis of the News Relater's line of questioning. This can be frustrating when they want to pursue the issue, and you don't feel it has the slightest relation to what you're doing.

✔ **The Hypothetical Questioner:** This interviewer loves to ask questions that begin, "Suppose. . .". (For instance, "Suppose you discovered an employee had harrassed a customer when delivering to her home.") Avoid answering hypothetical questions unless you've anticipated the made-up scenario and are comfortable in dealing with it.

✔ **The Pauser:** The Pauser's interviews are filled with silences, especially as you complete a thought. This tactic is meant to throw you. Instead, seize the moment as a chance to deliver your key message points. As you complete the first thought and meet the Pauser's empty look, smoothly transition into another thought.

✔ **The Gossip Monger:** The Gossip Monger brings up rumors about other companies and asks you to comment on them. Resist the temptation to respond. Don't comment on what others are doing or saying unless you're being interviewed to supply expert commentary on a given event.

✔ **The Limiter:** The Limiter hurls negative questions about a very specific topic and tries to keep you from bridging to a positive message — even after responding directly to the questions. When being interviewed by a Limiter, insist on bridging into more positive waters. Steer the discussion toward what you've done to resolve the problem and what you're doing to prevent it from happening again.

✔ **The Presumptive Negative:** The media is invariably skeptical, adopting what may sound like a negative stance when questioning the people behind institutions. Respond by challenging the form in which the question is asked and launch into a positive statement.

In any media interview, total and complete concentration is essential; you need a sharp antenna. Total concentration becomes imperative when you're dealing with antagonistic, hostile interviewers. So maintain a polite, distant, and measured stance.

On the air: Special tips for broadcast interviews

People who are cool and collected in almost any situation may get anxious when facing the prospect of a TV interview. But by following the basics, you can calm the butterflies in your stomach and deliver a credible performance that interests viewers and gets them on your side.

How to sit is very important. Here are some pointers for perfect TV interview posture:

✔ Cross your legs at the knee, not the ankle.

✔ Fold your hands one over the other (not clasped) on your lap.

✔ Lean forward slightly in your chair. This "attack" position helps keep you alert and concentrated.

What you wear is important as well; your wardrobe can speak volumes about you. And if you don't dress appropriately, your audience will focus on your clothes instead of your message.

TIP

Don't state the critic's position

When participating in a broadcast talk show with a guest who has an opposing viewpoint, your critic might attack you with an overwrought, emotional indictment of your company or product. If that happens, take a long pause and respond in a quiet, measured, and reasonable manner. The contrast should be evident to all.

Don't waste time restating your critics' views. Instead, use the time to state your case: "I'll let my critics speak for themselves. I can only tell you how our company feels about that."

Men should follow these wardrobe guidelines:

- ✔ Choose a dark suit in a solid color; avoid patterns or stripes, which appear too busy on the screen.

- ✔ Ties should be in muted tones.

- ✔ White shirts may be worn, but light blue is a better choice.

Women can use these general rules for on-camera dress:

- ✔ Pastels work wonderfully on television.

- ✔ Avoid wearing very bright or flashy jewelry; it doesn't televise well.

- ✔ Don't wear large or dangling earrings.

Whether you're male or female, choose comfortable, nonconstraining clothes so that you can focus on your message and not have to worry about your garments.

Before the interview

- ✔ Arrive early to familiarize yourself with the studio — at least a half-hour before your appearance. Once the interview begins, you don't want to be distracted or intimidated by the unfamiliar sights and sounds.

- ✔ Watch the program to learn the format, interviewer's personality, length of interviews, and attitude toward the industry audience.

- ✔ Read newspapers and watch television to catch late-breaking news.

- ✔ Prepare. Rehearse key messages and "gee-whiz" information — little-known facts that you can release to support your point.

At the studio

✔ Make friends. That's the bottom line. You want the media to believe you and write favorably about your company.

✔ Introduce yourself to the producer, host, or other contact person. Review the agreed-upon format and subject areas of the interview.

✔ Ask to see the studio for the set arrangements. Sit in the chairs to check comfort levels and lighting. Ask for changes if appropriate.

✔ Prepare your props.

✔ Allow studio personnel to put makeup on you. It will make you look better.

✔ Drink water or warm tea with lemon to loosen up your throat. Avoid milk products and powdered donuts.

✔ Take a few minutes to relax and refresh yourself.

✔ Remind yourself of the two or three messages you want to communicate.

✔ Remember posture, eye contact, and gesture rules.

✔ Give a full mike check.

✔ Be the Good Guy. Stay positive. Remember that you're trying to reach the audience, not the interviewer.

During the interview

✔ Stay focused and keep talking. Look the interviewer in the eye, even if she isn't looking at you. Unless otherwise instructed, focus on the person you're speaking to. If you look your best and maintain an alert, attractive presence, you'll come across as the kind of person who cares about yourself, your company, and your audience.

✔ Look into the camera lens as if you're looking directly at the person asking the question, and talk directly into it.

✔ Part your lips slightly when listening; your expression will be less stern.

✔ Sit up straight.

✔ If the subject is light, show your sense of humor. If it's serious, let your feelings show on your face. Anger is much trickier — generally, it's best to show dignity and calmness rather than going full-throttle on those feelings.

✔ Even if you think you've said something inaccurate, keep talking, perhaps correcting yourself in the next few sentences. But don't stop and say, "Can we do it over?" unless you've asked ahead of time if that is a possibility.

✔ Have fun! The interview will turn out best if you relax and enjoy yourself. Being enthusiastic about the subject will make the interview a pleasure for the host and the viewers.

You're the expert! You know more about your company — its history, its philosophy, its people, its products, and the issues it faces — than the reporter who is interviewing you or the audience. You're being interviewed because you're the expert. Your knowledge is your strength. Speak from that strength and succeed as an effective company spokesperson.

Being a little nervous is healthy and positive. That nervousness creates a heightened sense of awareness — it sharpens your antenna. So let yourself be a little nervous — not to the point of being immobilized, but just sensitized.

Then, if you've done your homework, come equipped with one or two communication objectives, anticipated key questions, and planned how you will use them as bridges to get your message across, you can feel confident that you will fare extremely well in any interview situation.

Promoting Yourself through Public Speaking

As a promoter of your organization, you're likely to speak to people other than those in the media. Public speaking — giving lectures, talks, papers, and presentations at public events, industry meetings, conventions, and conferences — is a PR technique that businesses use widely to promote their products or services.

Why is public speaking so effective as a promotional tool? When you speak, you're perceived as the expert. If your talk is good, you immediately establish your credibility with the audience so that members want you and your company to work with them and solve their problems.

Unlike an article, which is somewhat impersonal, a speech or talk puts you within handshaking distance of your audience. And because in today's fast-paced world, more and more activities are taking place remotely via fax, the Web, and videoconferencing, meeting prospects face-to-face firmly implants your image in their minds. If that meeting takes place in an environment where you're singled out as an expert, as is the case when you speak in public, the impression is that much more powerful.

Speaking is not ideal for every product or marketing situation. If you're trying to mass-market a new soft drink on a nationwide basis, television and print PR will be much more effective than speaking, which limits the number of people you reach per contact. On the other hand, a wedding consultant whose market is Manhattan would probably profit immensely from a talk on wedding preparation given to engaged couples at a local church.

Speaking is an effective PR tactic when

- Confidential matters are to be discussed.
- Warmth and personal qualities are called for.
- An atmosphere of openness is desired.
- Strengthening of feelings, attitudes, and beliefs is needed.
- Exactitude and precision are *not* required.
- Decisions must be communicated quickly or important deadlines must be met rapidly.
- Crucial situations dictate maximum understanding.
- Added impact is needed to sustain the audience's attention and interest or get them to focus on a topic or issue.
- Personal authentication of a claim or concept is needed.

Speaking is also the promotional tool of choice when you're targeting your PR efforts to a narrow vertical market in which many of your best prospects are members of one or more of the major associations or societies in that market. For example, in the household appliances business, you might consider getting on the roster to give a presentation at the annual housewares show in Chicago.

Finding speaking opportunities

Unless you're sponsoring your own seminar or other event, you need to find appropriate forums to which your company personnel can be invited to speak. How do you go about that?

First, check your mail and the trade publications you read for announcements of industry meetings and conventions. For example, if you sell furnaces for steel mills and you want to promote a new process, you may want to give a paper on your technique at the annual Iron and Steel Exposition.

Trade journals generally run preview articles and announcements of major shows, expos, and meetings months before the events. Many trade publications also have columns that announce such meetings on both a national and a local level. Make sure to scan these columns in the publications aimed at your target market industries.

You should also receive preview announcements in the mail. If you're a marketing manager or the owner of a small business, professional societies and trade associations will send you direct-mail packages inviting your firm to exhibit at their shows. That's fine, but you have another purpose: to find out whether papers, talks, or seminars are being given at the show, and, if so, to get your people on the panels or signed up as speakers. If the show's mail promotion doesn't discuss papers or seminars, call the organizers and ask.

Propose some topics with your company personnel as the speakers. Most conference managers welcome such proposals because they need speakers. The conference manager or another association executive in charge of the "breakout sessions" (the usual name for the presentation of papers or talks) will request an abstract or short 100- to 200-word outline of your talk. If others in your company will be giving the talks, work with them to come up with an outline that is enticing so as to generate maximum attendance but that also reflects accurately what the speaker wants to talk about.

Because many companies will pitch speakers and presentations at the conference manager, the earlier you do it, the better. Generally, annual meetings and conventions of major associations begin planning 8 to 12 months in advance; local groups or local chapters of national organizations generally book speakers 3 to 4 months in advance. The earlier you approach them, the more receptive they'll be to your proposal.

You can recycle your talks and give them to different groups in the same year or different years, tailoring them slightly to fit current market conditions, the theme of the meeting, or the group's special interests. When you create a description, outline, or proposal for a talk, keep it as a file on your computer.

Then, when other speaking opportunities come your way, you can quickly edit the file and e-mail a customized proposal or abstract to the person in charge of that meeting. I have a basic talk on PR that I have given half a dozen times over the past year at association meetings ranging from the American Pet Products Manufacturers Convention to the Hotel and Motel Association. I get at least one major new client every time I give the talk.

Because your goal is to sell your product or service, not educate the audience or become a professional speaker, you want to pick a topic that relates to and helps promote your business but is also of great interest to the group's audience. The presentation does not sell you directly, but sells you by positioning you and your company as the expert source of information on the problem your product or service addresses. As such, it must be objective and present how-to advice or useful information; it can't be a sales or product presentation.

For example, if you sell computer automated telemarketing systems, your talk can't be a sales pitch for your system. Instead, you could do something such as "How to Choose the Right Computer Automated Telemarketing Software" or "Computer Automated vs. Traditional Telemarketing Systems: Which Is Right for Your Business?" Although you want people to choose your system, your talk should be (mostly) objective and not too obviously slanted in favor of your product; otherwise, you will offend and turn off your audience.

I once spoke at a marketing meeting at which one of the other presenters, a manufacturer of such computerized telemarketing systems, was giving a talk. Although he was supposed to talk about how to improve telemarketing results with software, he proceeded to haul in his system and give a sales pitch. The comments from attendees were openly hostile and negative. I'm sure he didn't get any business, and this talk did not enhance his reputation, either.

Screening speaking invitations

On occasion, meeting planners and conference executives may call you and ask you (or a representative from your firm) to speak at their event, rather than your having to seek them out and ask them.

Being approached is flattering, but beware: Not every opportunity to speak is worthwhile. Meeting planners and committee executives are primarily concerned with getting someone to stand at the podium, and they don't care whether your speaker or your firm will benefit in any way from the exposure. So before you accept an opportunity to speak, ask the meeting planner the following questions:

- ✔ What is the nature of the group?
- ✔ Who are the members? What are their job titles and responsibilities? What companies do they work for?
- ✔ What is the average attendance of such meetings? How many people does the meeting planner expect will attend your session?
- ✔ Does the group pay an honorarium or at least cover expenses?
- ✔ What other speakers have presented recently, and what firms do these speakers represent?
- ✔ Did the group pay those other speakers? If so, why not you, too?

If the answers indicate that the meeting is not right or worthwhile for your company, or if the meeting planner seems unable or unwilling to provide answers, politely thank the person and decline the invitation.

Get on the mailing list

If you're not on the mailing list to receive advance notification of meetings and conventions of your industry associations, write to request that the associations place you on such a list. Their names and addresses are listed in *The Encyclopedia of Associations,* published by Gale Research and available at your local library.

Negotiating your promotional deal with the event sponsor

If you're asked to speak either for free or for a small honorarium and you're not offered a multi-thousand dollar fee like a professional speaker would get, you can use the group's lack of payment for your talk as leverage to negotiate for concessions. What kinds of things can you ask for? Anything that can help maximize the promotional value of your talk for your firm.

Tell the meeting chairperson that you would be happy to speak at no charge, provided that you receive a list of the members. You can use this list to promote your company via direct mail before and after your presentation. A pre-talk mailing can let people know about your upcoming talk and be a personal invitation from you to them. A post-talk mailing can offer a reprint or audio recording of your presentation to those who missed it.

At larger conferences and conventions, the conference manager provides attendees with show kits that include a variety of materials, such as a seminar schedule, passes to luncheons and dinners, maps, and sights of interest to out-of-town visitors. These kits are either mailed in advance or distributed at the show.

You can tell the conference manager, "I will give the presentation at no charge, but in exchange, we'd like to have you include our company literature in the conference kits mailed to attendees. Is that possible? We will supply as many copies of our literature as you need, of course." If he agrees, you get your promo pieces mailed to hundreds, even thousands, of potential clients *at zero mailing cost.*

Turn one speech into an extended campaign

A speech is an effective way of making yourself known to a particular audience (the members of the organization and, more specifically, those members who attend your presentation). But as you know, making a permanent impression on a market segment requires a series of contacts, not a single communication.

You can easily transform a one-shot speaking engagement into an ongoing PR campaign targeted to the membership of this particular group. One way, already discussed, is to get the mailing list and do your own mailings, plus have the sponsor include your literature in the mail-out kit. Another is to get one or more PR placements in the organization's newsletter or magazine. For example, tell the meeting planner that you will supply a series of articles (your current press releases and feature articles, recycled for this particular audience) to run in the organization's newsletter before the talk. This makes you known to the audience, which is good PR for your firm and also helps build interest in attending your program.

After your talk, give the editor of the organization's newsletter the notes or text of your speech, and encourage her to run all or part of it (or a summary) as a post-talk article so that those who could not attend can benefit from the information. Additional articles can also run as follow-ups after the talk to reinforce your message and provide additional detail to those who want to learn more, or to answer questions or cover issues you didn't have time to cover.

If the editor will not run a resource box with your phone number with the articles, talk to the meeting planner about getting free ads for your product or service. For a national organization that charges for ads in its magazine, the value of your free ad space should be approximately twice what your fee would be if you were charging for your talk.

The organization will do a program or mailing (or both) with a nice article about you and your talk. Usually, it prints more than it ends up using and throws out the extras. Mention that you would be glad to take those extra copies off its hands. Inserting those fliers in press kits and inquiry fulfillment packages is a nice touch.

Exchange your "fee" for a videotape of your talk

A professionally done audiotape or video of you giving a seminar can be a great promotional tool and an attention-getting supplement to printed brochures, direct mail, and other sales literature. But recording such presentations in a studio can be expensive.

One way to get an audio or video produced at low cost is to have someone else foot the bill for the taping. If an organization wants you to speak but can't pay you, and especially if its audience is not a prime market for you, say, "I'll tell you what. Normally I charge $X for such a program. I'll do it for you at no charge, provided that you can arrange to have it professionally videotaped (or audio-recorded, or both) and give me a copy of the master."

If the organization objects to the expense, say, "In exchange, you can copy and distribute the video or audio of my speech to your members, or even sell it to those who attend the meeting or belong to your group or both, and I won't ask for a percentage of the profits. All I want is the tape master when you're through with it."

Bargain for ownership of the audiotape

At many major meetings, it's standard practice for sponsoring organizations to audiotape all presentations and offer them for sale at the conference and for one year thereafter in promotional mailings. If you're being taped, tell the sponsor that you normally do not allow it but will as long as you get the master. (Also make clear that, although you will allow the sponsor to sell it and will waive any percentage of the profits, the copyright is to be in your name.)

If you use overheads, consider doing them in html format. Organizations are now starting to post speaker handouts on their Web sites if these visuals are supplied in html. You instantly expand the audience for your talk from dozens to perhaps thousands with this Web exposure.

If the group is a local chapter of a national organization, ask the meeting chairperson for a list of the other state or local chapters, along with the names, addresses, and phone numbers of the meeting organizers for each chapter. Then contact the chapters and offer to give the talk to their members.

Preparing and delivering your presentation

Of course, your objective is to sell. But be careful. People attending a luncheon or dinner meeting aren't there to be sold. They want to be entertained. Informed. Educated. Made to laugh or smile. Selling your product, service, or company may be your goal, but in public speaking, it has to be secondary to giving a good presentation. A "soft-sell" approach works best.

Say that your talk is primarily informational. You can organize it along the following lines:

 ✔ First, an introduction that presents an overview of the topic

 ✔ Next, the body of the talk, which presents the facts in detail

 ✔ Finally, a conclusion that sums up for the audience what they have heard

This repetition is beneficial because, unlike readers of an article, listeners of a spoken presentation can't flip back to a previous page or paragraph to refresh their memory or study your material in more detail. For this reason, you must repeat your main point at least three times to make sure that it's understood and remembered.

The talk should always be about the issue your product addresses, not about the product itself. For instance, when I had "The Juice Man" Jay Kordich giving talks nationwide to promote juicing, he talked about the nutritional benefits of drinking freshly made fruit and vegetable juices, not about the features of his machine or how to buy one.

Many other organizational methods are available to speakers. For example, if you're describing a *process,* you can organize your talk along the natural flow of the process or the sequence of steps involved in completing it. This would be ideal for a talk entitled "How to Promote Your Chiropractic Practice" or "How to Start a Fad or Trend."

TIP

Canned presentations

The trick to reducing preparation time is to have two or three "canned" (standard) talks that you can offer to various audiences. Even with a canned presentation, you need at least several hours to analyze the audience, do some customizing of your talk to better address that particular group, and rehearse once or twice.

If you're talking about expanding a communications network worldwide, you might start with the United States, then move on to Asia, and then cover Europe. If your topic is vitamins, covering them in alphabetical order from vitamin A to zinc seems a sensible approach.

Mastering the three parts of a talk

A talk has three parts: beginning, middle, and end. All are important. But the beginning and ending are more important than the middle. Most people can manage to discuss a topic for 15 minutes, give a list of facts, or read from a prepared statement. And that's what it takes to deliver the middle part.

The beginning and ending are more difficult. In the beginning, you must engage the audience's attention *and* establish rapport. Not only must members be made to feel that your topic will be interesting, but also they must be drawn to you, or at least not find fault with your personality.

To test this theory, a well-known speaker put aside his usual opening and instead spoke for five minutes about himself — how successful he was, how much money he made, how in demand he was as a speaker, and why he was the right choice to address the group. After his talk, he casually asked a member, "What were you thinking when I said that?" The man politely replied, "I was thinking what a blowhard you are."

How do you begin a talk? One easy and proven technique is to get the audience involved by asking questions. For example, if you're addressing telecommunications engineers, ask, "How many of you manage a T1 network? How many of you are using 56K DDS but are thinking about T1? And how many of you use fractional T1?" If you're speaking on a health topic, you might ask, "How many of you exercised today before coming here? How many of you plan to exercise after the meeting tonight? How many of you exercise three or more times a week?"

Asking questions like these has two benefits. First, it provides a quick survey of audience concerns, interests, and levels of involvement, allowing you to tailor your talk to their needs on the spot. Second, it forces the audience to become immediately involved. After all, when you're in the audience and the speaker asks a question, you do one of two things: You either raise your hand or don't raise it. Either way, you're thinking, responding, and getting involved.

Look for ways to engage the audience on an intellectual or emotional level. I often begin my talks on PR by reading the openings of the day's front-page stories in major media such as *USA Today* and *The Wall Street Journal.* Then, to the audience's amazement, I tell them which PR firms placed the stories and the key message points in each. Starting this way dramatically demonstrates the wide-reaching influence of PR, even into the uppermost levels of the major media.

While the beginning is important, don't neglect a strong closing, especially if you're there not just for the pleasure of speaking but also to help promote your company or its products.

Action doesn't have to be literal. If you simply want the people in your audience to mull over your ideas, tell them that this is what you want them to do.

Although you want a great opening that builds rapport and gets people to listen and an ending that helps "close the sale," don't neglect the body, or middle, of your talk. It's the "meat;" it's what your audience came to hear. If your talk is primarily informational, be sure to give inside information on the latest trends, techniques, and product developments. If it's motivational, be enthusiastic and convince your listeners that they *can* lose weight, make money investing in real estate, or stop smoking.

If your talk is a how-to presentation, make sure that you've written it so that your audience walks away with lots of practical ideas and suggestions. As actor and Toastmaster George Jessel observes, "Above all, the successful speaker is sincerely interested in telling his audience something they want to know."

When speaking, tailor the content to listeners' expertise. Being too complex can bore people. But being too simplistic or basic can be even more offensive to an audience of knowledgeable industry experts.

Matters of length and timing

Talks can vary from a ten-minute workplace presentation to a two-day intensive seminar. How long should yours be? The event and meeting planner often dictate length.

✔ Luncheon and after-dinner talks to local groups and local chapters of professional societies and business clubs usually last 20 to 30 minutes, with an additional 5 to 10 minutes allotted for questions and answers.

✔ For breakout sessions at major conferences and national expositions, speakers generally get 45 to 75 minutes. For a one-hour talk, prepare a 45-minute talk. You'll probably start five minutes late to allow for late arrivals, and the last ten minutes can be a more informal question-and-answer session.

✔ The luckiest speakers are those who get invited to participate in panels. If you're on a panel consisting of three or four experts plus a moderator, it's likely that you'll be asked to respond to questions from the moderator or the audience, eliminating the need to prepare a talk.

✔ Most executive speeches are about 20 minutes in length. A typed, double-spaced page of manuscript should take the speaker 2½ minutes to deliver. This means that an eight-page, double-spaced manuscript, which is about 2,000 words, will take 20 minutes to deliver as a speech. That's about 100 words a minute. Some speakers are faster, talking at 120 to 150 words a minute or more. So the 20-minute talk can really be anywhere from eight to ten typed pages.

The most important thing about a talk is to not exceed the allotted time. If you're given 20 minutes with an additional 10 minutes for questions and answers, stop after 20 minutes. People won't mind if you finish a bit early, but they will become fidgety and start looking at their watches if your time limit is up and you don't seem even near finished.

Here are some other tips for adding punch to your presentations:

✔ Write your own introduction and mail it to the sponsoring organization in advance of your appearance. (Also bring a copy with you for the master of ceremonies in case she loses your original.)

✔ Self-effacing humor works best. Poke gentle fun at yourself, not at the audience or the sponsor.

✔ Ask the audience questions.

✔ Don't give a talk; have a conversation.

✔ The presentation doesn't have to be great. Tell your audience that if they get one good idea out of your talk, it will have been worthwhile for them. Create a realistic expectation in the beginning, and the audience will be satisfied at the end.

✔ To announce a break, say, "We'll take a five-minute break now, so I'll expect you back in ten minutes." It always gets a laugh.

✔ To get the audience back in the room, go out into the hall and shout, "He's starting, he's starting."

- ✔ If panic strikes, just give the talk and keep your mouth moving. The fear will subside in a minute or two.

- ✔ Tell touching stories. If the stories are about you, be the goat, not the hero. People like speakers who are humble; audiences hate braggarts.

- ✔ Asking people to perform a simple exercise (stretching, Simon Says, and so on) as an activity during a break can increase their energy level and overcome lethargy.

- ✔ At the conclusion of your talk, tell your audience that they were a great audience, even if they weren't: "You've been a wonderful audience. [pause] Thank you very much."

The most important tip? Be yourself. Talk to the audience. Don't worry about being smooth, polished, funny, clever, dynamic, or dramatic. Because you aren't expected to be a professional speaker, coming off as a bit amateurish and inexperienced can even endear you to the crowd and get them on your side.

Think twice about using audiovisual aids

In 1970s, slides were all the rage in the corporate world. Nearly every presentation was an audiovisual presentation. Two managers could not get together for an informal chat without one pulling out a slide projector and dimming the lights.

Slides are still popular today, as are overhead projectors and PowerPoint presentations, but in my opinion, audiovisual aids are not necessary for most presentations. Most corporate presentations depend on PowerPoint or overheads, and they're boring.

Keeper of the time

Because most people can't concentrate on two things at once — giving a talk and watching a clock — try this trick: Ask someone in the audience to be the timekeeper and keep you on track. For example, if you're giving a 45-minute talk, ask him to shout out "Time!" every 15 minutes. The first two interruptions tell you where you are and how closely you're on track; the last tells you to stop and shut up.

Incidentally, rather than finding this shouting of the word *time* annoying, audiences like it. Make it fun, telling the timekeeper, "You must shout out 'time' in a loud, obnoxious voice!" Then, when he does and the audience laughs, ask them to rate, in a tongue-in-cheek way, whether the timekeeper was indeed loud and obnoxious enough. It gets a laugh every time.

Most professional speakers who earn thousands for a brief talk do *not* use audiovisual aids. I feel that businesspeople, especially in the corporate world, become dependent on the visuals and lose the spontaneity and relaxed manner that come with "having a conversation" rather than "making a presentation."

The problem with the corporate approach to visuals is that the audiovisual aid is seen as something that must run continuously and concurrently with the talk. So, although only 10 percent of the presentation requires visuals, the slide projector runs for 100 percent of the time, and the speaker fills in with word slides that are wasteful and silly. For example, if the speaker is going to talk for three or four minutes on branding, she hits a button, and the word BRANDING appears on the screen in white against a black background. Such a visual adds nothing to the talk and is, in fact, ridiculous.

A better approach is to have visuals that you can use when appropriate, and then deliver the rest of your talk unaided. For a small audience, you can give an unrehearsed, interactive feel to your talk by using flip charts and Magic Markers. The key: Don't prepare them in advance. Rather, draw as you speak, which adds excitement and motion. It also creates anticipation: The audience becomes curious about what is being created before their eyes.

Computer projectors and overhead projectors work for larger groups, but unfortunately, they're prone to mechanical failure. Errors in presentations, such as difficulty sorting through a pile of overhead transparencies or slides that are upside down or out of order, confuse and embarrass the speaker; they also cause the audience to snicker or lose interest.

Always arrive at least one hour before your speech is scheduled and request access to the room where you're speaking. Run through your slides or other audiovisuals once, quickly, to make sure that everything is working properly and that the materials are in the right order.

I have seen speakers who, interrupted by a jammed slide tray, lose their train of thought and never fully recover. Errors or mishaps with audiovisual support can be extremely disconcerting, especially when making a good impression is important or the presenter is uncomfortable with public speaking in the first place.

At times, high-quality visuals are needed to demonstrate how a product works, explain a process, show the components or parts of a system, or graphically depict performance. For instance, if you're trying to promote your landscape design practice by giving a talk entitled "How to Design a Beautiful Front Yard," you want to show pictures of attractive front yards that you have designed. If your speech is entitled "Advancing Science Using Supercomputer Generated Images," people will want to see color slides of those images.

In such cases, I suggest that you prepare overhead transparencies, a video-tape, flip charts, or similar displays that you can show briefly and then put away. If you use slides, turn the projector off and the lights on when the visuals are not in use.

A research study from 3M estimates that people retain only 10 percent of what they hear; by adding visual aids, the retention rate increases to 50 percent. And a report from Matrix Computer Graphics notes that 85 percent of all information stored in the brain is received visually. I'm not convinced that they're right, though. I can recall a number of memorable presentations — the speaker, the delivery, and many of the ideas — but I can't recall a single slide or visual from those talks.

If you do use slides, make them bold, bright, colorful, and easy to read. Slides and overheads are used to show, demonstrate, and create excitement. They're not a good medium for transmitting complex detail. Too much detail in a slide or overhead makes it unclear. To test the readability of a slide, hold it at arm's length. If you can't read the text, your audience won't be able to, either.

Giving your audience a handout

A handout can take one of several formats: hard copy of the presentation or overheads, brochures, article reprints, or reprints of the narration (with visuals incorporated, if possible). It can be the full text of your talk, an outline, just the visuals, or a report or article on a topic that is either related to the presentation topic or expands on one of the subtopics you touched on briefly in the talk.

Every handout should contain your company name, address, phone, fax, and, if possible, a full resource box with a brief summary of who you are and what you do — as should *every* marketing document you produce.

If the handout is the full text of your talk or a set of fairly comprehensive notes, tell the audience before you start: "There's no need to take notes. We have hard copies of this presentation for you to take home." This relieves listeners of the burden of note-taking, freeing them to concentrate on your talk.

Handouts such as transcripts of a speech, articles, reports, or other materials with lots of copy should be handed out *after* the talk, not before. If you hand them out before you step to the podium, the audience will read the printed materials and ignore you. You can hand out reproductions of visuals or pages with just a few bullet points in advance so that attendees can write notes directly on them.

Why do you need handouts? They enhance learning. But the main reason to give handouts is to ensure that every attendee (most of whom are potential customers, or you wouldn't be addressing the group) walks away with a piece of paper containing information about what you offer and how to contact you. That way, when the person goes to work the next morning and thinks, "That was an interesting talk; maybe I should contact them to talk about how they can help us," he has your phone number in hand. Without it, response to your talk will be zero or near zero; most people are too busy, lazy, or indifferent to track you down if they don't have immediate access to your contact information.

Why getting your handout into the audience's hands is so vital: the "green sheet" method

It's vital that you give a useful, interesting, information-packed talk that convinces prospects you know what you're talking about and makes them want to talk with you about doing work for them. But without the contact information immediately in hand, the prospect's interest and curiosity will quickly evaporate. Because you can't tell in advance who in the audience will want to follow up with you and who will not, your goal is to get everybody or as many people as possible to pick up and take home your handout material.

There are several ways to distribute handouts at your talk. The most common is to leave the materials on a table, either in the back of the room or at the registration table where people sign in for the meeting or your session. But this technique is not effective. Most people will walk right by the table without picking up the material. Many won't even notice the table or stack of handouts. Even if you point out the table and say that reprints are available, many won't take one. And you might feel embarrassed at the silence that follows your announcement; it makes you seem less authoritative, more of a promoter.

Another technique is to put a copy of your handout on each seat in the room about a half-hour before the start of your presentation. Most people will pick it up and look at it; about one-quarter to one-half will take it with them when they leave; and half or more will leave it on the chair. Disadvantages? People may read the handout and not pay attention to your presentation. Also, some people resent this approach, seeing it as too pushy and salesy.

The most effective method of distributing handouts is the "green sheet" method. It maximizes the number of attendees who take handouts, increases their desire to have the material, and, most importantly, eliminates any hint of self-promotion or salesmanship. Make the handout an essential supplement.

Here's how it works: Prepare a handout that expands on one of the points in your talk, covering it in more detail than you can in a short presentation. Or make the handout a supplement, covering additional points not discussed but related to the topic.

Another option is to do a handout that's a resource guide — for example, a bibliography of reference books on your topic, tables of technical data, a glossary of key terms, or a series of equations or examples of calculations.

The important point is that the handout relates to *but does not merely repeat* information covered in your talk; instead, it *expands* on it.

When you get to that topic in your talk, which should be about halfway or three-quarters through the talk, discuss the point and then say something similar to the following (adapting it to your topic and handout, of course): "I really can't cover in this short talk all the techniques related to this, so I've prepared a checklist of 25 points to consider when planning this type of project and reprinted it on this green sheet." Pause, hold up the sheet for everyone to see, and then continue: "I have plenty of copies, so if you want one, come up to me after the talk."

After your talk, you will be surrounded at the podium by a large crowd of people with their hands out to get the free green sheet. Try it — it works. Oh, and why a green sheet rather than plain white paper? Doing it on colored paper and calling it a green sheet seems to make it more special; also, instead of having to remember what's actually on the sheet (many people would not and therefore would hesitate to ask for it), people can just come up and say, "May I have a green sheet, please?"

Capturing attendee names for your prospect database

Say the conference organizer won't release a list of attendees or the people who go to your specific session, but you want to capture as many of those names as possible for marketing follow-up. In that case, offer your handout as a bait piece rather than giving it out at the session.

At the conclusion of your talk, discuss your handout and what it covers and say, "So if you would like a free copy of our free telecom security checklist, just write 'TSC' on the back of your business card and hand it to me. I'll mail a free copy of the checklist to you as soon as I get back to the office." The more enticing and relevant your bait piece, the more business cards you will collect. A really strong bait piece offer can get you the business cards of 25 to 75 percent of attendees or more.

My variation is to offer a free issue of my company's newsletter to everyone who gives me his or her business card. At the end of the talk, I get flooded with people handing me their cards to receive the free newsletter.

We send the newsletter and add the names to our database. They then get the newsletter mailed quarterly. Our database has grown, largely through this method, to 10,000 names. We now get one new client with every quarterly mailing of the 10,000 newsletters. The entire cost of the newsletter, including production, printing, and mailing, is paid for by the first month's fee from this new client (refer to Chapter 3 for details on PR firm compensation).

Part IV

Implementing Your PR Strategy

The 5th Wave — By Rich Tennant

SAFE LIVING MAGAZINE
Press Conference

In this part . . .

To turn your clever PR ideas into action, you've got to establish a good working relationship with the media, which is what I show you how to do in Chapter 12. The remainder of Part IV gives specific tips for increasing your PR coverage in specific media: radio (Chapter 13), TV (Chapter 14), print (Chapter 15), and new media, especially the Internet (Chapter 16).

Chapter 12

Media Relations: Getting Your Message Out

*E*ven the most brilliant campaigns and clever PR materials don't get results if they never leave your in-basket or hard drive. A vital step to generating PR is getting your PR documents into the hands of the right audience — the editors and producers who can make the decision to run them in their publications and on their programs.

Fortunately you don't have to hire an expensive PR firm to "buy" your way into these media contacts. They're readily available, as well as quick and easy to assemble. The two basic lists you'll work from are your personal contact list and your mass media list.

Compiling a Personal Contact List

I require many of my employees to compile what I call the personal contact list, also known as the "call list." It contains the names, publication or program, and contact information of both the editors and producers they know personally, as well as the media outlets they've found out about through experience or research. My employees should have at least 100 names on their personal contact list. When they're doing a PR program, they start calling the people on this list first to see whether they're interested in running the story we're pitching for our client. They call the people on their personal contact list even before they mail to media directory lists (which I cover in the next section).

Think of your personal contact list as your "house file." Just as you have a customer list from which you get great results whenever you send direct mail to them, you have a personal contact list of media outlets that are more likely to run your press releases than other editors and producers.

Using the Contact Form on the CD in this book, start compiling your own personal contact list now. Does your local chamber of commerce publish a business magazine for the region, and are you a member? Put the magazine and its editor on your list. Are you a member of an industry association? Its newsletter should go on your personal contact list. Other media to add to the list include your alumni magazine and your hometown newspaper.

Any time you're featured in or on any media, get the name of the writer or producer, and add it to your personal contact list. The journalist who has interviewed or written about you in the past knows your name and is therefore more likely to pay attention to future items from you. As an analogy, think of her as a customer who has bought something from a direct-mail piece you sent out. She's more likely to buy from you again than a stranger on a mailing list who has never purchased from you before.

Use the Contact Form on the CD in this book (refer to the Appendix) to compile your personal contact list of media outlets and personnel.

Developing a Mass Media List

Just as marketers mail to rented mailing lists to augment their customer mailings, you should mail to other media outlets beyond those on your own personal contact list.

Although these mass media lists will not generate quite as high a percentage of pickups (a *pickup* means that a publication used your press release and ran your story) as your personal contact list, you can still get very significant publicity results. And the cost to mail to a few hundred or even a thousand media outlets on these lists is fairly nominal.

There are several ways to distribute PR materials to the mass of media outlets available:

- ✔ You can buy major media directories, such as *Bacon's Publicity Checker* or *Gebby's All-In-One,* and type envelopes from the directory listings. Many media directories send you updates every six months or more to ensure that you're working with up-to-date information.

- ✔ You can order mailing labels from the media directories and affix them to your envelopes when you want to mail a press release or tip sheet. Ordering labels saves labor and ensures that you have the most recent address and correct editor or producer.

✔ You can send your press release to media services that can fax, mail, or e-mail the press releases to the media you select. Most of the major media directories, listed on the CD in this book, have mail, e-mail, or fax distribution services or some combination of these. This is the easiest, fastest distribution method.

I suggest that if you're doing your own PR, buy at least one of the major media directories listed on the CD. Even if you decide to buy labels or use electronic distribution services, you want a directory on your desk that you can look through to get an idea of the different categories of publications and programs you can choose from.

The PR industry connects with the media through a limited number of standard media directories and media distribution services, listed on the CD (refer to the Appendix) that comes with this book. The directories list thousands of media by category, and the distribution services will mail, e-mail, or fax your press release to the same media by these same categories.

Distributing Materials to the Media

You can distribute materials to the media in several different formats:

✔ **Mail:** The old standby, mailing your press releases in a #10 business envelope to the media, still works. In fact, you'd be hard-pressed to find an editor or producer who *objects* to this method of distribution. The drawback, of course, is that it's slower than electronic distribution and somewhat more difficult to time the delivery this way. So although mailing is fine for feature pieces, news and other time-sensitive releases — especially those tied to an event — are better delivered by another method.

✔ **Express delivery or messenger:** When the press kit consists of more than a text-only document and you want it to have maximum impact, send it by overnight courier or — for local media — messenger, although this method is obviously expensive. We sometimes messenger videos for local broadcast media, although as we discuss in Chapter 14 on television PR, a faster and better alternative to hand-delivering videos is satellite uplink services. If you have a particularly handsome or impressive press kit, mail it via the post office if timeliness is not critical, or messenger or express the kit if timeliness is of the essence.

✔ **Fax:** Fax broadcast is an extremely popular way to send press materials. With *fax broadcast* (also known as fax distribution), a single press release is simultaneously sent to multiple publications via fax. The CD in this book lists several fax distribution services that handle press releases. Almost all the broadcast media accept media alerts via fax, and most of the print media seem okay with it, too. Many major media distribution services recommend fax broadcast as the preferred medium of distribution for press releases.

 ✔ **Internet:** Can you e-mail your press release? Some editors love e-mail, and others hate it. So a mass mailing of a press release over the Internet to editors you don't personally know is risky. Ask editors which distribution method they prefer and whether they like e-mail. Note their preferences on your personal contact list.

Selecting PR Media

Media selection means choosing, from among your personal contact list and mass media database (directories or distribution services), the media outlets to which you want to send your press releases and other PR materials.

Because of the incredibly low cost per media contact of PR versus advertising, the winnowing-down process is somewhat different. In advertising, running an ad or commercial can cost thousands of dollars — even tens or hundreds of thousands of dollars — per insertion. So although you may want to run your ad in many publications, budget forces you to select only those few media whose subscriber or viewer demographics are the closest match with your potential audience. You think restrictively based on the finite budget you have to work with.

In PR, the cost per media contact is literally only the cost of mailing or faxing or e-mailing another copy of your press release to another media outlet: about a dollar or less per publication or program. The physical distribution is a minor cost component, and because the media don't charge you a fee to run your PR materials, you don't have to pay a pick-up cost.

Therefore, in PR media selection, think expansively rather than restrictively, as in advertising. As you study the media directories and scan the marketplace to see what's out there, add to your list any media outlet that seems to reach your target market in some way, even if these media are peripheral to your marketplace or industry rather than central to it. Remember all those publications you wanted to advertise in but couldn't because of your limited budget? All of them should be on the media distribution list to get your PR materials. PR is a great way of getting coverage in the media that you want to target but can't afford to target through advertising.

For instance, suppose that 5 magazines cover the aquarium industry and 100 magazines overall cover pets in some fashion. An aquarium manufacturer may be able to afford advertising in the one or two best-read aquarium magazines. But aquarium people also read pet magazines. A press release announcing a new aquarium filter could be sent, easily and inexpensively, to all 5 aquarium magazines and all 100 pet magazines, gaining broader coverage than can be affordably acquired with paid advertising.

Deliver us from e-mail

One of my staff members pitched a story to an editor at *The Dallas Morning News* via e-mail with a PC formatted attachment. He got back a stern e-mail telling him never to send an attachment for a number of reasons: They take up bandwidth. They cause e-mail to download much slower, wasting the busy editor's time.

And in this case, the editor couldn't read the document as he was not on a Windows or Mac-based system. In my experience, cutting and pasting documents into the body of an e-mail is the best method. You lose formatting, but you also remove the problem of the recipient's not being able to read an attached file.

In PR media selection, the general rule is, "When in doubt, *don't* throw it out." If you think, "Maybe some of the people watching this program *might* be interested in my product," add it to the distribution list. When in doubt, *send* it out. Even if one person watching the show becomes a customer, it's worth the first-class stamp it took to mail the release, right?

Turning the Press into a Client

A common misconception is that an adversarial relationship exists between PR and the press. Although there is a small element of truth in this — some journalists really do dislike PR people and prefer not to work with them — they are in the minority. Most journalists view PR people as resources who can provide both story ideas and access to sources (their clients) for stories they're working on. If you're a good resource, your relationship with the media will be a win-win situation.

As a PR agency partner, I see many PR firms that are advocates for their clients. That's fine. But I take a different approach. I see my role as not only helping my clients but also helping the media do their jobs. Treat the media as a customer — a consumer of your information — and then tailor information that they actually want and can use.

How do you do this? Much the same way you meet the needs of your customers. For instance, when a customer isn't happy, you ask what would make her happy? When an editor says that he isn't interested in running one of my stories, I don't hang up the phone in rage.

Instead, I ask him, "What type of stories are you interested in? What you are looking for?" Then I can note his preferences in my personal contact list and pitch my next idea in terms that will be attractive to him. For instance, if I'm promoting a product launch and the producer rejects a story because it doesn't have a local angle, I might find a retailer that carries the product or a customer who uses it in her town before my next call. As a result, the producer may want to send a camera crew to the local store for a short piece on the product, giving the story local color.

When a publication writes a story about you, send a note to the writer saying how much you like the article and what response you have received to the piece. Not only does your personal note flatter the writer, but also writers like hearing about responses — it tells them that people are reading their stuff.

Techniques for Breaking Through the PR Clutter

In Chapter 6, I give you my "bag of tricks" for coming up with creative PR campaigns. Now I'm going to dip into the bag again and look at some of my favorite techniques for breaking through the PR clutter in your media relations.

Surround sound

Some PR professionals and businesspeople have a misguided belief that the only way to reach a CEO is by getting a story on the front page of *The Wall Street Journal,* or that a chemical engineer will notice your product announcement only if it appears in *Chemical Engineering* magazine.

But are those assumptions really true? Do you read only magazines and newspapers focusing on your business or industry interests? Of course not. You read the sports page — or the comics. You probably don't limit your television viewing to shows about your business, either. You watch the news, ESPN, or the *Biography* series on A&E.

I naturally target my PR campaign to cover all the publications central to a market or audience, but then I spread out to cover all the other print or broadcast media that that target may read, hear, or see. I call this the "surround strategy" because, by taking this approach, I can surround the prospect with my story and message in multiple media. The message not only gets through, but it also reaches its audience through multiple exposures, thereby increasing credibility and making more impressions.

The lesson of surround strategy hit home for me on a flight where I sat next to the CEO of a big company. When the flight attendant handed out reading matter, I silently guessed whether he would pick *Forbes* or *Business Week.* Instead, he chose *USA Today* and began reading Section D, the Life section. When I asked him about it, he told me that was the first thing he read every day, at home or at the office.

Have a go-to guy

In Chapter 10, I talk about using pitch letters to establish someone in your company (an in-house employee or a hired spokesperson) as an expert in your particular industry or subject. I call this person the "go-to guy" because he becomes the source the media goes to first for commentary on that particular topic.

Donald Trump is currently the go-to guy in real estate. Dr. Ruth Westheimer (author of *Sex For Dummies,* published by IDG Books Worldwide, Inc.) is the go-to gal on sex. Donny Deutsch is the go-to guy in advertising. Alan Dershowitz is the go-to guy for the law, and Warren Buffett is the go-to guy on stocks (or at least for value investing).

Positioning someone in your company as a media go-to guy is a great way to break through the clutter, because if you're the source the media goes to first, you — and not your competitors — are the one constantly quoted in stories on your topic. In addition to multiplying your media exposure, this advantage will drive your competition crazy.

How many of you have noticed that someone is constantly quoted in your industry and complained, "Why does the media keep featuring this guy? He doesn't know a thing! I'm much more expert than he is!" When you're the go-to guy, you'll be the one the media calls, not the one complaining that the media called someone else.

Offer an exclusive

If I want to place my story in a specific publication or program, I offer that publication or program an *exclusive*. That means this media contact has first crack at running the story. If this media contact accepts, I won't release the story to any other media until it runs first as an exclusive with that publication or program.

The benefits are twofold. First, offering the exclusive increases the likelihood that my first-choice media outlet will run the story, because the media love exclusives. Second, if I get into a prestigious print publication through an exclusive, I make copies of the story and include it when I send the release or media kit to other publications after it has run.

When the other media, especially broadcast, see the reprint, they too become more likely to run the story. Reason: Pickup in a big national publication serves as a media "endorsement" of the story to the other media. Editors and producers see the reprint and think, "If *The New York Times* ran it, this must be legitimate." Just as testimonials from your customers help sell other customers on your products, endorsements from the media help sell other media on running your release or covering your event.

Go where the cameras are

As I mention elsewhere in this book, our campaign for Domino's Pizza received major TV coverage when Domino's sent pizzas to taxpayers standing on line at the main post office in Manhattan to file last-minute returns on the evening of April 15.

The technique we used in that campaign, "Go Where the Cameras Are," is based on the fact that it's easier to piggyback on a story or event the media are already covering in force than to entice them out for the sole purpose of covering your story. If cameras are already shooting and you walk in with something they can't help notice — in Domino's case, fresh hot pizza — it's as easy as moving a few inches to the right for those cameras to turn on you for a few seconds. And really, that's all you need.

Use timing in your favor

In Chapter 7, I discuss the idea of creating a PR campaign that ties in with a holiday, special event, or other calendar date. Even if that's not the central hook of your campaign, see whether you can work an element of timeliness into it. For instance, if you're doing a campaign to promote a nutritional supplement that lowers stress, why not give free samples in front of Macy's or another giant department store December 23, the last full shopping day before Christmas? Or at a college dorm during final's week? You get the idea.

Following Up: The Media Blitz

I tell my clients you need two ingredients to PR success, and that having media contacts is not one of them.

The two ingredients of PR success are creativity and hard work. I cover creativity in other chapters on creating PR campaigns, especially Chapters 5 through 7. The hard work comes in the media follow-up.

Many businesses send out press releases with no follow-up; others call only the one or two most important publications in their industry to see whether the press release was received and will be used. At our agency, we call more than one or two publications.

Specifically, we call every media outlet to which we sent the press materials — and we call them several times. Why? It's my experience that if you make a thousand phone calls, you can't help but get some media placements. So we make the thousand phone calls — for every press release we mail. And doing so pays off. The more you follow up, the more pickups you get.

"Did you get the materials I sent you?"

When you call an editor or producer, your first question should be, "Did you get the materials I sent you?" Approximately 50 percent say they don't have it. They don't remember getting the release or they misplaced it. Send it again by fax or e-mail (asking which the editor or producer would prefer) and then follow up later that day or the next day.

Working Your ABC Lists

I have a cold-calling technique for selling stories to the media. It's literally as simple as ABC. If you have a list of, say, 1,000 prospects to call, break it up into three segments — A, B, and C — as follows:

- ✔ **A — the prime prospects:** These are your most desirable targets — television networks, *The Los Angeles Times, The Wall Street Journal, Time,* and *Newsweek.* Include the major national media that would bring major prestige and credibility to your firm if they use your piece. This list should probably include about 50 to 100 names.

- ✔ **B — the smaller publications:** These are the small media that you don't view as essential to your PR campaign. These are the least critical and desirable media outlets, like your local *penny saver* (the free weekly newspaper every resident of your town gets). You should have about 25 to 50 names on this list.

- ✔ **C — the remaining 900-plus names:** This list includes everybody else.

First, call the B's to practice your pitch. Use feedback to refine your script to improve response to your next list, the A's. For instance, if the B's won't take the story because it's been done before, can you think of a fresh angle or twist to overcome that objection?

Next, call the A's. Do everything in your power (short of bribery, of course) to convince at least one of these media outlets to run the story.

Now, call the C's and let them know about the prestigious new pickups you have from the A list. The C's are influenced by big names and are more likely to run your campaign because of the endorsement of the A media.

Sticky Situations in Media Relations

In one case, a PR client was approached by the leading trade journal in his industry, which said it would write and publish a feature article about him in exchange for a big order of ad space. What's more, the publisher said, the client could get an even larger article and be featured on the front cover, if he paid a sum of several thousand dollars *in addition* to the cost of the ads. And this was from a highly respected industry publication readers valued for its editorial excellence, reporting, and objectivity. If only they knew!

Another colleague reports that a local business magazine, published by the chamber of commerce, offered to run a large, positive feature article about his business — an article that he could write and submit, and that would be run as written — if he joined the chamber. In fact, the chamber makes this offer to all potential members.

If you live in a small town, take a look at the local weekly "shopper" newspapers distributed free to all residents. Such newspapers are not reporting hard news per se but are really in the business of disseminating news about people and organizations in the community, including businesses. Send them a press release, and they'll publish it. Take an ad, and you get featured in editorial roundups highlighting local businesses and their services.

Because many publications do give editorial favors in exchange for your ad dollars, should you ever take the initiative in suggesting such an arrangement to the media? You should not — at least not when communicating with staff writers and editors.

Never say to an editor, "Please run my article; I advertise in your publication" or "I may place a lot of ads in your publication if you run my press releases and cover my grand opening." Such requests are likely to infuriate the editor. They demean the profession of journalism, insult the editor personally, and kill any chance that the editor will use your material now or in the future.

If the media outlet is one that allows advertising sales to influence editorial decisions, you'll find out when someone makes such a suggestion to you. It may come from the editor, but typically it comes from the publisher or advertising rep who says, "Run an ad with me, and I'll get your press release published" or the lesser promise of "Run an ad with me, and I'll personally place your press release on top of the editor's desk and try to get him to run it."

If you do decide to broach the subject of getting press coverage in exchange for placing your ad with the publication, bring it up with the publisher or advertising rep, not the editor. Say something like, "If I run these ads with you, what can you do for me editorially?" You'll quickly find out whether and to what degree the advertising department can influence the editor in favor of running the PR story of a particular advertiser.

Chapter 13

Tuning In to Radio

In This Chapter

▶ Understanding the advantages of radio over other media

▶ Landing a spot on a radio talk show

▶ Getting ready for your interview

▶ Impressing your audience while on the air

▶ Obtaining a tape of your interview

*A*lmost everyone listens to radio. But most people don't think of radio listening as an activity; they just do it. Radio listening is a natural part of just about everyone's lives.

"During the pre-test of our questionnaire, most people had difficulty thinking about radio as a leisure-time activity," notes John Crothers Pollock, president of the firm Research and Forecasts, Inc. "Radio is so closely integrated with all other activities people pursue — brushing their teeth, driving to work, walking down the street. Radio, rather than a leisure activity, is an integrated activity. It is so universal as to be indistinguishable from other aspects of daily concern."

Here are some additional facts about radio and radio advertising from the Radio Advertising Bureau in New York:

✔ Radio reaches 77 percent of consumers daily and 95 percent of consumers weekly.

✔ The average consumer spends almost five hours a day reading, listening to, and watching media. Forty-four percent of this time is spent listening to radio versus 41 percent watching TV and 15 percent reading newspapers and magazines.

✔ Eighty-two percent of adults age 18 or older listen to the radio while they drive.

✔ Radio, more so than other media, generates immediate purchases. More consumers buy products within one hour of hearing a radio commercial than within one hour of seeing a TV commercial or reading a newspaper or magazine ad.

✔ Consumers spend 85 percent of their time with ear-oriented media such as radio and TV, but only 15 percent of their time with such eye-oriented media as newspapers and magazines.

Radio is everywhere. It goes places other media can't. The time lapse between exposure to the promotional message and the retail reaction (that is, the time between when the buyer hears the commercial and goes to the store to shop for the product) is the fastest with radio: 2 hours for a radio commercial compared to 3½ hours for television, 3¾ hours for newspapers, and 4 hours for magazines. Radio has the fastest rate of return.

Studies show that the selective quality of radio has produced loyal listeners. This loyalty assures advertisers of a consistent audience of the type of listener that the radio campaign is designed to attract. And most large manufacturers have co-op advertising programs for radio through which the manufacturer reimburses the local advertiser — a supermarket, retailer, or other distributor — for a portion of the advertising expenditures.

Opportunities to get on radio talk shows are plentiful. In North America, there are 459 national radio talk shows, 251 syndicated radio talk shows, and 5,102 local talk shows. About a third of these shows are general interest; the others cover specialized topics ranging from agriculture and business to sports, health, personal finance, and travel.

Looking at the Advantages of Radio over Other Media

PR novices tend to focus on print media to the exclusion of radio and TV. As a result, the more seasoned PR professionals may be able to get broadcast coverage for their company or product that their competitors aren't.

Actually, it makes no sense to overlook radio producers in your PR campaign, because radio offers a number of advantages other media do not:

✔ **Economy:** Radio commercials are inexpensive to produce because the listener's imagination — and not a costly photographer or video production house — provides the picture. And radio time has a lower cost per thousand (refer to the sidebar "Figuring cost per thousand") than newspapers, magazines, and television. Of course, in this chapter, I show you how, through PR, you can get all the radio time you want absolutely free. So the cost is virtually zero.

✔ **Selectivity:** Radio offers a wide selection of program formats, each catering to a specific segment of the population. (I list various formats later in this chapter.)

- ✔ **Penetration:** Radio reaches nearly 99 percent of the consumer market.

- ✔ **Mobility:** Radio can reach customers just about everywhere, even at the point of sale.

- ✔ **Immediacy:** Advertisers can change their message quickly and easily. They can get new commercials on the air rapidly. A commercial can be written and taped or read live literally the same day, if necessary.

- ✔ **Flexibility:** Radio enables advertisers to talk to customers during the time of day and in an environment that's likely to induce a selling response.

- ✔ **Intrusiveness:** Radio can pervade a listener's mind, even when interest doesn't exist. Radio can and often does invade the mind of a preoccupied listener, forcefully delivering a message. Have you ever found a Top 40 sound running through your head? Constant exposure on the radio is the reason.

- ✔ **Audience:** Radio can reach virtually any segment of the consumer market, including people who don't frequently read newspapers (teens, for example). It reaches newspaper readers who don't read retailer ads because they aren't regular customers. It reaches prospects for your business whose names are not on the mailing lists you rent or who don't read unsolicited mail. And radio enables you to pinpoint your target audience by demographics, psychographics, and geography. A *psychographic* is a psychological characteristic of a target market. For example, market research shows that baby boomers are nostalgia oriented, so using spokespeople and images from their youth appeals to them when you're marketing products.

We live in an age of electronic information, with people reading less and watching and listening more. Therefore, getting on radio and TV enables you to reach additional prospects who may not read the newspaper or magazines.

Another advantage is that radio doesn't require intense concentration on the part of the listener. You can listen to the radio while doing other things, making radio especially appealing as a medium in today's time-pressured society.

Figuring cost per thousand

The comparative cost effectiveness of advertising medium is often measured in "cost per thousand" — the cost you pay for the media space or time per 1,000 subscribers, viewers, or listeners reached. For instance, if a 30-second radio commercial on a station reaching 100,000 listeners costs $500, your cost per thousand is $500 divided by 100, or $5 per thousand.

Who Do You Call? Getting on the Radio

You don't have to be a celebrity to be a guest on a radio show. Hundreds of radio shows are in need of interesting, informative guests. Celebrities do get lots of airtime, but at least as much airtime goes to people who, like you, have knowledge of a specialized subject of interest to a particular audience and can communicate this knowledge in an interesting, enjoyable, and clear way.

Radio talk shows are a great way to get your message to the world because they are always looking for interesting guests. Approximately 30 percent of radio and TV producers surveyed say that they're interested in booking guests who speak on topical issues; 16 percent are interested in having people speak about new products; and 12 percent like to book authors.

This book's appendix lists several directories of radio talk shows and their personnel, including the producers, receptionists, program managers, and hosts. To get on a radio show, you begin by contacting the producer, because the producer usually decides who the show's guests will be, especially at larger radio stations. At many smaller stations, the hosts are often their own producers and are therefore the ones you should contact.

Making a pitch for yourself

How do you go about pitching yourself as a potential guest? Here are some guidelines:

- Be brief. As in any sales call, you immediately say who you are and why you're calling and give reasons why the person should listen to you — why she should consider having you as a guest on the show. The most effective way to convince a producer that you would be a good fit with her show is to be familiar with the program. Turn on your radio and listen to the program a few times before calling to pitch your story. A radio producer is more likely to book you if, in addition to having a good story and being a good guest, you're a listener or even a fan. For more tips on pitching your story to producers, refer to Chapter 14 on television PR (the techniques are very similar).

- Don't pretend to be a publicist. If you're calling for yourself, say so. Don't try to overimpress or exaggerate, and don't lie. Producers can tell a phony immediately.

- If the producer isn't interested, thank her for her time, get off the phone, and call the producer of the next show you want to get onto. Don't argue with a producer who turns you down, and don't try to prove that you're a good potential guest; producers know what they're looking for in a guest. Don't ask producers who turn you down for a referral or recommendation to another show, either; they're not in business to be your publicists.

✔ You're unlikely to get booked for a show over the phone. Producers who are interested will ask you to send a package of information about yourself and your topic. That media kit can include such items as press releases, a personal biography, testimonials or endorsements, reprints of articles written by or about you, a sample of your product, and a *tip sheet* — a list of 10 to 15 suggested questions the host may ask you about your topic. In addition, if you have made prior appearances on radio or TV, you can include a list of them (with program names, stations, dates, and topic). I also recommend including an audiotape or videotape of a recent media appearance if it's impressive.

Persistent follow-up helps increase your success rate. Media people are busy. If you want to be on the show, persist. Follow up your initial contact with a phone call, a second phone call, and a note. If this follow-up still doesn't work, send another letter saying that you're going to stay in touch because the topic is important. Then stay in touch. Send clippings from print media featuring you, media releases, and articles you've written. Remember, one show can easily get you the attention of millions of people who can buy what you're selling. What you're seeking — publicity — is valuable. And you have to work to get it.

Being an accessible expert

A key ingredient of getting publicity in any medium, but especially on radio, is to be accessible, flexible, and accommodating. When the producer calls and says, "We got your material and are interested in having you on *The Joe Shmoe Show;* how does 10 a.m. on Thursday sound?" say yes. Give the media first priority, and accept the first suggested time or date unless you absolutely can't do so. If you're difficult, hard to schedule, and have a conflict with every date that producers suggest, they're going to get impatient, say, "Thanks anyway," and call the next candidate from the pile of hundreds of media kits they have received.

Although producers generally treat guests nicely, I recommend that you behave as if producers were customers of your business: You exist to serve their needs, not the other way around. This attitude gets results.

Making yourself accessible — anytime

A colleague of mine has a policy of being accessible to the media 24 hours a day, seven days a week, and it works: He gets one media placement or interview every day of the year. He says that once he was awakened at 4 a.m. by a phone call from the producer of a late-night radio call-in show. The scheduled guest was not available, and the producer asked whether my friend could do the interview instead.

"When?" my colleague asked sleepily.

"Right now!" the panicked producer begged. My colleague agreed and did the show from his bed, using the phone on his nightstand.

Preparing for Airtime

You've been invited to be a guest on a talk radio show. Now what? Don't go in cold. Do the following preparation, and your appearance will go more smoothly and be more successful for you:

- ✔ Familiarize yourself with the show on which you're going to appear. Know the host's name and manner of interviewing, the format of the show, and what is expected of you. Get to know the host's idiosyncrasies so that you can avoid surprise and potential embarrassment (for example, if you've written a book on liberal politics and didn't know that the host is ultra-conservative).

- ✔ Know the audience — who listens to the show? Ask the producer or contact the advertising sales department and ask for a media kit. Media kits, which are designed for potential advertisers, usually give details on the audience demographics such as age, income, family, and economic status.

- ✔ Take advantage of every opportunity to promote your appearance. For example, if you're going to be on a popular radio show broadcast in the Washington, D.C., area, call your Washington-based clients and let them know.

- ✔ Rehearse answering all possible questions that may be asked of you — not just the ones on your tip sheet (refer to the section "Putting together a tip sheet," later in this chapter).

- ✔ Know in advance the major points you want to make and the messages you want to get across. Practice saying them in short phrases that you can slip into the conversation in case the host doesn't ask questions whose answers help make your point.

✔ If you're on a call-in show, arrange for two or three friends to call in with prepared questions. These calls can get things going, save you the embarrassment of a quiet phone line (if people aren't calling), and ensure that you get to answer the two or three questions you most want to talk about.

✔ Have your toll-free number or local telephone number and mailing address ready.

✔ Take with you any materials you may need to refer to. If you're an author doing a call-in radio show, for example, have a copy of your book with you. If you want to support your opinions with facts and statistics but your memory is not great, jot down the key facts on index cards and have them handy.

✔ Have a free tip sheet, special report, booklet, or reprint that you can offer callers or viewers as a giveaway. This bait piece contains information that expands on one or more of the topics you discuss on the show. Having such a bait piece can make the difference between tremendous versus minimal lead generation from a radio appearance.

✔ Work on a definition of what you do and boil it down to a single brief sentence that you can say — for example, "My company, CTC, helps businesspeople improve their writing skills."

✔ For in-studio radio shows, leave for the interview early. This is one interview for which you absolutely can't be late. A client or recruiter can always wait, but an 11:00 a.m. show must start at 11:00 whether you're there or not. If the show starts at 11:00, you were told to be there at 10:00, and it takes an hour to drive in normal traffic, you may think that you should leave at 9:00. I recommend that you leave at 8:00 or 8:15 the latest . . . just in case. Nothing is as uncomfortable as being stuck in traffic at 10:45 for an 11:00 radio appearance. Trust me. I know from experience.

Boning up on your topic

Spend some time boning up on your topic before you go on the show. A radio appearance is the ultimate think-on-your-feet challenge. No matter how well you prepare, callers and hosts will ask questions on specific situations that require you to work out an answer instantly, on the spot, and present it in a clear manner, without hesitation, in 30 to 60 seconds.

Spend an evening reading through your press releases, press kit, book, article clippings, brochure, annual report, or whatever source material is the basis for your topic. Take notes on interesting highlights and jot these key facts and figures on a few index cards or a sheet of paper. Take this material with you. You can study it while you wait to go on the air and refer to it while on the air without the audience knowing that you're using a crib sheet.

Putting together a tip sheet

Radio program directors and show hosts are busy, and they often don't have time to read your material, study your press kit, do their homework, and prepare questions to ask you. Therefore, they'll appreciate it if you prepare the questions for them and submit them before your interview. A sheet of prepared questions is sometimes called a *tip sheet* because it tips the interviewer off about what he should discuss (refer to Figure 13-1).

Although putting together a tip sheet sounds like extra work, it's to your advantage to send one with your press kit in advance. By creating the questions, you can shape the interview — ensuring that the topics you want to cover are discussed during your appearance.

Questions for Robert W. Bly author of
101 Ways to Make Every Second Count

1. You write that there are three lists everyone should keep. What are they?

2. You state in your book that procrastination is the single biggest factor in people falling behind in their work. Give us your tips to overcome it. (Do you ever procrastinate? What works for you?)

3. Your discussion of knowing the value of time and money is so interesting and we loved your story about the two salespeople and their different sales goals. Can you tell us a little about the correlation between being productive and reaching an appropriate goal?

4. Most of us can relate to your statement that we're all running at full speed everyday with barely time to breathe, yet your book tells us we can add 10% more productive hours to our day! Can you explain how this works?

5. We're all inundated with material to read – magazines, journals, e-mails, reports, newsletters, memos, etc. What are your tips for helping us get through all of this material?

6. One of your chapters talks about being more productive through the right use of various communication tools. Can you talk about how we misuse or underuse the equipment in our office?

7. Tell us about virtual offices. How does yours work (and give us the ups and downs you experience)...

Figure 13-1:
Sample tip sheet for a radio interview to publicize a book.

Being interviewed at home

For call-in radio shows that interview you by phone from your home or office, arrange for absolute silence and no interruptions during the interview. Being interrupted is unprofessional, is annoying to the host and listeners, ensures that you will never be invited back, and can make you lose your composure and throw you off track. Put a DO NOT DISTURB sign on your door — a big one in large, bold letters. Let others know that you will be doing a radio show via phone and can't be disturbed for any reason.

Do you have call waiting? Use the call-blocking feature to shut it off, or have someone call you to tie up your second line and prevent your phone interview from being interrupted by the annoying call-waiting signal. If other phones in your home or office can ring within earshot, take them off the hook until after your interview.

Turn off your radio, too. You can't talk on the phone to a radio show and listen to it at the same time.

Finally, make sure that you have a glass of water handy and that the air conditioner or heat is not turned up too high. You want to be comfortable before you begin, because you won't be able to get up and change the thermostat once the interview starts.

Making a Good Impression during the Interview

Talking on radio is not the same as making a sales presentation to a prospect in your showroom or during a sales call. The key differences: (1) Your time on radio is strictly limited by the segment length defined by the producer, and (2) listeners prefer crisp, concise answers, and lose attention if you are windy.

Keeping all that in mind, here are some general tips for making your radio appearance a success:

- ✔ When asked a question, restate the question before giving your answer.
- ✔ Be brief. After 20 to 30 seconds, you're probably overanswering. If an answer goes longer than that, summarize.
- ✔ Use humor, but don't tell jokes. Short anecdotes are effective.
- ✔ Demonstrate that you're an authority by using facts to enumerate your points.
- ✔ Use dramatic statistics and findings to grab your audience's attention.

✔ Elaborate beyond yes or no responses. Make specific points, using examples to bring home each point.

✔ Don't come off like a stiff. Be relaxed and let your personality shine through during the interview.

✔ Use names — the person interviewing you and the people calling into the show. Later in the show, refer by name to people who have called in.

✔ Be positive and show enthusiasm and conviction.

✔ Don't repeat or paraphrase a caller's damaging question. It's okay to interrupt a question based on a false fact or premise.

✔ End each segment with an upbeat, summarizing benefit of following your advice or using the product you are selling.

Defining the limits of your expertise

The host and listeners expect you to be an expert in your topic; that's why you're there. However, part of being an expert is to know how far your expertise extends and where it ends. This honesty impresses hosts and listeners instead of turning them off. I have two specific strategies for handling questions that throw me off balance and to which I don't have a good answer (or can't come up with one on the spot):

✔ **Decline to answer based on limits of expertise.** For example, on a recent radio appearance in which an expert talked about how to be a more effective salesperson, a caller asked about managing a sales force and specifically whether the expert knew compensation schemes that rewarded salespeople for getting repeat business from existing accounts. He immediately answered, "Michael, I'm sorry, but my expertise is selling techniques, not management of salespeople. I know nothing about management and have no idea how to compensate a sales force. You might try asking colleagues who are sales managers at other companies in your industry."

✔ Say, **"I don't know the answer to that question, George, but if you call me at my office tomorrow, we can discuss it further. I will then research it and get the answer for you or put you in touch with someone who knows. Host, may I give George my office number?"** This technique demonstrates that you're a helpful source of information and gets you off the hook of having to know it all.

Asimov the expert

The late Isaac Asimov, prolific author of more than 400 books on science, history, literature, and other topics, tells an amusing story in his book *Opus 100* (published by Houghton Mifflin) about the media's expectations of an expert. His publisher booked him on a radio talk show to promote his latest book, *The Human Brain*. When the interviewer asked him a question about the brain, he answered, "I don't know."

"What do you mean you don't know?" asked the interviewer. "You wrote a book on the human brain!"

"Yes," Asimov replied, "but I've written hundreds of books on dozens of topics, and I can't be an expert on all of them. I only know what's in the book, and in fact, I can't even remember all of that!"

Exasperated, the interviewer said, "So you're not an expert on anything?"

"Oh, I'm an expert on one thing," said Asimov.

"On what?" asked the host.

"On being an expert," Asimov replied. "Do you want to talk about that?"

The host declined.

Handling surprise gracefully

Being a guest on a radio talk show is not always a winning situation. Getting yourself on the show, preparing, and doing the interview take a lot of effort and time. For small-business people, time is money — you don't do publicity for the fun or glory; you do it for the sole purpose of publicizing your product or service, generating leads, enhancing your visibility and reputation, and making more sales and profits. (At least that's my motivation.)

So when you go to all this trouble and the media appearance doesn't work out, you tend to get upset. But don't let it show. Instead, handle the situation gracefully: Never yell or complain, and always leave people thinking well of you. This positive behavior increases your chances of getting more and better media opportunities. Negative behavior will give you a reputation as a difficult person and make media people want to avoid you.

Most media appearances go well, but horror stories do exist. One friend recalls driving two hours in torrential rains to keep an appointment to appear on a radio show. When he arrived, another guest was sitting in the interviewee's chair. "Whoops," the assistant program manager said. "I must have forgotten to make a note after we talked, and I guess I forgot to schedule you. Can you come back next week?"

Another horror story happened to my friend Richard Armstrong. He was thrilled when his publisher booked him on the Bob Grant show, a top-rated talk show in the New York City area, to discuss his new book on politics, *The Next Hurrah*. Unfortunately, when he got there, he discovered that he was not the sole guest; another author would be on at the same time. The author was celebrity George Plimpton. Worse, Plimpton had just written a book on baseball and wanted to discuss baseball, not politics. The show made no sense, with Plimpton talking about baseball and Grant and Armstrong discussing politics (with Plimpton also commenting on politics but obviously disinterested in doing so). But Armstrong performed like a pro, meaning he didn't whine about it and discussed his topic during the show to the best of his ability and as much as the host would permit.

Don't make product pitches on the air

Some experts tell you to plug your product or service when on the air. I disagree. People don't want to hear about your book, video, or accounting firm; they want to get solutions to pressing problems. So rather than talk about yourself, your product, or your service, focus on the listeners — what they need, what they want, and what their problems and concerns are.

For example, Bob Bly, my coauthor, was recently a guest on a number of call-in radio shows to promote his book *Selling Your Services: Proven Strategies for Getting Clients to Hire You (or Your Firm)* (published by Henry Holt). Repeatedly, the hosts would say, "Tell us about your book, Bob."

He answered, "I'd be happy to talk about the book, Mr. Host. But what I'd really like to do is help your listeners overcome their fear of making cold calls, overcome the objections they're getting from prospects, feel more confident about selling, and get better results. So, those of you listening out there, when you call, we'll go through your particular selling situation and solve the problem right over the phone!"

The hosts were delighted with this approach, as were the listeners. Bob created a much more interesting, useful show by working with the listeners as if they were clients, rather than saying, "my book this" and "my book that," as 99 percent of authors do. And what about promoting the book? No problem: The host did that for him, because he was enthusiastic about the information and wanted to help listeners get more of it.

The benefits were twofold. First, Bob came across as a credible, respectable expert, not a self-interested author trying to get the listeners to buy a book. Second, the host promoting the book is more effective than the author promoting it because it amounts to a third-party endorsement: the host saying that the book is great and telling his listeners that they should order it.

Radio is warm and intimate. You must personalize what you know, reach out, and talk directly to your prospects as friends, entirely honestly, as if you're having a conversation. The fact that you can't see the people you're talking to is irrelevant. Those listeners must feel the force of your personality.

Getting a Tape of Your Guest Appearance

Whenever possible, get a tape of each radio and TV appearance you make. These tapes have a number of uses:

✔ You can use them to convince producers of other radio and TV shows that you're a good guest — entertaining, pleasant, bright, and informative, with information relevant to their audience. Producers are somewhat reluctant to book guests who are experts but have no or little experience in broadcast media. An audiotape of a good performance can eliminate that reluctance.

✔ Listening to the tapes can help you improve your performance so that you're better the next time.

✔ You can use the tapes as marketing communications tools. For example, if you're a consultant who specializes in quality and you were on a radio show to discuss quality, you can make copies of the tape and send it to clients and prospects.

✔ You can give copies of the tapes to your parents. They'll be thrilled. (The extra copies are for mailing to Uncle Ned and Grandma Nellie.)

How do you get a tape? Before your scheduled interview, call the producer and say, "May I ask a favor? I would love to get an audiotape of the broadcast. If I send you payment, would you be willing to tape the show and mail the tape to me? If not, no problem, of course." Most will agree and, further, will not charge you for the tape (but you should always offer to pay). Others may ask for a nominal sum to cover the cost of duplication and mailing, usually just a few dollars.

Although it's best to get an original tape from the studio (because originals give the best-quality duplications), you can arrange to tape your appearance yourself. Some stereo systems allow direct recording from the radio to a blank cassette. Putting a cassette recorder near a radio and picking up the sound from the speaker usually results in a poor-quality recording that's not good enough for duplication.

Chapter 14

Getting PR on the Tube

• •

In This Chapter

▶ Clarifying how broadcast PR is different from print

▶ Segmenting the medium

▶ Assembling material for your TV media kit

▶ Using b-rolls and VNRs

▶ Selling your story to producers

▶ Getting TV publicity on a tight budget

• •

*T*he Handbook of Advertising Management, edited by Roger Barton, says, "Television is the closest thing to the ideal salesman — a real person — available within our current media environment. It moves, it talks, it demonstrates, it is in the home."

According to the Television Bureau of Advertising, TV is the primary news source for 69 percent of Americans, making it No. 1 ahead of newspapers, which only 37 percent of Americans ranked as their primary news source. Perhaps even more surprising is that Americans picked TV as their most credible news source: In a Roper-Starch survey, 53 percent of Americans said they would be most inclined to believe TV when receiving conflicting reports from different media versus only 23 percent who said they would believe newspapers first.

As a nation, we love to watch television, with 98.2 percent of all U.S. households having at least one TV. The Television Bureau of Advertising also reported that in 1999, TV households averaged almost 7½ hours of viewing a day compared to only 4½ hours in 1950.

Not surprisingly, then, the television commercial is one of the most popular selling tools used by advertisers today. The viewing public is bombarded with 320,000 commercials per year, up 20 percent from 1985. More important, according to the Television Bureau of Advertising, adults rate TV advertising as the most authoritative, most believable, and most influential of the advertising media.

Many small companies automatically dismiss television because of the high cost. But as David Ogilvy writes in *Ogilvy on Advertising,* "Inexpensive commercials can be highly effective if they come directly to the point and offer something of genuine interest."

PR is the most inexpensive TV commercial of them all, overcoming television advertising's cost constraints. For the same dirt-cheap dollar or so that it takes to send a media kit to your local paper, you can send the same media kit to CBS and reach millions of viewers that same evening. This chapter takes a look at how to do a PR campaign aimed at the broadcast media and get results from it.

Understanding How TV PR Differs from Print

The same public relations campaign that you design for newspapers, magazines, and radio can work in TV, too, provided that you *add a visual element* to the campaign.

How, for example, would you get local television stations to feature Fred DeLuca, chairman of Subway Sandwich, if you sent him on a media tour across the country, as we did? By adding a visual element. We had Mr. DeLuca traveling to various cities, where he was available to go on the air and demonstrate to viewers how to build a perfect sub sandwich. Every time he traveled, we would send a media alert or press release to local television stations and get him on at the very least one TV station.

TV is a visual medium, so campaigns with an inherent visual element work better on TV than those that do not have a visual component. An event that has lots of action can make a good short segment for a feature spot on the TV news, for example.

My PR agency's "World's Fastest Pizza Maker" contest for Domino's Pizza, with its pizza-twirling contestants and winner, was a natural for TV (although it worked well in print, too).

Another campaign with a strong visual element to appeal to television was our "Smelly Socks" contest for sneaker maker British Knights. Consumers were invited to send in their smelly socks, which would be judged in a contest, and the winner would get free British Knights sneakers. The visual gimmick was that one of the judges was a dog (actually, my dog).

We sent media alerts (covered later in this chapter) to the New York AP Day Book (also discussed later in this chapter) and all local TV stations. The news cameras ate up the video of me, the British Knights chairman and marketing director, and my dog sniffing the socks as we judged which were the foulest. The story aired on both Fox and WABC.

The most boring visuals are "talking heads" — people being interviewed on camera. Some people have the ability to be engaging on the air; even more do not. Unless you're a totally dynamic personality, do not go on and on with video of yourself chatting. Find something you can show or demonstrate, like how to make the perfect sub sandwich or inspect your furnace or build a compost heap in your backyard.

The most engaging visuals are dynamic, showing lots of action — for example, hot air balloons with the client's logo launching into the skies over a local park while a fair sponsored by the client is going on below.

The more unusual the visual, the more it will catch a producer's eye and engage the viewer. The chairman of Empire Kosher Chickens talking about food safety is okay. Having him talk about food safety as he walks through a poultry processing plant is better. Having him give the same talk while standing in the middle of a football field with a thousand chickens strutting around him — something I actually did — is engaging video.

Are there exceptions to the rule of needing a powerful visual element? Just one. You can get away with straight video only with a personality who has strong charm, charisma, or appeal on camera. TV producers will have you on — and ask you back — if you are one of those rare individuals who is a great guest.

Author Matthew Lesko, whom we once handled, was such a "great guest." His personality was so dynamic, his enthusiasm so contagious, that he lit up the screen, even though he was basically a "talking head" without a strong visual element. If you've seen Matthew on TV as a guest or in his infomercial, you know that he is super-animated — and almost hypnotic to watch.

I'll never forget when we got Matthew on David Letterman. As Matthew grew more and more excited discussing his topic (which is the seemingly mundane subject of how to get free information from the government), Letterman laughed louder and louder, finally commenting, "Matthew, could I suggest decaffeinated coffee?" Similarly, Matthew was talking excitedly on *Larry King Live* when Mr. King, grinning, interrupted him and pointed out, "Matthew, I haven't even asked you the question yet!"

If you are a great guest — photogenic, enthusiastic, appealing, and maybe a bit unusual — you may be a "natural" for television, able to get by just on your own appeal. But that's rare. For most clients, I advise improving the odds with a clever campaign built around an engaging visual element.

For a publishing client, I promoted the book *The OJ Legal Pad* by having a Judge Lance Ito lookalike give out copies of the books on the courthouse steps during the O.J. Simpson trial. When O.J. accepted a copy of the book from our lookalike on those steps, the video made the evening news.

Did we plan or prearrange with O.J. to accept a copy of the book? That would have been impossible. Rather, it was a case of, as scientist Louis Pasteur once said, chance favoring the prepared mind. I am a media hound, and a public relations professional, so of course I watched the trial every day. I knew camera crews were on the courthouse steps every day. So although I couldn't guarantee my client that O.J. would take the book, the odds were in our favor.

Elsewhere in this book, I discuss the PR tactic of "going where the cameras already are." The *OJ Legal Pad* was a prime example. And, because we thought of it first, there was virtually no competition from other marketers for attention — the media's or O.J.'s. After our promotion made the evening news, of course, the courthouse steps were jammed with publicists trying similar stunts.

Sorting Out the TV Shows

Not all TV shows are the same. By recognizing the different kinds of shows and their programming, you can increase your chances of getting coverage by offering them a story that fits in with their format. Here are some of the types of shows you can pitch stories to:

- ✔ **News programs,** such as the local and national TV news, look for short feature segments of interest. Local news programs obviously prefer a local angle.

- ✔ **News shows,** such as *60 Minutes, 20/20,* and *Dateline,* do longer feature segments, often focusing on an important issue, trend, or a family's or individual's story.

- ✔ **Talk shows** range from local cable TV to *Good Morning America, Oprah,* and *Today.* Stories they look for vary from host to host and show to show. For example, Oprah Winfrey likes heartwarming stories, self-help, and fun; Jay Leno looks strictly for funny stories.

In Chapter 12, I talk about how I see my role as a public relations professional to be not only an advocate and partner for my client — the business seeking exposure — but also for the media in getting them stuff they can use. I practice this philosophy especially in TV PR. When a TV show is considering a segment on you, think of the show as your customer. Provide whatever assistance they need to make the segment come off.

Recently, my firm worked with the *Oprah* show on behalf of our client, IKEA, on a segment. Viewers wrote in to tell Oprah their home decorating horror stories. The show picked two viewers, and IKEA experts redecorated and refurnished their homes. Managing the entire process from start to finish took four months, but to get on *Oprah*, it was worth it.

Targeting a Specific Show for Your PR Campaign

How do you go about targeting shows for your PR campaign? Here's the step-by-step:

1. Watch TV.

   You will quickly be able to figure out which programs are a good fit for your PR efforts, and which your target audience is watching.

2. Once you have found a program you think you may want to get featured on, watch it a number of times. Pay attention to the format and the types of segments it runs.

3. Think of a way to fit your message into the show's format and, even better, one of its regular segments.

4. Prepare a press kit to mail to the show.

   What should be in it? The two documents discussed later in this chapter — a pitch letter and a media alert — are essential. You might also include a press backgrounder, your bio, articles published about your company — anything that might help sell your story to the producer.

5. Send the press kit.

6. Follow up with a phone call to the producer.

   Ask whether he would be interested in running the story. If not, why not? How does it not meet his needs? If he is not interested in this story, what kind of stories is he looking for? Elicit information on why you're being rejected so that you have a better chance of getting a positive response to your next story idea.

7. When you are rejected, be gracious and end the call pleasantly.

   Do not sacrifice what could be a valuable long-term relationship with an important media outlet in a fruitless attempt to badger the producer into running your story. It probably won't work, and it may very well alienate the producer for life.

Many PR novices tell me that calling the producer is the step that causes them the most anxiety. "How can I call a TV producer whom I don't even know?" they ask me. "After all, I am nobody to them." The secret is that the person who makes the call may get on the show, but the person who never gets up the courage to make the call is definitely *not* going to be on the show!

When I started doing PR for Matthew Lesko, I was a kid in my 20s fresh out of college and with zero public relations experience. Since I didn't know any better, my first day on the job, I picked up the phone, called the *Larry King Live* show, and asked if they would like to have Matthew — who was then largely unknown — on the show. And guess what? They booked him! When people asked Matthew back then how he got on Larry King, his answer was, "A 20-year-old who does not know that 'no' is a possibility."

Don't accept no as a possibility. Or, at least consider that no means "no, not now" — it doesn't mean "no forever." I always keep calling. As a PR pro seeking placement for my client's products and services, I always strive to turn a no into a maybe, and a maybe into a yes.

Preparing Your TV Media Kit

You can use the same press releases and media kits that you prepare for other media (refer to Chapter 9) when pitching PR to TV, without modifying or customizing them for television. In addition to your standard media kit, a few other formats are especially effective. You can use them as stand-alone pieces or add them to media kits going to TV producers.

Article reprints

Whenever you get coverage in major print media, such as *The Wall Street Journal* or *The New York Times,* make reprints (with the paper's nameplate at the top of the page). Include the article reprints with all media kits mailed to broadcast media. A TV producer will be more likely to run a segment on your story if a national and well-respected print publication has already covered it. Producers figure that if *Time* or *USA Today* ran the story, it must be legitimate.

A lot of cross-pollination exists between print and broadcast media. Pay attention to the media. You will soon notice that stories you read in *USA Today* in the morning you then hear on the radio driving home from work at night. We recently did a promotion for our PR firm that played off the TV show *Survivor,* asking CEOs what they would do if stranded on an island. CNBC picked up the story directly from *The Washington Post* article about our survey.

Those in the TV world see an article reprint from a major paper as a legitimate media endorsement of the story. I always try to get one big print placement in the beginning so that I have an article reprint to include with my outgoing media kits.

Articles that appear in a magazine or newspaper are the copyrighted property of the publisher, as is the publication's nameplate. Be sure to get permission before photocopying either piece.

Media alerts

A *media alert* is a short, one-page notice that looks like a cross between a standard press release and a wedding invitation. It quickly hits the highlights, using a graphic format that makes it easy to scan, and sticks to the facts without puff or elaboration. As you can see in Figures 14-1 and 14-2, media alerts focus on the basic "5W's and one H" of journalism — who, what, when, where, why, and how.

The most common method of delivery is to fax the media alert to the television producer; the media directories and distribution services on the CD-ROM make it easy to do this. But sometimes we deliver PR materials in an unconventional manner: To introduce a new deep-dish pizza for Domino's Pizza in the Washington, D.C., market, we delivered the press releases to the four network affiliates by messenger; the press releases were taped to pizza boxes containing hot deep-dish pies.

Figure 14-1 shows a media alert used to announce a promotional event. Notice that the times for photo opportunities are given. TV crews don't want to waste their time standing around or fighting to get the star or celebrity on camera. You should set aside a specific time when camera operators can shoot video of the featured attraction and specify this time in your alert.

For Carvel Ice Cream, my firm did a promotion in which Carvel gave away ice cream to reward the schools with the best attendance records. The message was that Carvel cares about kids and families. Figure 14-2 shows the media alert sent to broadcast media for this campaign.

Pitch letters

In Chapter 8, I discuss writing pitch letters to get journalists to interview you for stories about your topic, product, or industry. You also use pitch letters to persuade TV producers to do features about you on their shows.

Figure 14-3 shows a pitch letter that my firm sent to a local news show to attain an on-air interview with our client, Jose Cuervo, an expert in tequila. The appeal was to do a feature segment on planning great outdoor parties. Timing is important for stories like these. We sent this pitch letter in June, when people are starting to think about outdoor parties and backyard barbecues; it probably wouldn't have worked if we had sent it in the middle of winter.

MEDIA ALERT:

****

WORLD SERIES CHAMPION

Orlando "El Duque" Hernandez

SMOKES A VICTORY CIGAR FOR CHARITY

****

Yankee Pitching Sensation "Teams" Up With Club Macanudo and Hoyo de Monterrey at an Auction To Benefit The Institute of International Education

WHO: Orlando "El Duque" Hernandez, Club Macanudo and Hoyo de Monterrey
***Other notable attendees include: Oscar de la Hoya, Montel Williams and Star Jones*

WHAT: "The First Annual **Club Macanudo** Charity Auction,"
benefiting The Institute for International Education, will feature "El Duque." The auction, conducted by Christie's, will offer a number of exclusive items including: pre-Castro Cuban cigars, autographed Yankee paraphernalia, and signed boxes of the new Hoyo de Monterrey Seleccion Royale "Duque."

WHERE: 26 East 63rd Street (Between Park & Madison) New York, NY

WHEN: TODAY -- 7:00 p.m. to 10:00 p.m.

7:00 - 7:30 PM Photo Opportunity
Orlando Hernandez puffs on a victory cigar as he is bestowed his own personal "El Duque" humidor presented by General Cigar CEO, Edgar Cullman, Jr.

7:30 - 10:00 PM
Orlando Hernandez meet and greet. Auction of autographed items for charity.

CONTACT: Jessica Wolff
Jericho Communications -- (212) 645-6900 ext. 123

Figure 14-1:
Sample media alert announcing an event for television.

If you watch TV news, you sometimes see meteorologists showing outdoor footage — people throwing Frisbees, walking dogs, or jogging in the park — as they do the weather. Or they may appear in person with a microphone and a camera at an event. These spots are called *remotes*. In the movie *Groundhog Day*, for example, Bill Murray plays a TV weatherman doing a remote on Groundhog Day in a town called Pucsatawny.

MEDIA ADVISORY AND PHOTO OPPORTUNITY:
NEW YORK CITY'S P.S. 20 TOPS IN ATTENDANCE AMONG TRI-STATE'S ELEMENTARY SCHOOLS
****

**Carvel Ice Cream To Donate Ice Cream Cakes For Party
In Recognition Of 94.19% Attendance During '97-98**

WHO: P.S. 20 and Carvel Ice Cream

WHAT: Carvel Ice Cream donating ice cream cake for entire student body to celebrate PS 20's '97-98 school year attendance record

In April, Carvel Ice Cream invited tri-state area elementary school principals to send in their school's attendance record in an effort to reward local schools for high attendance rates and help winning schools -- those with the top 50 attendance records of all entrants -- celebrate the close of the school year, an important milestone in children's lives.

WHERE: P.S. 20, 166 Essex Street, between Houston and Stanton

WHEN: Monday, June 22;

Delivery at 9:30;

Party from 10:30 to 12:30

WHY: A school's attendance record is a sign of dedication to learning and excellence. This program lets Carvel Ice Cream recognize the completion of another school year as a milestone in these students' lives -- which is the very essence behind our Lil' Love cakes -- while reinforcing the importance of school attendance, a powerful message for kids.

For information on Carvel's Attendance Recognition Program or to cover P.S. 20's celebration, please call Emily Sills at 212/645-6900.

Figure 14-2:
Media alert
for Carvel
Ice Cream.

I find that pitching a PR idea specifically for live remote coverage is an effective strategy. The reason it works is that live remotes are becoming increasingly popular, and therefore it's not something you have to convince the producer to add to her show — she's already sending out crews every day to shoot live remotes and is looking for a fresh angle for her daily live remote.

Ms. Gwen Edwards
News 12 Connecticut – Morning Edition

Dear Gwen:

So you're planning a party…You've set the date, compiled your invite list, and purchased the perfect summer outfit, but you have no idea how to make this backyard bash stand apart from the rest.

Time to separate the tomatoes from the tamale. Ana Maria Cesaña, an expert in the tequila industry and a native of Tequila, Mexico, is available to show you and your viewers how to spice things up and throw the fiesta of the summer.

A Brand Development Manager for Jose Cuervo International, Ana Maria knows all there is to know about planning a party that will transport your viewers from their smoggy city apartments to a South-of-the-Border celebration. Following are a few of the things Ana Maria can share with your viewers:

Secrets of the perfect Mexican margarita (frozen, on the rocks, flavored, etc…)
Different types of tequila; what they are and how to mix them
How to decorate, from piñatas to cacti
How to make authentic Mexican dishes, including salsa, guacamole and 'frijoles maneados'
The perfect siesta soundtrack

We look forward to helping make the heat of the summer a little more bearable for you and your viewers. If you have any questions or would like to book a "How to Plan the Perfect Summer Fiesta" segment with Ana Maria Cesaña, please call me at 212-645-6900, ext. 122….

Figure 14-3:
Sample pitch letter for a feature segment on a local news show.

By suggesting a live remote that involves your company, you meet the producer's need for an interesting story while getting the cameras that are already in the field to focus on you and your message. Figure 14-4 shows a pitch letter sent to a meteorologist who does on-air weather (TV and radio) for ABC in New York City.

Bill Evans, Meteorologist
WABC-TV

Dear Bill:

In the midst of millionaire mania Crunch Fitness is offering themselves as an outlet for all Americans to vent their frustration about this current craze and get into shape at the same time. Just in time for the summer, Crunch will award 10 free weeks of either boxing or kick boxing lessons to the winner of their millionaire contest – "Who Wants to Kick a Millionaire's Butt?"

As a prelude to summer why not conduct a live remote from a Crunch Fitness gym with a kick boxing instructor. The instructor will provide tips and discuss the following:

Boxing and kick boxing techniques.
How to shape up fast for summer.
The latest fitness trends.
The creative elements behind the campaign.
Which millionaire would viewers would most like to pummel with in the ring.

If you are interested in conducting a live remote from a Crunch Fitness gym or would like to interview Mark DiMassimo, President of DiMassimo Brand Advertising and creator of the contest, please feel free to call me at 212/645-6900 ext. 109….

Figure 14-4:
Sample pitch letter for a live remote spot on local TV weather.

If the media wants to do a live remote, cooperate fully. For a live remote at an IKEA store featuring IKEA's chairman, we were inside the store at 4:30 a.m. helping the TV crew set up for a 7 a.m. spot on a morning show. Why is this important? When we got to the store, we found that there was an automatic AC timer that had turned on the air conditioning, the noise from which would have made the live remote inaudible. Because we were there to handle it personally, the problem was fixed, the show went on, and IKEA got the PR coverage.

There's an old saying: "God is in the details." Well, TV is a detail-oriented medium. The TV crews that show up expect your site to be "TV-ready" — no odd noises, no lighting problems, no logistics hassles. If things aren't just right, the shoot won't come off.

For events, you can use either a pitch letter or a media alert. Figure 14-5 shows a pitch letter that my firm did inviting TV producers to a fun event featuring TV personalities of yesteryear. The event got coverage on national network TV.

> **Dear Dave,**
>
> They entertained and educated millions of children during the '60s, '70s and '80s...and now they're back!
>
> On Saturday, November 15, 1997 on Long Island, the original "**Captain Kangaroo**," Bob Keeshan; Bob McAllister of "**Wonderama**" and "**Kids Are People Too**;" and Tom White and Donna Moore of "**Zoom**" will join with Children's IKEA to present "Let's Rewind and Play."
>
> The gala event will be an interactive, educational and fun playland (tons of activities, giveaways, etc.) for children and adults headlined by performances from these icons from the past. And it's all to benefit children's development-related charities.
>
> We are delighted to invite you and your audience to attend this first-ever event. So, if you're interested in spreading the word to your audience, stopping by, or arranging any interviews with the celebrities or IKEA spokespeople, please call me at 212-645-6900. I'll be happy to help you.
>
> Enclosed you'll find in-depth details on the event and the introduction of Children's IKEA...plus some other "goodies" for your enjoyment. We hope you'll come "rewind" and "play" with us.
>
> Sincerely,
>
> **Crista Rizzuti**

Figure 14-5:
Pitch letter
for an event.

B-rolls

So far in this chapter, I've talked about paper documents. But TV is a visual medium. Should you create video PR materials and send them to TV producers? Yes. Will they use them? Yes.

Producers have limited crews and limited budgets. Much as they'd like to, they can't always send a crew to cover your event or story. Without video, they're less likely to use the story (although on-air personalities doing the news mention many stories that aren't accompanied by video clips). Good video of the product or event increases the odds of your getting coverage.

Typically, I hire a video production company (a number of which I list on the CD-ROM) to shoot the event. The company sends a crew — usually a camera operator and a producer or director — to take footage. The result is a b-roll: a quick video compilation designed to give a TV producer footage of a story that he can use to create a feature segment on the event or product.

B-rolls are best produced by professional video production companies using professional-quality video. TV producers generally won't use home video shot on VHS unless it is a news event of extraordinary value or extremely rare footage, like a hurricane, earthquake, or the Rodney King beating.

The b-roll is shot on the day of the event, preferably early in the day. The production company edits the video to contain several different segments on the event, ranging from 30 seconds to a few minutes. Some of these segments may be question-and-answer interviews, and others are merely sound bites — snippets showing people making brief comments. The video also contains action shots, such as kids throwing pies or riding roller coasters.

Immediately after completion of editing, you send the b-roll to the appropriate TV producers. If you're targeting local TV shows, you can make quick duplicates of the b-roll and deliver the tapes via messenger for possible airing that day.

A number of TV production companies you can hire to do b-rolls are listed on the CD-ROM at the back of this book. What will it cost? Production for one b-roll will run $2,000 to $5,000. Add satellite uplink service to distribute your video to TV producers (refer to the next section), and you're looking at a package price of around $15,000 to $22,000.

Just follow the instructions to view a sample b-roll we did with baseball player Cal Ripken for Itsy Bitsy. The event was the introduction of a new line of toys, "Just Like Dad's," at FAO Schwartz, the famous New York toy store.

Satellite feed services

What if you're targeting national media or other media not in your town? Overnight shipping won't work in most cases, because an event held today will only be covered today; by tomorrow, it's old news. In such cases, the solution is to use a satellite feed service. These services, which are listed on the CD-ROM, take your b-roll video footage and uplink it to a satellite. (I'm not sure of the exact technical method, but for our purposes here, it really doesn't matter.)

TV producers are then given the coordinates of the satellite. They can download the video from the satellite and use it on their shows that day. With a satellite feed service, you can distribute your b-roll to TV stations throughout the entire country on the same day you shoot and edit it.

VNRs

A VNR (video news release) is a more elaborately produced video than a b-roll. Instead of consisting of a series of short clips, a VNR is one entire feature story, usually running 30 seconds to 3 minutes. It's meant to be run in its entirety, although many producers use only a portion of the video.

B-rolls are the format of choice when you have a current event, a hot announcement, or another story for which immediacy is paramount. VNRs are more complete pieces used for feature stories rather than hard news. The trend today in PR is away from VNRs in preference of b-rolls. Reason: B-rolls are cheaper to produce than VNRs, and TV stations like them just as much.

The video production companies mentioned earlier (and listed on the CD-ROM) can produce a VNR for you. Production costs for such a video run $10,000 to $20,000. Add satellite uplink distribution, and the total package price is around $20,000 to $30,000. Yes, that's a lot more than a press release, but it's a lot less than most TV commercials.

To view an actual VNR, insert the CD-ROM and follow the instructions to view the two sample VNRs: One is from Progressive Watercraft Insurance, promoting the "Keys . . . Please" boating safety program. The other is from "Kiss Your Feet," an IKEA event in which the store returned all the profits from sales one October day to its employees as a bonus.

Pitching Your Story to Producers

How do you approach a TV producer? In much the same way that you approach a magazine or newspaper editor (refer to Chapter 10), with just a few differences.

- ✔ If you're trying to impress a producer with whom you have no prior relationship, a nicely packaged media kit sometimes helps.

- ✔ If you want to increase your chances of getting coverage on a particular TV show, offer the producer an exclusive on your story — give the show first crack at running it. If the producer accepts, she gets to run the story first; then you're free to give the story to other shows and stations.

Offer an exclusive only if the story is breaking news or something else important enough to warrant it. When my agency did PR for best-selling author Peter Golenbock's book on a college basketball scandal, *Personal Fouls,* the media considered it a big story. We got continual coverage by offering a new exclusive angle on the story to a different media outlet each day.

✔ When time is of the essence — and this is frequently the case for TV producers, who produce segments daily and often focus on the day's news — fax press releases and media alerts. The best way to make sure that a producer knows about your event is to fax a media alert and then follow up with a phone call. The first thing you want to know is whether the producer got your media alert. If he received it, ask whether he needs additional information or wants to interview anyone.

When you follow up, ask the producer whether you're catching him at a bad time. If the producer is busy, ask when would be a better time to call back.

Don't give up if the response is negative. Ask, "Why isn't this for you?" When the producer gives the reason, you can often find a way to overcome the objection and get him to air your story.

✔ Don't push too hard to sell your story to the media, though. Yes, you'd like to get it on the air. But you're also building a relationship with that producer. Being too aggressive can turn him off and ruin your chances for future placements.

Look to target TV segments that others aren't pitching. I already gave the example of remote shots for TV weather. Another underpitched segment is monologues. Using the TV media directories listed on the CD-ROM, call shows like *Live with Regis Philbin* or *The Tonight Show with Jay Leno.* Ask who's in charge of writing the monologues and send feature material to that person. These shows can always use good jokes, and if what you send fits, you just might hear it on the show that day.

Once, we did a humorous campaign for Domino's Pizza in which we gave free pizza to college seniors who came in with rejection letters from potential employers. Johnny Carson talked about it on his monologue on *The Tonight Show,* and pizza sales for Domino's soared the next day.

Many TV shows plan their shoots for the day by consulting the *AP Day Book.* Each day, the *AP Day Book* wires stories and events to TV producers around the country. I recommend that you send all your TV media alerts to the *AP Day Book;* doing so can increase TV coverage of your events and campaigns.

Finding the right angle

For one campaign, my firm's job was to publicize a tool called RotoZip, which you use to smooth small dents in your car. Media interest was mild. But when I had the wife of the company owner demonstrate the tool, the story began to get TV coverage. The idea of a woman fixing her own car instead of relying on a man to do it seemed to be the angle producers were looking for.

The AP (Associated Press) has bureaus in major markets throughout the U.S., and each bureau has its own day book covering its region. AP bureaus are listed in major media directories, such as *Bacon's Publicity Checker,* listed on the CD-ROM in the back of the book.

Doing TV PR on a Shoestring

Don't have $10,000 to $30,000 to spend on a b-roll or VNR? Relax. There are many less expensive, yet just as effective, ways to use TV PR to make you and your product famous.

My coauthor, Bob Bly, has an office in Dumont, N.J., that's just a mile or so up the road from Napolitano's produce in Bergenfield. There are many produce stands in the New York tristate area, but Napolitano's is one of the most successful and best-known. Why? Because it's the home of "Pete Your Produce Pal." A spokesman for the store, Pete appears on New York television as the produce expert on a morning show.

The publicity costs Pete not a dime out of pocket — the TV station produces his show and makes him famous. And there's no reason you can't use a similar strategy of getting yourself and your product on local TV.

How can you, like Pete Your Produce Pal, get covered by local TV? Here are a couple techniques I have used with success:

✔ **Come up with an angle that appeals to a TV audience.** You don't need to produce a b-roll or VNR. If you have an angle, the producer will have you come to the studio and be interviewed — or, better yet, have you do some kind of demonstration on her set. For Jeff Star, cofounder of Camp Beverly Hills Clothing, we got major TV coverage by positioning Jeff as the "Clothing Psychologist." On the air, he would look at someone and then recommend a wardrobe based on the person's personality.

✔ **Pay attention to the media.** Certain segments on TV repeat every year; in the trade, we call them "evergreens." For instance, you can bet that next Thanksgiving, hundreds of local stations across the country will have a chef visit the set to show how to make Thanksgiving dinner. A food company could send a pitch letter offering to have its chef do the segment with some unique recipes featuring the company's products. If the producer is looking for a new chef for this year's segment — and that's often the case — you may just become the station's new holiday gourmet.

Chapter 15

Getting More Ink
(Print Isn't Dead Yet)

*T*he Internet has changed the way business is done in the United States, and it's now transforming the way we live. It's hot.

But print media such as newspapers and magazines are viewed differently by many people. Some say that print is not only "not hot" but also in danger of disappearing entirely. A few of these skeptics predict that printing words on paper will become as rare as carving commandments on stone tablets.

I disagree. Print is still alive and well. More than 8,000 magazines and 6,900 daily and weekly newspapers are published in the U.S. Nearly 60 million newspapers are sold every day!

So, to promote your business interests, you still want to reach print journalists and get your business covered in their publications. This chapter tells you more about how to do that successfully.

Cracking the Journalists' Secret

Journalists, like all of us, have too much to do and not enough time to do it. If you give them a good story idea, you automatically improve the odds of getting into print. If you give the story to them written, packaged, and ready-to-go, your chances of getting ink increase dramatically. The best way to deliver such a story is in the standard PR document called a press release.

Chapter 9 covers the structure and style of a press release. In this chapter, I focus on how to fill your release with content that gets editors to print it and publicize your product, service, organization, or offer.

Knowing What Not to Do

Many PR practitioners waste an enormous amount of time churning out routine, standardized press releases that, almost invariably, land in the editor's wastebasket. Figure 15-1 shows a typical example.

FROM: XYZ Company, Anytown USA
CONTACT: Paul Paterson at 555-5555

For immediate release

JOE JONES PROMOTED TO EXECUTIVE VICE PRESIDENT AT XYZ COMPANY

ANYTOWN, USA- Joe Jones has been promoted from vice president to executive vice president at XYZ Company. In his new position, he will be responsible for managing U.S. operations as well as long-range strategic planning for all business units.

Before being promoted to executive vice president, Mr. Jones had served for 5 years as vice president for the ABC Division of XYZ Company.

Prior to joining XYZ, he had been a program manager for Another Bigco in Sometown, USA, and had also worked as staff analyst at SmallCo in Another-town, USA.

Mr. Jones holds a B.S. in systems engineering from Nice College and an M.BA. in finance from NightSchool U. He is a member of Tau Beta Beta Rho and the Society for Systems Engineering.

Mr. Jones currently resides in Anytown with his wife, Janet, and his three children, John, Jamie and Jack.

Figure 15-1:
A ho-hum, dead-end press release.

Most publications receiving a press release like the one shown in Figure 15-1 will ignore it. Oh, sure — one or two industry publications will run a one-line mention of Joe's promotion, as will his alumni magazine. And if he lives in a small town, the weekly newspaper may run a short feature article with his picture and the text of the release. But except for some warm fuzzies around Joe's house, the result is minimal visibility for Joe's company — zero leads, inquiries, or new business. In short, the time and money invested in preparing and distributing the release yields virtually no return.

Perhaps 90 percent of all press releases are similar to this fictional example, generating a similar lack of interest, media coverage, and benefit. Press releases of this type, despite their popularity, are ineffective for a number of reasons:

- ✔ The topic is a nonevent. Hundreds of people get hired or promoted every day. So there is nothing to differentiate the announcement from the other dozen or hundred or more the editor receives that week.

- ✔ The topic is not meaningful. The promotion is important to Joe Jones and his family — but that's about it. The release contains nothing to interest an editor or a reader.

- ✔ The announcement does not help promote Joe's firm or sell the firm's products, other than by mentioning the company name. (Journalists, of course, have no interest in promoting your product, but in your role as your company's PR person, you should.)

- ✔ There is no reason or incentive for the reader to pay attention — no benefit or usefulness in the information presented.

- ✔ There is no call to action, no response for readers to take if they want to do business with Joe or his firm.

Despite this lack of effectiveness, the "Joe Jones Promoted" press release is the most commonly used and most popular; approximately eight of ten releases are structured just like it. (Other common company themes are expanded facilities, new hires, awards won, other honors, corporate reorganization, openings of new facilities, and company anniversaries.)

Such press releases remain popular with publicists for two reasons. The first is that they're easy to write and can be prepared quickly without much effort, research, or creative thought. The second reason has to do with the way PR firms and professionals traditionally have earned their keep.

Many PR firms work on retainer: In exchange for a fixed monthly fee, they produce a set number of releases and articles. Or they devote a certain number of hours per month to developing and disseminating PR materials on behalf of their clients. To fulfill this obligation, the outside PR firm (and often, the inside PR manager) looks around the company, asks, "What's new?" and writes and distributes releases on these topics.

If a lot is going on during a particular month, the releases have substance and will work. If nothing noteworthy is happening, the PR person still has to produce X number of press releases. That's when bland releases are hatched on nonevents such as Joe Jones's promotion or Sam Smith's election as treasurer of the fraternal club.

Think twice about sending press releases on new hires or promotions. Such releases offer little benefit to your company, and their publication can cause headhunters to call the employees featured and lure them with job offers.

There are only two situations where I think sending out new hire or promotion press releases is to your advantage. The first is when you hire a big gun for a top executive position. Having the big shot on your team makes the company sound better, especially to investors.

The second situation in which I recommend new-hire press releases is in the dot-com sector and related businesses. Venture capitalists buy resumes, and if you announce to the press that you've just hired the former founder of Big Dot-com as CEO of your Little Dot-com, that can help get the venture capital cash flowing into your coffers.

Catching an Editor's Eye with a "Creative" Press Release

"Creative" press releases are more effective than routine press releases. A *routine* press release is an almost mandatory write-up of an event, usually important to the organization issuing the release but mundane to the media and the general public. In routine press releases, the facts drive the release — something happens or exists, and the publicist, searching for a topic, finds it and writes about it.

A *creative* press release has a "hook" — an angle or slant designed to get the attention of the media (so they will publish the story) and the public (so they will read it). We use the term "creative" because the publicist, instead of just working with the facts as they exist, either creates or helps shape the story hook, with an idea that is not obvious from the story itself.

But the creative release is always built around a genuine story, a real event, important information, or other "meat." If it's just an angle with nothing behind it, the release will get attention but be rejected as a publishable story.

An effective release, however, doesn't begin with the product or the point the publicist cares about; rather, the publicist must build the story around something that would interest prospects — the readers of the publication or listeners of the program.

Too many people write press releases from the product marketer's point of view. They put out story after story about things that are of interest only to the company and its managers.

You do this either in the mistaken belief that others care about you and your company as much as you do (which isn't true) or to stroke someone's ego. Often an executive orders the PR department or agency to put out a release on a person or his or her accomplishments as a way to recognize and honor that person. It may flatter the subject of the release, but editors don't care . . . and neither do your prospects.

As with any effective marketing effort, good public relations focuses on the prospect, not the product. As far as PR goes, think about not what is important to you; concentrate on what is important to your prospects. What are their problems, their needs, and their most pressing concerns? What information, advice, products, services, tips, or guidance do they require to improve their lives, do their jobs better, or save time and money? What information do you have that they would want to know and read about in a magazine or hear on the radio or see on TV?

A press release should not be created merely to stroke the client's ego or serve some internal requirements to have certain topics covered in releases. Press releases succeed when they're focused on what appeals to media people and interests their audiences the most.

Using a "Hook" to Snare Attention

You can choose from numerous ways to make a press release more creative. I list and discuss ten "hooks" that you can attach to your release that have proven successful time and time again in luring attention from the mass media. (Others tactics are discussed in Chapters 4, 5, and 6. Adapt these formulas to your own PR campaign, or invent your own idea.)

- Free booklet or report
- Telephone hotline
- Special or timely event or gimmick
- New product or service
- New literature
- Tie-in with current trend, fad, or news issue
- Survey results
- Free giveaway or trade-in tied to product
- Calls to action
- High-visibility advertising

When writing your own release, you can closely copy the format and style of the example releases in this book, substituting details specific to your topic. For example, I have used the format for a "free booklet press release" to promote numerous products and services — always with substantial results.

Free booklet press release

Th free booklet press release works as follows: You write a booklet, report, or tip sheet on a topic relating to your product or service. For example, if you're selling seeds by mail, write some gardening instructions and offer them as a free reprint. If you sell spices, offer a booklet of free recipes. You then send out a release that (1) announces the publication of your new booklet or report, (2) describes some of the useful information it contains, and (3) offers the booklet free to readers of the publication or to the audience of the radio or TV show.

All three elements are critical. Editors are primarily interested in what's new, so if you're offering a new booklet on a topic, your headline should always begin with "New Free Booklet," followed by a description of the topic, contents, or issue the information addresses.

Next, your press release should repeat (either word for word or edited) some key points highlighted in the booklet or report. This technique makes it easy for the editor to run your release as a "mini-feature article" on the topic.

Just saying that you have a booklet available may get you a small mention. But if you allow editors to reprint some of its contents, by putting such material in the release you send, they're more likely to run longer, more in-depth pieces featuring all the useful information you've provided.

"But if all of the information in my booklet is revealed in the article, then people will have no reason to send for my booklet!" you might protest. That sounds like a logical objection. But experience proves the opposite is true: The more the articles describe the contents of your booklet, the more people will read the article and send for the booklet. "The more you tell, the more you sell." That's an old saying favored by mail-order ad copywriters, but it also applies to free booklet press releases.

Experience has shown that even if the entire text of a booklet is reprinted in an article (or an ad), people still want to get that text in booklet form. Why? Perhaps people don't like to tear out an ad or article, and they find that booklets and reports are a more permanent medium.

Do not assume that the editor will read your booklet and pull out pertinent material for an article. The press release should be a self-contained mini-article ready to use as is so that the editor doesn't have to refer to any enclosures or other materials.

Finally, your free booklet release must call for action. In the last paragraph, you say, "For a free copy of [title of booklet], call or write [your company name, address, and phone number]."

Many editors include that contact information and a call to action when running your releases, and you will get many requests. Some editors, however, will not print such contact information. But you have no control over that. However, if you don't include contact information and a call to action, *no* editors can tell their readers how or where they can request your booklet, and without such information, no one will contact you. So, always close with the call to action.

Should you include a copy of your free booklet with the press releases you mail?

Including a sample of the booklet may be desirable, but it isn't necessary. I have had great success mailing press releases that didn't include a sample copy of the booklet or report being offered.

The main benefit of leaving out the sample booklet is cost savings: Including a sample booklet can add another 10 to 70 cents or more per release being mailed, depending on the cost to print the booklet and the weight of the booklet (which increases postage). For example, a tip sheet or slim pamphlet adds less cost than a bulky special report, book, or manual. If the extra 10 cents to 70 cents per piece is significant to you, omit the sample booklet and pocket the savings.

Be sure to put a line after the close of your release that says, "Editor: Review copy of [title of booklet] available upon request. Call Joe Jones at [insert phone number]." Some editors may insist on seeing a copy of the booklet before they'll promote it in their publication, so offer to send a copy free to any editor who requests it. The editor can get the information instantly via fax or e-mail.

If your free booklet is slim and inexpensive, or if cost is not a factor, include a sample copy with each release you mail. Doing so certainly can't hurt. And some editors may pay extra attention when they open the envelope and see your report or pamphlet.

Some sample new booklet press releases follow.

Sample release: Free tip sheet on how to market software

Your free booklet need not be an actual booklet with cover and staples; you can offer a free report, fact sheet, audiocassette, or other free information in your release.

A release shown in Figure 15-2 offered a free tip sheet on how to market and sell software. The purpose was to get publicity, establish the author as an authority in software marketing, and get leads from potential clients for his copywriting and consulting services.

The tip sheet was an 8½-by-11-inch sheet of paper printed on two sides; each side contained a reprint of a brief how-to article the author wrote on the topic of selling and marketing software.

The press release was sent to 50 advertising and marketing trade journals and several hundred computer magazines and journals. Eight or nine of these publications picked up this story, generating hundreds of inquiries and resulting in two new clients and consulting assignments.

The cost of printing and mailing the release was less than $200, including postage, and the initial assignments generated amounted to more than $9,000 in revenue from copywriting and consulting fees.

In addition, a number of people requesting the tip sheet ordered more of the author's tip sheets, books, and reports, resulting in thousands of dollars in product sales.

The author requested $1 and a self-addressed stamped envelope from the reader. This was done not to "qualify" the prospect but to eliminate the labor of addressing envelopes and to cover costs.

If I were doing a similar PR mailing for corporate clients or entrepreneurs, I'd probably advise them not to require a self-addressed stamped envelope and to send the tip sheet free of charge — unless they were strapped for cash and needed a "self-liquidating" promotion (one that pays its own cost in revenue generated).

Note in the last paragraph of the release the key code "Dept. 105" in the address. By counting the number of requests for this tip sheet addressed to Department 105, you know exactly how many responses were generated as a result of mailing this press release to the media.

Some practitioners take this a step further and put a different key code on each individual press release; the key code indicates the specific publication the release was sent to. Therefore, the press release going to *Computer Decisions* would have been key coded "Dept. CD," while the next copy, being mailed to *InfoWorld,* would have been key coded "IW."

FROM: Bob Bly, 174 Holland Avenue, New Milford, NJ 07646
CONTACT: Fern Dickey, 201 385-1220

For immediate release

**NEW TIP SHEET SHOWS ESTABLISHED
AND START-UP SOFTWARE PRODUCERS
HOW TO MARKET AND PROMOTE
THEIR PRODUCTS EFFECTIVELY**

New Milford, NJ - With the glut of software products flooding the marketplace, it's essential to produce mailings, brochures, ads, and other printed materials that quickly, clearly, and dramatically communicate the key functions and benefits of your software to potential buyers.

That's the opinion of Robert W. Bly, a New Milford, NJ-based consultant specializing in software marketing and promotion. He is also the author of a new tip sheet, "How to Sell Software," which presents advice on how both established and start-up software producers can effectively advertise, promote, and market software for PC's, mainframes, and minicomputers.

One of the most difficult marketing decisions facing software sellers says Bly, is whether to use a one-step or two-step marketing approach-that is, whether to sell the product via mail order directly from the ad or direct mail piece, or instead to generate a sales lead which is followed up by mailing a brochure or sending a sales person for a face-to-face meeting.

"PC software products in the $50 to $299 price range are good candidates for one-step mail order selling," advises Bly. "In the $399 to $899 price range, you may want to test a one-step vs. a two-step approach and see which works best." And at $1,000 and up, says Bly, the two-step lead generating method is best. "Few people will send payment for a $1,999 software package without some extra convincing by a salesperson, free trial, or demo diskette," he notes.

Some additional software marketing tips from the fact sheet:
- Early in your ad copy, tell the prospective purchaser what type or category of software you are selling. "People are usually in the market for a product to handle one of the known, identifiable, major applications-project management, word processing, accounts payable," says Bly.
- Talk in terms the reader can visualize. Instead of writing "56 KBPS modem," say "The SuperSpeedy modem transmits data at a rate of 56,000 bits per second--about a third of a second for a full page of text"....

For a copy of Bly's software marketing tip sheet, "How to Sell Software," send $1 and a self-addressed stamped #10 envelope to: Bob Bly, Dept. 105, 174 Holland Avenue, New Milford, NJ 07646.

Figure 15-2:
You can dramatically increase response to your press releases by offering something useful the reader can send for.

The advantage of individual coding of releases keyed to publications is that it lets you know how many responses were generated from each publication, not just the entire mailings. With this knowledge, you can fine-tune your distribution list, hitting only those publications that generate a high level of response. The major disadvantage of key-coding each release with a different key is that it's time-consuming: You have to do it one release at a time. I don't think it's worth the time and trouble, but do whatever seems best for you.

Sample release: Recession-fighting business strategies booklet

The release shown in Figure 15-3 was one of the most successful new booklet releases prepared by my coauthor, Bob Bly, and it's a good model for anyone offering free information via press release: The format is easily adapted to any information offer and has worked for everyone who has tried it.

This press release was mailed to 300 business magazines, 50 advertising and marketing magazines, 80 syndicated newspaper columnists who write on business topics, business editors at the nation's 500 largest daily newspapers, and a few other publications. Because a sample booklet was included with the release, the total cost for mailing approximately 950 releases was a bit under $1,000.

The release generated dozens of pickups, ranging from brief mentions to magazines that reprinted almost the entire text word for word. I don't know the specific number of pickups because Bob didn't use a clipping service to keep track of all the placements.

Virtually every pickup included information on how the reader could order the booklet. From this press release alone, Bob sold over 3,000 booklets at $7 each, for a gross of more than $21,000. The follow-up sales included several consulting and speaking assignments, half a dozen speaking engagements, and additional sales of other booklets and reports.

The release works for two reasons: First, because the topic was timely — the release was issued during the worst of the recession of the early 1990s — it was a hot topic with inherent media appeal. Second, it precisely follows the three-part formula of (a) announcing the availability of a new booklet, (b) excerpting highlights so that editors can run a mini-feature article on the subject, and (c) providing contact information and a call to action.

The only way in which it violates the formula for the free booklet release is that the reader must pay $7. "I did this because my primary motivation was to make money selling this booklet as well as a line of related booklets and reports I offer, and I felt the need for such a booklet was so great that the $7 charge would not prevent people from ordering," Bob told me.

FROM: Bob Bly, 174 Holland Avenue, New Milford, NJ 07646
CONTACT: Bob Bly, phone 201 385-1220

For immediate release

NEW BOOKLET REVEALS 14 PROVEN STRATEGIES FOR KEEPING BUSINESSES BOOMING IN A BUST ECONOMY

New Milford, NJ-While some companies struggle to survive in today's sluggish business environment, many are doing better than ever-largely because they have mastered the proven but little-known strategies of "recession" marketing."

That's the opinion of Bob Bly, an independent marketing consultant and author of the just-published booklet "Recession-Proof Business Strategies: 14 Winning Methods to Sell Any Product or Service in a Down Economy."

"Many business people fear a recession or soft economy, because when the economy is weak, their clients and customers cut back on spending," says Bly. "To survive in such a marketplace, you need to develop recession-marketing strategies that help you retain your current accounts and keep those customers buying. You also need to master marketing techniques that will win you *new* clients or customers to replace any business you may have lost because of the increased competition that is typical of a recession."

Among the recession-fighting business strategies Bly outlines in his new booklet:

- *Reactivate dormant accounts.* An easy way to get more business is to simply call past clients or customers- people you served at one time but are not actively working for now-to remind them of your existence. According to Bly, a properly scripted telephone call to a list of past buyers will generate approximately one order for every ten calls.
- *Quote reasonable, affordable fees and prices in competitive bid situations.* While you need not reduce your rates or prices, in competitive bid situations you will win by bidding toward the low or middle end of your price range rather than at the high end. Bly says that during a recession, your bids should be 15 to 20 percent lower than you would normally charge in a healthy economy.
- *Give your existing clients and customers a superior level of service.* In a recession, Bly advises businesses to do everything they can to hold onto their existing clients or customers-their "bread-and-butter" accounts. "The best way to hold onto your clients or customers is to please them," says Bly, "and the best way to please them is through better customer service. Now is an ideal time to provide that little bit of extra service or courtesy that can mean the difference between dazzling the client or customer vs. merely satisfying them"....

Figure 15-3:
This release generated more than 3,500 orders for a booklet at $7 each.

For a client selling a consulting or advisory service, however, I suggest not charging for the booklet or asking for a nominal sum if the objective is to generate sales leads for the service.

Sample release: Free article reprint

Figure 15-4 shows another variation on the free booklet theme. This company published an article on its specialty, collections, in a trade journal. It made reprints of the article and offered it as a "free special report" in a press release sent to other publications within the same industry. Interestingly, many of these publications used the release, and not one voiced an objection to printing what was essentially an offer to send an article reprint from a competitor's publication.

From this I learned that *any* published article can be offered as a reprint through a free booklet press release and that other magazines will run the offer. You can print somewhere on the booklet cover or at the bottom of the tip sheet that the article was "reprinted with permission from Vol. 5 No. 10 of *XYZ MAGAZINE*" without fear that this will discourage rival magazines from using it.

In the release, however, call your reprint a "special report" if it's a lengthy article, a "monograph" if it's a scholarly or scientific article, or a "tip sheet" if it's a short (one- or two-page) article. These terms sound more important than an "article reprint," so more readers are likely to request it.

Special event, gimmick, or timely issue

The press is always looking for a story that captures the public's imagination. Therefore, if you have a special event, timely issue, or unusual human-interest story, or if you can add some sort of hook or angle to your release, you'll have a better chance of gaining coverage.

Editors are interested in stories that are substantial and of value yet have an unusual twist or gimmick to them. If you can be a bit different (albeit in a relevant way), you will get noticed.

Sample press release: Empire State Building location

Figure 15-5 shows a news release that's a perfect example of a story with an offbeat angle. This company rents mailboxes — a pretty mundane business. But the angle for this story was the unusual, prestigious location of its mailbox address: the Empire State Building.

FROM: RMCB, 1261 Broadway, New York, NY 10001
CONTACT: Russell Fuchs, 800 542-5025

For immediate release
**FREE REPORT FOR DIRECT MARKETERS
PRESENTS 12 NEW WAYS TO COLLECT OLD
BILLS**

New York, NY, January-A new special report, published by
Retrieval-Masters Creditors Bureau (RMCB), a nationwide
agency specializing in the collection of low-dollar amount, high-
volume accounts receivable, reveals 12 key strategies for using
an outside collection agency to turn past-due accounts into paid-
up customers.

The 8-page report, "How an Outside Collection Agency Can
Improve Your Conversions," is available free of charge to
circulation directors, publishers, direct marketers, business
executives, advertising professionals, entrepreneurs, and
students. the cost to the general public is $5.

Although the report originally was written to show circulation
directors how to improve subscription collections, Russell Fuchs,
president of RMCB, says the information is applicable to direct
markets selling virtually any product or service through the mail
- including publishers, book clubs, mail order firms, continuity
plans, and catalog marketers.

Why should direct marketers, whose invoices typically reflect a
low dollar balance, be interested in working with collection
agencies to improve collection results? " Whenever you extend
credit to the customer and allow him or her to say 'bill me,' you
typically have a nonpayment rate ranging from 5 to 35 percent or
more," says Fuchs. "Experience shows that a competent
collection agency can convert 21 to 25 percent of those
delinquent accounts into paid-up customers."

Here are some of RMCB's suggestions on how to use a
collection agency to improve collection results:
• *Vary the letterhead.* Fuchs says that sending a dunning letter on a
  third-party letterhead-either in an internal billing series or the
  collection agency's billing cycle-lifts response virtually every
  time.
• *Vary the dunning cycle.* To extend the billing series and increase
  net recovery rates, collection agencies will vary the timing
  between efforts, typically from 14 to 28 days. "This is a proven
  response-booster," says Fuchs.
• *Make sure "white mail" is given special handling.* "Promptly
  acknowledge and resolve every nonpayment and partial payment
  response," warns Fuchs. "Your collection agency should have a
  special 'correspondence response department' whose job it is to
  communicate with customers who dispute invoices, make partial
  payments, or have other responses out of the ordinary"....

Figure 15-4:
Offers
of free
information
work well
in PR.

FROM: Empire State Communications, 350 Fifth Ave.
New York, NY 10118
CONTACT: Arthur Goodman, phone 800 447-0099

For immediate release
NOW BUSINESSES NATIONWIDE CAN ESTABLISH A BRANCH OFFICE IN NEW YORK CITY'S PRESTIGIOUS EMPIRE STATE BUILDING- FOR A LITTLE AS $35 PER MONTH

New York, NY - Want to give your company added prestige and impress your customers? NYC-based entrepreneur Arthur Goodman has a suggestion: a "branch office" in New York's most distinguished and memorable location: the Empire State Building.

Goodman's company, Empire State Communications, provides mail receiving, fax, telex, and telephone service for businesses nationwide that want to establish a branch address in New York without physically having an office there. And the price is right: Empire's service starts at $35 per month.

"Our service allows firms nationwide to immediately and inexpensively establish a New York presence at one of Manhattan's most memorable-and impressive-addresses," says Goodman. "The Empire State Building is a status symbol worldwide. And the address is easy for your prospects to remember; no multidigit P.O. box number is necessary."

What types of companies use Goodman's Empire State service? " It's for small out-of-town companies that want to convey an image of a larger, more substantial firm through a prestigious New York City address, as well as large corporations that feel they should have a New York City location but don't want the expense of renting costly office space," he says.

How does Goodman's service work? For a small monthly fee, Goodman's clients obtain the right to use his Empire State Building address as their own in letterhead, business cards, and advertisements. "We act as their New York office," says Goodman. "They can receive mail, phone calls, telexes, and fax transmissions, just as if they were physically located in New York.

"In fact, your prospects and customers will have no way of telling that you don't actually have a big, fancy office in the Empire State Building," he adds.

Mail received at the Empire State location is forwarded daily by Goodman to any location his clients specify--usually their headquarters' corporate mailroom. According to Goodman, the Empire State Building is one of the few buildings in the United States with its own post office branch and private zip code (10118)....

Figure 15-5:
Editors look for an unusual hook or angle, such as the "unique zip code" that makes this office space special.

Mentioning that the Empire State Building is one of the few buildings in the country with its own private zip code and post office is a nice added touch, as some editors like to include a bit of trivia or little-known information in their articles.

Sample press release: Entrepreneur seminar

A special event, such as a convention, sale, grand opening, trade show, or seminar, is also a good topic for a press release because it's timely. When The Communication Workshop decided to hold a seminar on the topic of being an entrepreneur, it sent out the release shown in Figure 15-6 to local and national business magazines.

Although this release was *not* wildly successful, it did catch the attention of a reporter at *Nation's Business,* who featured The Communication Workshop prominently in a cover story on entrepreneurs in the United States.

A successful promotion that my PR agency did for our client IKEA was the "Sharing the Caring Program." In addition to being an event-driven PR promotion, it's a good example of the PR principle of "show, don't state."

Like many giant retailers, IKEA sometimes gets resistance when opening a major store in a new area: The neighbors don't want a big store in their neighborhood because of the traffic and noise.

A mediocre PR tactic would be sending out a release saying, "We care about the neighborhood," with some bland statements from the CEO. In the "Sharing the Caring Program," IKEA demonstrates that it cares about the neighborhood and its people by sponsoring a free family-day fair offering education and services to help residents live better lives — everything from lead testing to health check-ups. Which do you think gets more coverage in the news — the free family fair or the usual corporate claptrap?

Telephone hotline press release

Telephone hotlines — numbers people can call to get free advice and information from a live operator, tape recording, or voice mail system — are extremely popular with consumers and therefore with editors. People like the convenience of being able to dial a phone number and order a product, ask a question, or get free assistance or advice.

Telephone hotlines are available on every conceivable topic, from cancer and lawn care, to gambling and auto safety. Although some hotlines are nonprofit, many are sponsored by companies that use them as a way of generating leads, sales, inquiries, visibility, and publicity.

FROM: The Communication Workshop, 217 E. 85th St.,
New York, NY 10028
CONTACT: Gary Blake, 718-575-8000

For immediate release

NEW NYC SEMINAR SHOWS "ORDINARY PEOPLE" HOW TO BECOME SUCCESSFUL ENTREPRENEURS -- WITHOUT SPENDING BIG MONEY OR TAKING BIG RISKS

NEW YORK, NY, October 30th--Computer whiz kids, choco-late-chip-cookie bakers, and other young hot-shot millionaire success stories have become media darlings. But what if you're a regular guy or gal, not looking to make a million but just wanting to make a go of a modest small business of your own?

Take heart. Two local entrepreneurs-Gary Blake and Bob Bly, co-authors of the new book OUT ON YOUR OWN: FROM CORPORATE TO SELF-EMPLOYMENT (New York: John Wiley & Sons)-have created a new one-day seminar on BECOMING AN ENTREPRENEUR.

The seminar teaches would-be entrepreneurs that you don't have to be a Ted Turner or a Victor Kiam to start your own business. Anybody can do it-and succeed- without a lot of money, without being a genius, and without taking big risks.

Says Bly, "Although I always disliked corporate life, I was the person people would have voted 'Least Likely to Take a Risk.' But by following a few simple principles, I successfully made the transition from a 9-to-5 job to self employment. I didn't have any money in the bank or a great new product. Yet I quadrupled my corporate salary within 3 years."

Adds Blake, 42, director of The Communication Workshop, a management consulting firm, "It's traumatic to leave the world of weekly paychecks; we know because we've done it. Our seminar on BECOMING AN ENTREPRENEUR helps people progress from just dreaming about quitting to realistically assessing their options, making plans, and then acting on those plans."

The first BECOMING AN ENTREPRENEUR seminar, which costs $85 per participant, will be presented in midtown Manhattan on January 24th. The seminar is aimed at people who are not satisfied with corporate life but may not have the impetus, self-confidence, or focus to break loose. BECOMING AN ENTREPRENEUR gives a blueprint for entrepreneurial success, guiding each participant toward confronting the positive and negative aspects of being your own boss....

Figure 15-6:
This press release made the front cover of *Nation's Business.*

One of the best ways to promote such a hotline is through a press release. Editors may print short blurbs and articles announcing your hotline, describing the information available to callers, and giving the phone number. Such announcements can generate hundreds or thousands of phone calls, plus lots of media coverage.

Sample press release: PR hotline

Alan Caruba, a New Jersey PR counselor, wanted to gain some publicity for his business. The challenge: Caruba is one of hundreds of independent PR counselors, and nothing is newsworthy about being in the PR business per se.

Alan's solution? Create a PR hotline through which he can offer his consulting service on an hourly basis via telephone to smaller firms that either need quick advice or cannot afford to pay the traditional large monthly retainer that most PR firms charge.

Another interesting quirk: Alan accepts MasterCard and Visa, which is an unusual way to charge for professional services. His release on the topic, which gained wide publication and generated many inquiries to the hotline, is shown in Figure 15-7.

Sample press release: The Advertising Hotline

Years ago Bob Bly wanted to promote himself as an authority in advertising. Unlike the big ad agencies, however, he knew that merely sending a release announcing his latest projects or clients would not be effective. The business of J. Walter Thompson, one of the world's largest advertising agencies, is of interest to the trade press and *The New York Times;* the business of one lone freelance copywriter is not.

The solution was to create news by instituting the Advertising Hotline. The idea is simple: a nationwide telephone hotline that business people can call to get quick tips and advice on how to improve their marketing.

Implementing the idea was even easier: Bob just set up a phone line in his office and attached an answering machine with a long outgoing message. Hotline callers were treated to a 2-minute prerecorded "mini-seminar on tape" on a different topic each week. Figure 15-8 shows the release announcing Bob's hotline.

Bob sent the release to 50 trade publications covering advertising, public relations, promotion, marketing, and sales. Attractively printed Advertising Hotline Rolodex cards were mailed with releases to give editors the impression that the hotline was a real and ongoing activity.

THE CARUBA ORGANIZATION
Box 40, Maplewood, NJ 07040
201 763-6392

For immediate release

CHARGE PR ADVICE TO YOUR CREDIT CARD "PR HOTLINE" -- NEW BUSINESS SERVICE

Maplewood, NJ-Mike Wallace of "Sixty Minutes?" is at the door with a camera crew! What do you do now?

"Most public relations does not involve a crisis," says PR counselor Alan Caruba of Maplewood, NJ. "In fact, good PR can avert such problems while helping to promote products, services, and causes of every description."

Caruba notes that "many business and professional people neither need, nor want, to retain a full-time a full-time public relations agency or counselor. What they need is good advice from time to time." That's why Caruba created the "PR Hotline," a telephone service (201 763-6392) that allows anyone with a PR question or problem to call. One can charge the service to either a MasterCard or Visa.

At $50 for the first forty minutes or $75 for up to a full hour, "a lot of very specific analysis and advice can be provided," says Caruba. "Public relations can be local, regional, or national in scope. It can represent a single project or a long-term program."

Caruba has been dispensing advice and service to corporations, associations, small business operations, and individuals for more than twenty years. He is a member of The Counselors Academy of the Public Relations Society of America and frequently lectures and writes on the subject.

Figure 15-7:
Editors like to run short items on telephone hotlines their readers can call.

FROM: The Advertising Hotline, 174 Holland Ave., New Milford, NJ 07646
CONTACT: Amy Sprecher, 201 385-1220

For immediate release

NEW NATIONAL TELEPHONE HOTLINE PROVIDES FREE ADVERTISING AND MARKETING TIPS TO AD AGENCIES, CORPORATIONS, AND SMALL BUSINESS

New Milford, NJ, December 4th-The "Advertising Hotline," a new nationwide telephone hotline, has been establish to provide free advice, information, and tips on adverting, direct mail, publicity, and other forms of promotion to ad agencies, PR firms, large corporations, and small business. The Hotline number 555-5555.

"Clients and their agencies today need solid, reliable information on what works in advertising-and what doesn't," says Bob Bly, the Hotline's director. "As a freelance copywriter, I have hundreds of people calling me asking questions such as: 'How can I get more inquiries from my quarter-page trade ad? How can I write a direct mail package that will get a good response?' I set up the Advertising Hotline to give these folks some of the answers."

Unlike many other information sources, Bly points out, the Advertising Hotline is free. "A lot of companies can't afford to hire consultants, and it takes time to read a book, listen to an audiocassette, or attend a seminar," notes Bly. "The Hotline is free and takes only five minutes of the caller's time."

In the months to come, callers who phone the Advertising Hotline at 555-5555 can listen to taped "miniseminars" on a variety of subjects. Scheduled topics include: "10 Ways to Stretch Your Advertising Budget," "How to Write Winning Sales Letters," "12 Questions to Ask *Before* You Create Your Next Advertising Campaign," "New Ideas for Your Corporate Newsletter," and "Selling Financial Services by Mail." The current topic can be heard right now by calling the Hotline at 555-5555....

Figure 15-8:
This press release generated 5,000 telephone hotline calls within a few months.

Eighteen publications ran stories based on the release. At least five ran almost the entire release, practically word for word. This publicity generated thousands of phone calls to the hotline within 12 months.

You don't need to have a hotline number that is a toll-free 800 or 888 number or that spells out a word (such as 800-AUTO-SAFETY). You can be successful by using an ordinary toll number that is staffed by employees or that uses electronic voice mail or an answering machine to deliver its message.

You can use this same type of release to promote your Web site, but the editorial pickup probably won't be as significant. That's because relatively few telephone hotlines are being promoted compared to the huge number of Web sites. And the more common something is, the less the media is interested.

New product press release

The most popular type of press release is the new product release, which is a simple announcement of a new product. The product doesn't need to actually be brand-new to qualify for a new product release. Enhancements, upgrades, new models, new features, new options, new accessories, new grades, new sizes and styles, and new applications can all form the basis for a release of this type.

New product releases are typically featured in the new product sections of publications. Editors run short two- or three-paragraph descriptions of the products along with a photo or drawing, if provided along with the release. This type of coverage, although routine in nature, provides additional exposure for your product, builds awareness, and can generate numerous inquiries at low cost.

Figure 15-9 is an example of a new product release that's effective because it ties in the new product announcement with current news — in this case, the controversy over genetically engineered foods, a hot topic as of this writing.

The new product release can work for any new product, whether it ties into a newsy hook or not. Figure 15-10 shows a release that was extremely effective for an industrial product that most of us would view as dull and boring.

This release was picked up in more than 35 trade journals; many ran the entire three-page release word for word. Result: 2,500 requests for a technical brochure on the product generated within six months. Total promotion cost: under $500.

Figure 15-11 illustrates another new product release, this one for a software product.

For Immediate Release

INTRODUCING THE WORLD'S FIRST-EVER BABY FOOD THAT IS 100% PURE

Earth's Best Introduces the Only Organic Baby Food that Contains No Genetically Engineered Ingredients

UNIONDALE, NEW YORK - Parents will do everything in their power to ensure the safety and well-being of their children. And, it is the responsibility of companies who make children's products to do the same. Earth's Best, a leading brand of all natural, organic baby food, is pleased to announce that as of January 1, 2000, all of their baby food will be made without genetically engineered ingredients.

In simple terms, genetic engineering is the process of taking genes from one strain of plant, animal or virus and inserting them in another with the goal of reproducing characteristics of the original species. Some of the most common foods affected include canola, corn, soybeans and potatoes -- all popular ingredients found in baby food.

"At Earth's Best, we believe that consumers have the right to be informed. That is why we are labeling our Earth's Best Baby Food GMO-Free," said Irwin Simon, Chief Executive Officer, and a fan of Earth's Best since before it became part of the Hain Food Group. "Four years ago when my daughter was born, like all new parents, I wanted the very best for her. She started solid foods with Earth's Best, and now my twin boys are Earth's Best babies."

One of the major hazards associated with genetically modified foods includes unpredictable health effects such as food allergies brought about by the introduction of new genes to any organism or plant. Other concerns include damage to the environment as new genetic information could cross into other related life forms and cause the possible extinction of the species. In addition, unknown animal genes inserted into foods may jeopardize strict vegetarian or religious dietary constraints.

It is estimated that about 60-70 percent of the food found in grocery stores has been genetically modified by scientists. Many believe if a product is certified organic, it is GMO-Free, however that may not be the case. Farmers may be subject to unintended and undesirable cross-pollination due to genetically modified seeds from nearby farms. Earth's Best products will undergo a rigorous testing and affidavit program to ensure their products purity....

Figure 15-9: New product release with a news angle (generically engineered foods).

KOCH ENGINEERING COMPANY, INC.
CONTACT: Mike Mutsakis, 212 682-5755

For immediate release

**KOCH ENGINEERING DEVELOPS
DRY SO2 SCRUBBING SYSTEM**

Koch Engineering Company, Inc., of Wichita, Kansas and New York City, has developed a dry SO2 scrubbing system for cleaning flue gas in coal-fired boilers.

The system uses a line-based dryer and a baghouse for SO2 and particulate removal. To design dry scrubbing systems tailored to individual applications, Koch Engineering has a fully integrated dry scrubbing pilot plant available for test and evaluation of customer coal and chemicals.

"Koch Engineering is the only manufacturer in the dry scrubbing business that has a dry SO2 scrubbing pilot plant operating off a dedicated pulverized coal-fired boiler, a large-scale semiworks spray dryer, and a commercial-scale system now in operation," says David H. Koch, president of Koch Engineering. "No company is better equipped to design, scale up, fabricate, and install complete dry scrubbing systems for industrial boilers."

The Koch dry SO2 scrubbing system, he added, uses a two-fluid nozzle in the spray dryer rather than a rotary or centrifugal atomizer. This results in increased reliability, simpler maintenance, and reduced initial investment ...

Figure 15-10:
This release was picked up by 35 publications. Several used it word for word.

New literature press release

The new literature release is used to announce the publication of a new product brochure, capabilities brochure, data sheet, catalog, or any other literature on a product or service.

When you come out with a new product, you can send out a new product release first and then follow up a month or so later with a new literature release (announcing publication of the product brochure or data sheet). In this way, you get two PR opportunities for each new product instead of just one.

For immediate release

UNIQUE ACCOUNTING SOFTWARE PACKAGE CAN BE EASILY MODIFIED BY USERS TO FIT THEIR BUSINESS PROCEDURES -- WITH NO PROGRAMMING!

Kingston, NY -- PLATO Software recently released an upgraded version of its modifiable business and accounting software package, P&L-Pro Version 6.0.

What makes P&L-Pro unique is that it's the only affordably priced accounting software that can be modified by the user with no programming required, claims Richard Rosen, president, PLATO Software.

"Most low-end, off-the-shelf business software forces you to adjust your business procedures to accommodate the limitations of the program," says Rosen. "As a result, you cannot get the software to do things your way. Some high-end business software packages are designed to be modifiable, but these start at $10,000 to $25,000 and up for a complete system."

P&L-Pro, by comparison, is a complete and affordably priced business and accounting software package that can be modified by users, even non-programmers, to precisely fit their procedures and operations. Base price starts at approximately $100 per module.

How P&L-Pro works:
Most business software, according to Rosen, is created using complex programming languages, and therefore can only be altered by computer programmers.

P&L-Pro, however, was built using Alpha Four, an easy-to-use database management system. As a result, users can add functions to or modify their copies of P&L-Pro directly, without help from a programmer or software consultant.

The new version, P&L-Pro 6.0, features faster and simpler bank reconciliation, check entry, application of payments to invoices, screen entry, and statement preparation. It also includes two new modules, Payroll and Inventory Control, which @md added to the existing modules of General Ledger, Accounts Receivable, and Accounts Payable @md make P&L-Pro a complete business and accounting software package that is fully modifiable by the user....

Figure 15-11:
New product release for a software product.

If your literature contains how-to or reference information — for example, it tells how to specify a product, select the proper grade, install the right attachment, or the like — your release should highlight that fact.

Figure 15-12 shows a sample new literature release.

Figure 15-12:
Trade
journal
editors
frequently
run new
literature
releases.

> **NEW CATALOG AND REFERENCE MANUAL OFFERS WIDGET BUYERS GUIDANCE IN PROPER SELECTION, INSTALLATION OF WIDGETS**
>
> ANYTOWN, USA--Smith Widget Co., announced today the publication of its new 32-page widget catalog and buyer's guide.
>
> The catalog, available free, contains complete specifications for more than 400 grades and models of widgets for standard and custom industrial applications.
>
> It also contains charts, graphs, cross-reference tables, and other technical data enabling engineers to correctly specify, order, and install the right widget for their application, said Joe Smith, president of Smith Widgets.
>
> [List some of the highlights of features of the catalog here.]
>
> For a free copy of the Smith Widget catalog, call or write: Smith Widget, Dept. PRC-1, Anytown, USA, 555-5555.

Tie-in with current fad, event, or news

Although not always easy to do, tying in your release with a fad, current event, news story, or trend can help you maximize your publicity pickups.

For instance, after the first run of the enormously popular TV game show *Survivor,* my PR firm did a survey to find out the differences in survival instincts and strategies between CEOs of brick-and-mortar companies versus CEOs of dot-coms. The objective: to get our name known and demonstrate knowledge of the dot-com marketplace. The survey was featured in the Japanese edition of *The Wall Street Journal.*

In 1997, virtual pets became popular, and Bob Bly sent out the release shown in Figure 15-13. Within three days of mailing it, six newspapers had called Bob for an interview; one sent a photographer and reporter to his home and did a front-page story.

FROM: Microchip Gardens, 174 Holland Avenue, New Milford, NJ 07646
CONTACT: Bob Bly, phone 201-385-1220

For immediate release

MICROCHIP GARDENS, WORLD'S FIRST "GIGAPET CEMETERY," OPENS IN NORTHERN NEW JERSEY

When 7-year-old Alex Bly's gigapet died after he dropped it in the toilet, he couldn't find a place to bury it. So his father, NJ-based entrepreneur Bob Bly, created Microchip Gardens -- the world's first gigapet cemetery -- in the family's suburban backyard.

Now if your child's gigapet dies and can't be revived, instead of unceremoniously tossing it in the trash, you can give it a proper burial in a beautiful, tree-lined resting place.

For fees starting at $5, based on plot location and method of interment (burial, mausoleum, cremation), Bly will give your dearly departed gigapet an eternal resting place in Microchip Gardens, complete with funeral service and burial certificate. "Even gigapets don't last forever," said Bly. "There are pet cemeteries for dogs and cats; now gigapets have one too."

To help owners get the most pleasure from gigapet ownership, Bly -- author of 35 published books including *The "I Hate Kathie Lee Gifford" Book* (Kensington) and *The Ultimate Unauthorized Star Trek Quiz Book* (HarperCollins) -- has written an informative new booklet, "Raising Your Gigapet." The booklet covers such topics as purchasing your first gigapet; taking the pet home; care and feeding; and play and discipline. Gigapet burial rituals and the origins of Microchip Gardens are also covered.

To get your copy of "Raising Your Gigapet," which includes complete information on the Microchip Gardens gigapet cemetery, send $4 to: CTC, 22 E. Quackenbush Avenue, Dumont, NJ 07628.

Figure 15-13:
This press release got my coauthor, Bob Bly, on the front page of a local daily newspaper.

What's the lead story in the news this week? Who's the hot celebrity? Which trend is all the rage? With a bit of creative thinking, you can probably think of a way to tie your organization or product into that story.

Survey results press release

It's ironic: Journalists consider themselves in the news business, yet aside from investigative and news reporters, most journalists — trade journal editors, columnists, feature editors — have a tough time finding anything that's really new. Most of what they find is recycled and has been done before. So when you present them with real news, they'll bite — and publish.

At my PR firm, our favorite strategy for creating real news — new information — is to take a survey. It's easy to do; anyone can take a survey and tabulate the results. By doing so, you create new facts, based on numerical results, and journalists love hard numbers.

Trade-in press release

Another promotional gimmick that works wonders in PR is to publicize a trade-in. The classic example is my firm's promotion for British Knights sneakers: We offered a free pair of sneakers to coach potatoes who mailed in their TV remote controls. At my agency, I use the trade-in gimmick often. The only requirement is to have a logical reason for the trade-in: For example, you want to give people sneakers and get their remote controls so they'll exercise more and watch TV less.

For Calyx & Corolla, a national florist, my firm did a trade-in for Mother's Day: Send in a toy gun (to promote nonviolence) and get free flowers (see Figure 15-14).

Call to action press release

Create a cause or a call to action and publicize it. One example is the Strike Back promotion, described in Chapter 1, that got me front-page coverage in *USA Today*. All I did was urge baseball fans to boycott baseball games one day for every day the major leagues remained on strike.

Another example was the "cursing for chips" promotion we ran for a snack food manufacturer. At the time, New York City Mayor Rudolph Giuliani was running a campaign to improve the quality of life for New Yorkers. We said that living in New York was stressful, so one way to improve the quality of life would be to reduce stress. We encouraged people to "blow off steam" — by swearing aloud. They came to a booth on a busy street corner in Manhattan; if they swore in front of us, they got a free bag of potato chips.

Contact: Lauren Weinberg
Jericho Communications
212/645-6900 x 110

THIS MOTHER'S DAY, GIVE YOUR MOM THE GREATEST GIFT OF ALL…A TOY GUN

Calyx & Corolla Asks Children Nationwide to Help Prevent Gun Violence by Trading in Their Toy Guns for Flowers

SAN FRANCISCO, CA April 25, 2000 – Every year, over four thousand children are killed unnecessarily by guns. Calyx & Corolla, The Flower Lover's Flower Company, is lending its support to mothers around the nation who are fighting to keep guns out of the hands of children. Over the next several weeks, Calyx & Corolla is inviting children to participate by trading in their toy guns for a flower for their mother this Mother's Day.

"Flowers are a symbol of peace, harmony and the very best of nature, as are our children," said Ruth M. Owades, CEO and Founder of Calyx & Corolla. "Calyx & Corolla is pleased to offer this trade-in to encourage children to exchange their toy gun for a token of peace, a flower for their mother."

The first 1,000 children who turn in their toy guns can receive a gift for their mothers this Mother's Day, compliments of Calyx & Corolla. This gift, a spray of dendrobium orchids and a classic glass bud vase, will be sent directly from the grower, via FedEx. Participating children should send a toy gun and name, mother's first and last name, address, and phone number (for proper delivery) to:

Attn: The Greatest Gift of All
Jericho Communications
304 Hudson Street, Ste. 700
New York, NY 10013

In addition, Calyx & Corolla has created a special Mother's Day bouquet and will donate a portion of the proceeds to benefit the Million Mom March organization. For additional information, please log on to www.calyxandcorolla.com/mmm.html or call 1-800-800-7788….

Figure 15-14:
I think it's the cleverness of trade-ins that attracts editors and readers to these stories.

High-visibility advertising

Sometimes advertising is so outrageous or memorable that it creates its own PR buzz. One example is the famous "Mama mia, that's a spicy meatball" commercial for Alka Seltzer. More recently, Priceline.com attracted a lot of media attention with its TV commercials featuring actor William Shatner singing old rock-and-roll songs. Priceline.com has gotten a lot of media buzz simply because the spokesperson is William Shatner and the commercials are so offbeat and unusual.

Another example is the Hair Club for Men's slogan, "I'm not only the Hair Club president; I'm also a client." It has been repeated so many times that it's almost become a national phrase: Jack Nicholson quotes it to his reflection in the mirror when his hair starts to grow back after he becomes a werewolf in the movie *Wolf.* And in the film *That Old Feeling,* when Bette Midler sees ex-husband Dennis Farina and notices he has a fuller head of hair, she asks him point-blank, "Hair Club for Men?"

Hair Club President Sy Sperling took advantage of this by using both TV commercials and radio publicity to get himself and his famous slogan in front of the public as much as he could. In fact, he hired a publicist whose sole function was to book Sy as a guest on talk radio shows as frequently as possible, and at one time Sy was doing at least one show every week.

Comments Sperling: "The general public may be skeptical of advertising, but they love celebrities. Our entire culture is celebrity-oriented. Therefore, by publicizing myself, and turning myself into a semi-celebrity, HCM had the services of a full-time celebrity spokesman, me, without paying big fees to a ball player, rock star, or other endorsers.

"By making myself the spokesperson, I became the one person in the United States who, more than any other, was identified with hair replacement. I am recognized on the street or in social situations all the time. We spent millions on TV commercials to create that image, but now it's self-perpetuating: Every time I'm on a talk show or in the news, it's a free commercial not for me but for the entire Hair Club operation. Few CEOs are as recognizable or have this promotional value to their company. Frank Perdue comes the closest, probably because he physically resembled the product he sells (chickens)."

Chapter 16

Employing New Media: Web Sites and E-Mail

The Internet is changing the way business is done, and public relations is no exception. Surveys show that one-third of the public logs onto the Internet to get news at least once a week. If you're not online, you have no idea of what's being said about you on the Internet or how your brand or image is holding up in the new digital economy.

For a company doing PR, the major application of technology on the Web is the "virtual press rooms" — sections of company Web sites designed specifically for use by the media.

Some of the most media-friendly Web sites address their need for speed as well as content. When you're a reporter on deadline, you don't want to click through three or four pages of content just to find an executive's name, a financial statistic, or a product specification.

Everybody knows it makes sense to be customer-driven when designing a Web site, especially if you're doing business online. But that's no excuse to forget other major audiences, including the media. In this chapter, I provide a plan for you to serve the media well at your site.

Designing a Media-Friendly Web Site

If you're a manufacturer or a service provider, plan to design extensive informational options and databases — options that make it easier for your company and your products to get mentioned as accurately and thoroughly as possible. A chemical manufacturer, for example, might allow journalists to access chemical formulas, research studies, applications briefs, and material safety data sheets for each of its products.

What informational options am I talking about? The headings that follow can serve as a quality check of sorts. And remember, as you expand your Web site, don't sacrifice *ease of access* and *speed*.

Company background/history

Often lumped under a section titled "All About XYZ Company," this information may sometimes include so many different pieces of information that you should consider making it a separate section. Here are some types of information you can include:

- What the company does
- Mission statement
- Industries/applications
- Philosophy
- Founders and an explanation of how the company got started
- Historical markers and milestones
- Philanthropic events and charity sponsorships

Another key piece of information you can offer is a list of customers. Case histories or customer success stories are also valuable. Obviously, if part of what you offer new clients is confidentiality, posting a list of customers and the projects you performed for them violates that confidentiality, unless you note on the site that all customers listed have given their permission.

Key management

Read business articles and you notice that journalists like to give descriptions of key players of the companies they are writing about. So, make executive bios available to journalists on your Web site. Be sure to provide

✔ Where managers hail from

✔ Individual biographies/background

✔ Responsibilities

✔ Contact information

✔ Hot links to their e-mail addresses

It's amazing to me how many companies hide contact information. A high percentage of sites have addresses and phone numbers on their sites, but a large number are almost impossible to find. Most journalists need this type of basic information.

Always have an e-mail and phone number available for the PR director or whoever is the company's main contact for the press. You can also list key personnel, but be warned: Web sites are a ripe source of information for headhunters who want to steal your employees. So if recruiters are actively raiding companies for people, you may opt not to list your personnel on your site.

The top three things journalists want to find quickly when they visit a site are deep financial information (for public companies), a file of historic press releases, and readily available e-mail/phone/address contact information.

One survey of editors shows that only 60 to 75 percent of companies are offering these basics. When asked how often they're required to phone, fax, or e-mail a company for information that could have been offered on its Web site, all answers ranged from 25 to 50 percent of the time.

Press release archive

Archiving all of a company's press releases for online retrieval on a Web site has become common practice. On larger corporate Web sites, some search engines give the visitor the option of excluding press releases from the documents being searched by key word — otherwise, the results would be overwhelming. If you decide to offer a press release archive online, I suggest you include these parts:

✔ Chronological listing (most recent first) of release announcements, including the date of the release followed by the title

✔ Downloadable photos of your products

✔ E-mail link and phone number of your PR manager or main media liaison

✔ E-mail hot links to press contacts, resources, or quoted sources, when applicable, within the body copy

Financial information

More and more publicly traded companies are making their financial data available online. At a minimum, you should include

- ✔ Key current financial data for the year and by quarter (taken from annual and quarterly reports)
- ✔ Historic financial information

An added bonus, especially for financial reports and stock analysts, is charts backed up with Excel spreadsheets showing the financial history of the company.

Increasingly, larger public companies are putting both their annual reports and their proxy statements online. Be aware of how your print document translates for the Web. For example, in the Alaska Airs annual report, articles are printed over a background of color photographs — tough to read, especially on the Web. To solve the problem, the Web designer moved the text to the side to make it readable.

When posting annual reports, proxy statements, and other financial data on the Web for analysts, shareholders, and the financial press, use html format rather than plain text (ASCII). The reason? ASCII is unattractive and difficult to read, while html documents look very professional and are easy to read.

Another problem with ASCII documents is the lack of navigation capability: ASCII documents do not have hyperlinks. By comparison, html documents can have hyperlinks to each section. An up-front index lets shareholders immediately click to the section they want to read. Without navigation links, the shareholder or journalist can get lost in a lengthy document.

Product/service catalog

Customers and prospects come to your Web site for product information, so there should already be plenty of it for journalists to reference. The product information available to the media on your site should include:

- ✔ Product or service descriptions and specifications
- ✔ Up-to-date pricing and availability
- ✔ Mini product photos you can click on for larger views and more information

Article/white paper library

As I mention elsewhere in this book, the coverage you receive from major media helps establish credibility with other media and makes them more comfortable in running your story. Therefore, your Web site should give journalists access to press clippings and other evidence of the major media coverage you have already received. You should

- Include html or pdf color images of the covers of major magazines where your company has been featured in a cover story.
- Provide hot links to these articles if they are posted online at the publication's Web site.
- Provide a hot link to the author's e-mail.

Trade show list

Journalists want to know where you'll be and the industry events where you will be speaking or exhibiting. Your Web site is an ideal place to post

- Shows that the company attends, promotes, or sponsors
- Hot links to releases associated with shows
- Hot links to specific trade show sites or sponsor sites
- An option to schedule a booth visit

Locations/facility information

In cyberspace, it's easy to forget that people want you to have a physical presence, not just megabytes of text and images on a server. Be sure to include

- Maps to headquarters and major regional facilities, including sales offices
- Hot link to mapquest.com for more detailed directions
- Site capabilities (what is manufactured there or major activities/ services)
- Number of employees at each facility
- Hot link to e-mail address of facility manager or key authority for each site

Avoiding "Speed Traps" on Your Web Site

Nothing annoys Web browsers faster than s-l-o-w sites. Here are two suggestions to keep your site easy and fast:

✔ Don't use snazzy graphics that take too long to download (keep your users' systems in mind). Not everyone has DSL or a Pentium III. Some people are actually using a 28 Kbps modem and a 486 PC!

✔ Don't emphasize entertainment (animation, special effects, graphics) over content (information), especially on business-to-business sites.

Keep in mind that most editors are too busy to waste time navigating poorly designed sites. With reporters, having a well-designed site is even more crucial. Come deadline time, an easily navigated Web site may mean the difference between being included in an article or excluded.

Speed is essential — have I made that point? The plain fact is, media surfers are almost always on deadline. Designers should make sites easy to navigate. Information shouldn't be more than one or two clicks away. Fast downloading is important, as is ease of navigation. Pretty pictures aren't important, and the speed of download can be affected by the server as well as by the type and complexity of graphics.

Want some examples of companies that editors praise for their media-friendly sites? Take a look at

✔ Applied Materials (www.appliedmaterials.com)

✔ Microsoft (www.microsoft.com)

✔ Broadsoft (www.broadsoft.com)

✔ Sterling Publications (www.sterlingpublications.co.uk)

✔ Intel (www.intel.com)

✔ Motorola (www.motorola.com)

The Three C's of E-Success

Internet specialists talk about the three C's of e-business: commerce, content, and community.

The first C, commerce, refers to the Web site's ability to permit the consumer to buy online. Without e-commerce, an e-mail can only generate online leads or offline purchases; you cannot have true one-step mail order on the Internet.

The second C, content, refers to the information and services available on the Web site. Web sites that display only product information are not as interesting to Internet users as Web sites that offer useful information and tools. (An example of a tool is a page I saw on a health Web site. After you enter your height, it displays your ideal weight.) The better your content, the more users will favor your site.

The interactivity and graphic nature of the Internet may, on the surface, make it attractive as a marketing tool. But Web surfers are drawn by content, not graphics. Animation and Day-Glo colors may make a Web site lively and inviting, but content-rich sites are what attract browsers and keep them long enough to become buyers.

Are you tuning in to the term *content?* What people used to call *editorial* is now content, according to *Hotline,* the monthly newsletter of the Newsletter Publishers Association in Washington, D.C. *Hotline* observes that on the Web, much of the content is created not by professional publishers or writers, but by users, buyers, and consumers — people sharing and talking with each other, rather than a publisher deciding and controlling what they read. "The power of content," the article concludes, "comes from someone with interests or experiences similar to yours writing you about it."

The third C, community, refers to the relationship that users have with the Web site and each other. It's the online equivalent of a neighborhood bookstore, café, or coffee shop. Web surfers begin to feel your site is a good place to go and spend time, especially with other visitors. People who study Web world more than I do say there are three communities out there:

✔ Internet communities that serve as a marketing and advertising tool

✔ Extranet communities designed to strengthen relationships with trade partners or customers

✔ Intranet communities that facilitate knowledge sharing within an organization

Chat rooms and forums can help build this sense of community. When you see people in postings talking not just to the person who originally posted the message, but also by name to each other — as they argue a point or share opinions — you know you're on a site with a strong sense of community.

A good example is iVillage.com. The use of the word "village" in the name instantly creates an image of an Internet community. The Web site caters to a variety of interests, including news, health, parenting, personal investing, pets, relationships, travel, and even a book club aimed primarily at women. You can send instant messages to other members, participate in chats, post notices on boards, and even have your own members' page. Another example is TechRepublic, a community of IT (information technology) professionals, which you can visit at www.Trfree.com.

CyberSite Inc. oversees about 20 communities of interest. Its most popular community is AncientSites, which is aimed at pre-medieval history enthusiasts and has 90,000 registered members. It offers free information as well as related products through affiliate programs. One e-mail, promoting ancient coins, generated a 74 percent click-through rate, with a 3 percent conversion rate. "It (the community of interest) is a superior environment for selling merchandise," says CyberSite's COO Keith Halper.

To make your Web site a success, community may be the most important C. The greater the sense of community, the stronger the relationship between the users and the Web site. Therefore, the users who have opted in and are on your e-list (and you can get almost all of them to opt in by requiring them to register to use chat rooms, forums, and other favorite site features) have a great relationship with the site. This maximizes their receptiveness to and willingness to receive e-marketing messages sent both by you and by other companies you allow to rent your e-list.

Too often we don't realize that our business or Web site is much more interesting to us than it is to the mass of Web surfers on the Internet. However, the more content and utility you offer, the more visitors will grow to like your site, and the greater awareness you'll gain.

Remember to measure Web surfer activity. Those who visit and buy know you better than those who visit sporadically or never buy. Factors you can measure include hits (visits to the Web site), page views (the specific pages visitors click to), duration (amount of time spent on site), and conversions (number of click-through visitors who make a purchase).

You can track traffic by time of day, day of week, and day of year. Use this data in network planning to ensure sufficient bandwidth to handle peak periods. Remember what happened to Internet toy retailers when they got more Christmas orders one year than they could handle? Customers were irate, and the share prices of those dot-com companies plummeted.

The bottom line is, don't assume a closer relationship between your site and visitors than actually exists. Your customer dictates the depth of the relationship, which must be based on what she needs, so don't try to bond with every visitor to your Web site. Just get to know your customers and then keep getting to know them. If you nurture these connections over time, real relationships will develop.

Designing a "Sticky" Web Site

A "sticky" Web site is one that people want to linger on, spend time with, and revisit frequently. The stickier the site, the more business it will generate (if it's an e-commerce site and not just an advertising site consisting of product literature posted on Web pages).

If you have the first C, commerce, taken care of, you'll increase your stickiness and sales by strengthening the other two Cs, content and community. If the content is relevant and interesting, people will use your site more — and buy more. If the site has a real sense of community, they'll visit often to see what's happening.

National Geographic increased e-commerce by surveying its gift shop to determine the most popular item. It turned out to be greeting cards. As a result, its next e-campaign featured a set of wild animal cards, with four cards displayed per page. An e-mail encouraged prospects to click onto the site to view the sample cards. The prospect could then choose to e-mail electronic versions of any card to a friend. People liked what they saw, and the opt-out rate to the e-mail was less than 0.04 percent. The click-through rate was 32 percent, and the campaign added 25,000 new names to the *National Geographic* e-list within three weeks.

Brainstorming More Ways to Make Profit Online

Here are your marching orders to put the Web to work promoting your business:

- ✔ **You must have a Web site.** There's no way around this today. You need a site if only for added credibility. But it also enhances customer service and sales. In a recent study conducted by Thomas Register and Visa USA, 30 percent of businesses said their primary reasons for moving to e-commerce were speed and convenience. In addition, the survey respondents indicated by a margin of 2 to 1 that they would give preference to a supplier who could accept online purchasing transactions.

  - • A Web site establishes instant credibility. It provides anytime access to you and the information about your services, making life easier for you and your prospects.

- ✔ **You must give people a reason to visit your site.** Internic, the governing body that controls Internet domain names, reports that there are more than 1.5 million Internet sites. So why in the world should anyone take the time to see yours? If you have your picture, your brochure, or a cute saying, who cares? People care only about themselves. If you don't give them an appealing reason to zip over to your site, why complain if they don't visit it?

- ✔ **You must give people options to buy.** If you don't list your products and services at your site, with different ways to make purchases, you will miss sales. Remember that people are still extremely nervous about buying anything online. Give them both online and offline options to buy, including a toll-free phone number, street address, and fax number.

✔ **You must constantly change your site.** You may get people to visit your site once, but how will you get them to return? Make sure to continually add new content. That's what keeps them coming back again and again. So, present special offers, news, and additional products to buy.

✔ **Get listed with search engines.** Only 6 to 12 search engines really count, and virtually all of them use spiders, or robots, that go out and find your site. You can and should manually register your site with Yahoo, Lycos, Alta Vista, Excite, Go, Netscape Search, AOL Search, MSN Search, Snap, HotBot, Google, and Infoseek.

  • If you want your site to be listed with search engines, pay your Webmaster to select the best candidates and make the submissions manually. Internet services that offer to have your site automatically registered with numerous search engines for a nominal fee can generate a flood of poor-quality inquiries and spam.

  • Provide the search engines with 10 to 20 key words you want your site to be listed under, and rank them in importance. When in doubt, have more key words rather than fewer. Hits related to less important terms can add up.

Have content-rich, text-rich pages, not just graphics. Search engine robots — software that travels the Web to find content and register it automatically with the search engine — find pages by words, not by pictures.

One study shows that only 42 percent of today's 800 million Web pages show up on any of the 11 major search engines. That's down from 60 percent of 320 million Web pages in 1997. Web pages are proliferating faster than the search engines can keep up. So don't become too dependent on search engines to drive traffic to your site. Instead, use PR to promote your URL to your offline customers, and forge alliances with reciprocal links to Web sites of companies whose products complement your own.

✔ **Use your sig file to promote your Web site.** Your "sig file" is that four- to eight-line paragraph at the end of every one of your e-mail messages. The Internet allows you to promote yourself in your sig. It's your opportunity to list your Web address and give people a reason to visit it.

  • Because your e-mail messages travel the Internet, get seen by potentially thousands of people, and are usually archived at giant databases like www.dejanews.com where they can be retrieved, you never know who will see one of your messages or when. If your sig file has your Web site address in it, you just promoted your Web site.

✔ **Print your Web site address on everything.** Every ad you run, commercial you air, business card you hand out, catalog you mail, and press kit and brochure you distribute should contain your Web site address. Use the offline world to promote your online presence.

✔ **Participate in online discussion groups.** Join e-mail discussion groups where your target prospects gather. Do a search at www.liszt.com to find the groups for you. Hang out at the site to get a feel for the nature of the group, and then post relevant responses to the list. As you do, you will be promoting yourself and your business. And if your sig has your Web site address in it, every time you post a message, you will be promoting your Web site in a perfectly acceptable manner in conformance with Internet etiquette. You'd be surprised at how many journalists sit in on or monitor discussion groups dealing with their area of coverage.

✔ **Cross-promote yourself in partnership with related Web sites.** Offline, we call it networking and co-op marketing. You can do the same thing online. Find Web sites that serve the same market you do and join forces with them. Maybe advertise on their site. Maybe exchange links. Create online allies to help you make money online.

✔ **Always give your Web site address in media interviews.** Whenever you're speaking to the press, but especially in broadcast media, tell listeners they can get more information on your topic at your Web site, and give the URL. Some media have policies limiting "plugs" and the mention of toll-free numbers, but right now, no one stops you from mentioning your Web site. I guess because the Web is perceived as an information medium and toll-free numbers are perceived as marketing devices, the media have fewer qualms about airing Web information. Take advantage of this policy now by always mentioning your Web URL. Things may change later as more and more journalists realize that the Web is rapidly becoming a marketing tool, not just a free speech medium.

✔ **Experiment.** The Internet as a vehicle for commerce is relatively new. Most of us are applying everything we have ever learned about marketing to this new medium. We have to think out of the box, stretch our minds, and create new ways of doing business online. We have to be willing to take risks and try new ideas. Some of this may cost money. Or time. But as Flip Wilson said, "You can't expect to hit the jackpot if you don't put a few nickels in the machine."

Is your Web site overdesigned?

The more graphics you put into your Web site, the slower the pages download to the viewer. According to Zona Research, Web pages take anywhere from 3 to 11 seconds to download, depending on the user's modem and Internet connection. The average viewer will "bail out" — click off the site onto another — if a page takes more than 8 seconds to download. Zona estimates these bail-outs cause e-businesses $4.35 billion annually in revenue. Speed makes the difference: One site decreased the bail-out rate from 30 percent to 8 percent just by reducing its download time by 1 second per page. One survey found that 84 percent of Web sites examined downloaded too slowly.

Just the FAQs

Add a Frequently Asked Questions (FAQ) page to your Web site. This section is a page listing, in question-and-answer format, of the most commonly asked questions and a brief answer to each. The benefit? You will get fewer e-mails asking you the same basic questions if you have this information instantly available online. A FAQ page saves you time, keeps your customers happy, and increases your sales.

Driving Traffic to Your Web Site

Successful Web site owners report that they spend 70 percent of their marketing budget on media outside the Web to direct prospective customers to their sites. Here are a few techniques you can use to boost your site traffic:

- ✔ **Put your URL on all promotions — direct mail, catalogs, card decks, fax marketing, space advertising, press releases, invoices, and renewals.**

- ✔ **Use search engines.** Write a short, compelling title and description tags for each page. Focus on one keyword phrase and use this phrase in page description tags, headlines, body copy, and alt tags. The keyword makes it more likely that someone doing an Internet search on the subject will be directed to your page.

- ✔ **Encourage prospects to register with you to build your e-mail database.** Offer a resource and document center, free demos, catalogs, samples, a drawing, or a free e-mail newsletter subscription. One of my firm's clients, Internet herb and vitamin marketer AllHerbs.com, sends out a regular e-mail newsletter to its database of 700,000 members. The e-mail newsletter — which generates a response rate of 30 percent — is a mishmash of useful information about herbs, useful facts, and special offers. For instance, Allherbs.com's Valentine's Day offer was free, all-natural chocolates with any purchase of $40 or more.

- ✔ **Consider testing banner ads** (those tiny little ads that pop up on the screen unsolicited by you when you're on the Internet). Try offering some of your content in exchange for a free banner ad. But test cautiously. Banner ads have been steadily declining in effectiveness, with click-through rates averaging only half a percent.

✔ **Send out press releases promoting your new site and the information it contains.** These press releases can focus on content (free information visitors can get on the site), community (online forums and discussion groups), or commerce (breadth of product line or special offers).

✔ **Link your site to other sites.** Set a goal of submitting a certain number of link requests per week. Search on your keywords to identify the relevant sites to which you want to link and then submit to those. Consider associations, magazines, consultants, and complementary sites.

✔ **Build strategic partnerships and alliances.** List your products on another company's site in exchange for a small royalty on any sales. For example, a site selling gourmet pancake batter can list another site's maple syrup. Consider submitting articles for an e-mail newsletter in exchange for a Web link and additional promotion.

✔ **Make it "sticky"** (refer to the "Designing a 'Sticky' Web Site" section, earlier in this chapter). Offer your prospects a reason to keep coming back. Good content, free resources and tools, contests, and drawings work well.

 • If people aren't flocking to your Web site, do a little offline (paper) promotion. Example: Print postcards introducing your Web site and send them out to everyone on your mailing list.

 • Internet direct mail is a powerful tool for driving people to your Web site. You can also use e-newsletters or e-zines.

✔ **Include your Web address on letters after the signature line.**

✔ **Develop a bookmark with your Web address on it and mail it with fulfillment of your products.**

✔ **Offer a weekly update of some sort to keep people coming back.** Write an e-mail newsletter you can push to your prospects to remind them about your Web site.

The early bird gets the URL

Register your Internet domain name early. When in doubt about a name, register it anyway. Registration is cheap when you get the name directly from Internic, the governing body that controls these names. But if someone else registers the name you want, you may have to pay dearly to get them to sell it to you. Recently, drugs.com sold for $823,456. And a Texas entrepreneur recently sold business.com to a California company for $7.5 million. Two years earlier, he had bought the name from someone else for $150,000. My coauthor Bob Bly registered bly.com a year or more before he was ready to put up a Web site just to secure the name. Sure enough, a number of Blys approached him later to say that they wished they had gotten it first! To register a domain name, go to www.networksolutions.com or ask your Internet access provider.

Should You E-Mail Press Releases?

According to a poll, 55 percent of editors prefer getting printed press releases sent via regular mail; 25 percent prefer e-mail; and 15 percent prefer faxes.

A number of editors I've talked with tell me that they do not open all their e-mails, and sending releases via snail mail is too slow. For this reason, we send most of our press releases via fax broadcast. Doing so gives you speed and immediacy nearly equal to e-mail but without the two big e-mail problems: fear of opening an e-mail because of virus concerns and difficulty opening an e-mail because of file format incompatibility.

For materials that can't be sent via fax, such as press kits, we send them via regular first-class mail. The cost, including postage, envelope, and paper, is less than $1 apiece for each publication to which we send the kit.

When an editor lets us know that he's willing to accept releases via e-mail or even prefers it, we change our database so that any future releases sent to him are transmitted via e-mail. Keep a separate mailing group on your address book of editors and publishers whom you know prefer receiving press releases over the Internet, and e-mail your releases to this group separately.

E-mailing press releases works best when you want to follow up a press release mailing (sent via regular mail) with a phone call. Then, when the editor expresses interest but says that he doesn't remember getting or didn't save the original release, you can e-mail him a copy instantly and then follow up later that day to confirm receipt of the e-mail.

Send e-mail press releases as pasted-in text messages or attached files in common formats such as text (ASCII), WordPerfect, or Microsoft Word. Avoid any file formats that the editor may not be able to open. (Example: A few corporations use Lotus WordPro, and many editors do not have it.) If the editor has the least bit of trouble opening your attachment, she'll click Delete faster than you can say, "Not interested."

Part V
Creating Buzz

"Tarzan's paintings good, but no one come to gallery. Need to put buzz on street. That when Tarzan call in elephant stampede down Bleeker Street."

In this part . . .

*N*ow is the time to turn up your PR efforts to full heat. One way is by staging special PR events, as outlined in Chapter 17. In PR, timing is everything, and Chapter 18 helps you take advantage of timing to maximize your PR results. Sometimes the heat you face is negative, so I include Chapter 19 to guide you in coping with any PR crisis. Finally, Chapter 20 shows you how to measure your PR results and return on PR investment.

Chapter 17

Staging Publicity Events

. . . .

. . . .

*W*ho says publicity stunts are passé? Outrageous staged events designed solely to show up on the evening news still get the job done when they're clever and fun.

A case in point: Stan Heimowitz, owner of Celebrity Gems in Castro Valley, California, recently successfully dramatized in the streets of San Francisco the fact that IntraLinux, a small software company — Heimowitz's client — is challenging Microsoft, the industry giant.

Outside the Moscone Center in San Francisco, where Microsoft was launching its new product Windows 2000, a Bill Gates look-alike was matched against a Penguin (IntraLinux's mascot) in a boxing ring whose four corners were held up by Penguinettes, young women dressed in penguin costumes. The Penguin defeated the faux Gates, naturally, while a plane towing a banner that read "IntraLinux" flew overhead. This creative bit of street theater made its point to onlookers and the media alike.

Publicity stunts go back at least to the days of showman P.T. Barnum, who announced that his circus had arrived in town by hitching an elephant to a plow beside the train tracks. This stunt raised such a ruckus that plowing a field with an elephant is still against the law in North Carolina.

Suspense became an element in a stunt featured on the front page of *The Los Angeles Times* in 1980 when the paper challenged Bob Allen to make good on his boast that he could be dropped into any city with $100 and 72 hours later own several properties without paying down payments. Although readers wondered whether Allen could really do it, the author of *Nothing Down* indeed pulled it off.

Attention-getting can go highbrow, too. In 1989, actor Norman George, who portrays Edgar Allen Poe in a one-man show, persuaded the city of Boston to rename Carver Street, where the creator of "The Raven" was born, in honor of the poet in connection with the 180th anniversary of Poe's birth.

Publicity stunts and milder special events aren't ever a sure thing. Your parade can get rained on, and a breaking news story elsewhere can pull the media away. When Massachusetts retailer Rick Segel sponsored a gala contest for the Best Hairdresser of Medford, the fur coats that bore contestants' numbers got switched, causing prizes to be awarded to the wrong people. Two judges walked out, and fistfights almost broke out among the hairdressers.

Despite the risks, Stan Heimowitz had such a hoot with his IntraLinux Penguin versus Gates bout that he floated himself as a publicity-stunt impresario to PR and ad agencies. The whole event cost just $3,700, Heimowitz says, including the actors and costumes. Compare that to the cost of a color magazine ad — as much as $10,000 or more — that gets two seconds of a reader's attention!

Drawing Crowds and Gaining Publicity

Special events — such as grand openings, pony rides for children, barbecues and square dances, picnics, and Halloween parties — are effective publicity vehicles in two ways:

- They help market your company, product, or service to the public. People attend the event, come to your store for the free hot dogs or ice cream, and then browse and buy while they're there.
- They're promotable and can get you a lot of press coverage. Many editors like special events and cover them.

If the event involves free food, gifts, rides, or other giveaways, many editors at least announce it in their papers, typically in a schedule of events or things-to-do-this-week column.

If the event is based on a clever gimmick or angle, many editors not only put it in the calendar but also may give it broader feature coverage, both as a preview as well as a post-event story. This leverages the time and effort spent putting on the event, because you not only promote yourself to those who attend but also, through the publicity, reach thousands of additional prospects who did not come.

Spiderman snares kids but loses sales

It's important to maximize the selling opportunity at special events. For example, a local department store advertised that Spiderman would be at the store's grand opening to pose for photos with the kiddies and give away autographed comic books. When we got there, the line of parents with children to see Spiderman went around the store, with a 50-minute wait.

Spiderman stood in front of the toy department, where he shook hands and posed with young fans. To my amazement, no Spiderman or other superhero toys or comic books were displayed near him! In fact, no such display was set up anywhere in the toy department! The store blew an opportunity to sell thousands of dollars' worth of Spiderman and superhero action figures, dolls, costumes, and other comic book paraphernalia. Don't you make this same mistake.

Also, the only announcement of Spiderman's appearance came in free-standing newspaper inserts and ads. The store didn't drum up any free publicity. You might say, "What do you expect? It's just a guy dressed up in a Spiderman costume. No news there."

Here's where being creative and clever could have made the difference. What about writing and distributing a press release in the form of a tongue-in-cheek, question-and-answer interview with Spiderman? If such a release had been sent with some action photos of Spidey striking a dramatic pose or shooting a web, I guarantee that at least one local editor would have enjoyed and run this release as a feature article, thus generating publicity for the store.

Here are some quick suggestions for creating special events that not only draw big crowds but also gain publicity:

- ✔ Tie the special event into current events or news. For instance, a store selling 1950s and other nostalgia items could have had an Elvis Presley memorabilia sale tied into the U. S. Postal Service's widely publicized introduction of the Elvis stamp.

- ✔ Tie the special event into a holiday, anniversary, or other observance. Virtually every day is the anniversary of some famous person's birth or death; the anniversary of some important event; or a holiday, commemorative day, or day of recognition. For example, you might give 25 percent off any item in your store to left-handed people on National Lefty Day.

- ✔ Involve local celebrities. For example, invite the DJ from a popular local radio station to serve as the master of ceremonies and to sign autographs. Celebrities draw crowds and generate press coverage. Stores often call on celebrities to help promote grand openings.

- ✔ Make your own news. When a union of social workers was not getting a lot of press for its strike against a state agency unwilling to grant them a small wage increase, I suggested that they make a video greeting card and send it to the agency's director. On the video, families served by the agency pleaded with the director to end the strike, because the scab workers who were replacing the striking workers did not know the families and their special needs. The PR angle? We sent the video greeting card not only to the agency director but also to all local TV news programs.

✔ Feature an unusual, interesting, or creative event as part of the day. For example, to promote your pizza parlor, you can truck in ingredients and attempt to get everyone present into the *Guinness Book of World Records* by having them help you make the world's largest pizza.

Figuring the Cost and Setting a Budget

The biggest drawback of events is their cost, and the second biggest drawback is the sheer amount of work they take to put on. When planning an event, the best place to start is your budget because it will dictate the scope, size, and even the creative approach to your event.

Once a client asked me to submit ideas for a promotional event. Figuring he was thrifty, I presented several concepts that would work on a modest budget. He became enraged: "I want *big* ideas," he told me. "Come up with something really spectacular." When I came back with the spectacular ideas, he paused a second and then said, "These are great, but we can't afford them." You need to establish a budget first and then frame an event you can do within your budget.

I've worked with event budgets ranging from $30,000 to $1 million. With a million-dollar budget, you can afford to do a travel promotion with an appearance by a pitcher from the baseball team that won the last World Series. When your budget is smaller, you may have to stick to something simpler — hot-air balloon rides or just hot dogs in the parking lot.

The biggest plus of events is their unique ability to dramatically demonstrate a message and make it come alive. PR is the art of demonstration. You just can't say you're environmentally friendly or technically savvy; to get the public to believe you and the press to quote you, you have to demonstrate that these claims are so. Consider this example: When the Park Central Hotel in New York City wanted to communicate the message that the improvements being made at the hotel would improve the quality of service for guests, it offered a day of free "personal renovations" in the lobby, where visitors could get hairstyling, massages, and manicures (more later on that event).

Controlling Event Costs

A general guideline is that a special event always costs at least ten times more than a strictly print promotion (for example, mailing a press release). There's no getting around it — events cost time, money, and effort.

ZINGER

Fine smokes feed old folks

Cigar smoking, once a hot trend, has faded in recent years, and our client, Club Macanudo — a New York City cigar club — wanted to demonstrate that cigar aficionados are people with taste who appreciate the finer things in life. Our agency created the "Ultimate Cars, Premium Cigars Road Rally" in which participants in 25 luxury and collectible cars drove through New York's Westchester County.

At each rest stop, drivers were given a fine cigar to smoke. Onlookers could see happy people driving beautiful cars, smoking and enjoying their cigars. The event proceeds — which included the entry fees plus sales of humidors to the crowd attending the event and its awards banquet that evening — benefited City Meals-on-Wheels, a nonprofit organization providing food to elderly New Yorkers. The event was covered in *The New York Post* and *The New York Daily News* and on WB Channel 11 among other media.

However, you can take several steps to control costs and keep the event budget at a reasonable level:

- ✔ Keep the event local. Hold it in your own town or the nearest city, not the city where the annual industry meeting is held 2,000 miles away.

- ✔ Allow only essential personnel to attend. Having executives travel to the show or conference wastes your budget and their time.

- ✔ Be a scrooge about expenditures. For example, at events where wine is served, I tell the waiters to ask attendees whether they want more wine instead of automatically pouring more in the glass. The savings are considerable.

- ✔ Shop around for everything. You would be shocked to discover how prices for seemingly comparable services and items vary. For instance, many "second tier" celebrities who are very well known and are crowd pleasers will work for a fraction of the cost of a superstar with a slightly bigger reputation who doesn't buy you much extra as a draw.

Determining Your Event's Theme and Concept

Demonstrating a key message should always be the reason for and key objective of any promotional event. Look at your product or service. Identify the key messages you want to communicate. Now get creative and, using the methods outlined in Chapter 6, brainstorm ways to use events to demonstrate these messages.

Here are some examples:

- ✔ Carvel Ice Cream wanted to modernize its image as a place that really cared about kids. To animate the message, it brought free ice cream to 55 schools in the New York tristate area with the best attendance records.

- ✔ To support the launch of IKEA's line of a.i.r inflatable furniture, I helped conduct the IKEA a.i.r Open Golf Tournament benefiting the Asthma and Allergy Foundation of America (AAFA). We covered a golf course with room settings by using the inflatable furniture and other IKEA furniture. Soap opera stars Jackie Zeman and Julian Stone were on hand to raise money to send 100 children with asthma and allergies to the AAFA's summer camp. Media coverage included *The Los Angeles Times,* Reuters, CNN, and local affiliates of all major networks.

- ✔ Another client of mine, the Park Central Hotel in New York City, wanted to publicize a $50 million renovation. That may sound like a big deal, but it's actually far from a record in the world of high-priced hotel renovations. To draw attention and press coverage, the hotel sponsored a "Renovate Yourself"day in its lobby. People could come in for a free facial, manicure, hairstyling, massage, shoe shine, and even a consultation with a plastic surgeon who used a video imaging system to show people what they'd look like before and after a face lift or tummy tuck. The event — and the hotel's renovation — got coverage on all four network affiliates, national TV, and a feature story in *The Daily News.*

Events like these can help elevate you above your competition; you're playing on a different field. The creative theme and the fact that you're doing an event are what set you apart from your competitors who may publicize a company only by doing the usual press release (for example, "Hotel Undergoes $50 Million Renovation") — yawn.

With a little creativity, you can apply this kind of thinking to come up with an event to publicize your own business. First, decide the key message that you want to communicate and whom you want to reach. A local dry cleaner, for example, may want to compete with other dry cleaners — for example, a national chain — by showing that the local store is a cornerstone of the community.

Next, think of a way to demonstrate the message. In the above example, how can you prove — not just say — that you are a part of the community? Perhaps you can make some kind of donation or offer a service.

Now, decide how you tie that donation or service to your product or service. A dry cleaner cleans, so perhaps the dry cleaner can sponsor a "Clean Up Happytown Day." Residents come to the messy downtown park for a cleanup effort; the dry cleaner provides the garbage bags, entertainment, and refreshment for the volunteers. And what does a dry cleaner clean? Clothes. So maybe the dry cleaner invites local residents to bring in old clothes, which the dry cleaner then cleans and donates to a local shelter.

Planning the Event and Logistics

Although a clever theme and a creative approach can make your event, poor planning can break it. Event planning is a detail-oriented task, so assign someone on your team who's good at details to handle it.

Here are a few tips to help you plan your event:

- ✔ Determine the number of attendees, the location, and the exact time and day of the event early in the planning process. Many of your needs depend on the season, weather, time of day, and day of week that you hold your event.

- ✔ Visit the event site as early as possible in the planning stage, both before and during the creative process. Take your team to the site for part of the brainstorming process.

- ✔ Do a mental walk-through of the event from start to finish. Write down each of the major steps and the tasks involved with each. Prepare a schedule with deadlines, and assign people to each task. Specify when every detail will be completed and by whom. Double-check timing on everything that must be ordered. Allow time for delays; they happen more often than not.

- ✔ Communicate regularly with all vendors, participants, and volunteers to make sure that they're on schedule. Ongoing communication helps them maintain a comfort level and makes them less likely to pull out. If they do pull out, you'll know about it in time to find a replacement.

- ✔ During the mental walk-through, visualize the event. Do you need sound, lighting, décor, signage, tents, a stage, a band shell, heat, air conditioning, entertainment, music, toilets, dressing rooms, water, security, food, drinks, storage for supplies, a coat room?

- ✔ Make a rough floor plan of the event. Make sure that you have enough space. Keep updating the floor plan as the event proceeds.

- ✔ Leave out no details, no matter how small. The success or failure of an event is in the organization and the precision of details. If everything is perfectly organized and all the details are correctly done, your event is more likely to be a success.

- ✔ Write everything down. Make detailed checklists. Go over them again and again. The more often you review them, the more details you can add.

✔ Make an agenda or timeline for the event itself. Everything must be perfectly timed, in many cases to the second. Have rehearsals until you get the timing right.

✔ At a pre-event meeting, give all staff and participants an information package. The package should contain any press releases (refer to Chapter 9) regarding the event, an overview, the event agenda or timeline, the responsibilities of each person, staff schedules, a layout or map of the event, a schedule of breaks for the staff, location of rest areas, and location of food and beverages. Give out uniforms at that time if they are to be worn.

A word about timing. You may ask, "How can we make sure our event isn't ruined by a hurricane or overshadowed by a scandal or crime that steals the headlines that day?" The answer is: You can't. Unforeseen events happen all the time, and there's nothing you can do about them. That's what makes events so risky.

For example, a lot of planning went into an event my firm scheduled for Earth Grains, a client introducing a new bread product in the California market. All three local network affiliates had vans on the way to cover our event. Then a sniper starting shooting into a crowd from a rooftop ten blocks away from our event. The vans turned around to cover the sniper, and not a single station ran the Earth Grains story that evening.

I am fond of telling clients who want to do an event that, if they name any major news event — war, an airline crash, political scandal — I can tell them about one of our special events that the headlines preempted that day. It's just a risk you take.

The "Meeting Planner's Checklist" on the CD contains a list of the questions to ask and requirements to address for planning anything from a small breakfast seminar to a theme-day event for thousands. Also on the CD is the article "20 Tips for Great Events."

Publicizing Your Event

The tools discussed throughout this book for reaching the press — the telephone, e-mail (Chapter 16), press releases (Chapter 9), pitch letters (Chapter 10), and meetings — apply equally to promoting events. Because events are more time-critical than many other promotions, I suggest that you e-mail or fax your materials for faster delivery and a slightly greater sense of urgency.

Should you create some sort of clever invitation to lure the press to your event? If the concept doesn't intrigue them, they won't go, no matter what you send. But if the event is appealing, they'll come. A press release announcing the event does fine as an invitation.

As for TV coverage, watch the evening news. On most local affiliates, the last story is always a light feature piece. If your event catches the producer's interest, this is the spot in which it will probably run.

Measuring Event Results

My measure of a promotional event's success is simple: If it doesn't get major press coverage, it's a failure.

The event itself is important, but it's the PR effort to promote the event that makes or breaks it. As I discuss in Chapters 9 and 12, the key is strong press releases widely distributed to the appropriate media outlets and diligent telephone follow-up to all of them, with an eye toward convincing as many as possible to cover the event.

I don't care how many people came or the impression you made on them. Given the time, expense, and sheer work involved in sponsoring an event, it's only worth the cost and trouble — in my mind — if you get media coverage.

Thousands of people turned up to watch the IKEA a.i.r Open Golf Tournament. Throughout the golf course, in the open air, pieces of IKEA's new inflatable a.i.r furniture were blown up and displayed.

When bad news happens to good events

Events are risky because coverage of your event can be preempted by the news of the day, and that's a factor you cannot control. As I mention earlier, this has happened so frequently that if you name a world crisis, I can probably tell you the PR event I was having that day.

Baseball player Cal Ripken Jr. appeared one morning for my client Itsy Bitsy Entertainment at a major licensing trade show in Manhattan (you can see the event on the CD-ROM). I learned the night before his appearance that Vice President Al Gore was coming into the city! Fortunately, Gore arrived in the afternoon. Had he come in the morning, I guarantee the press would have covered the Gore visit and ignored our Cal Ripken promotion. Fortunately, that was not the case, and the event helped Itsy Bitsy make the front page of *The New York Times* business section. But it could have easily gone sour; we were extremely lucky.

Those thousands of people in attendance saw the new furniture, but the real benefit was the press coverage, which gave us more than 40 million media impressions. (A *media impression* means that a person saw, read, or heard about the product in the media. If a TV news story covers an event and the viewership is 100,000, that counts as another 100,000 media impressions for that campaign.)

A large, well-attended event can attract as many as 5,000 people, but a well-publicized event can reach hundreds of thousands more through media coverage. Attaining that press coverage is the real objective of promotional events.

The shorter the event, the smaller the window of opportunity for the media to cover it. Whenever possible, I make an event two days to maximize opportunity for media coverage.

Chapter 18

Spotting and Seizing Opportunities

. . . .

In This Chapter

▶ Getting the timing right

▶ Capitalizing on current news and events

▶ Making the most of changing conditions

▶ Searching for an opening

▶ Finding ways to get noticed quickly

. . . .

Woody Allen is frequently quoted as saying, "90 percent of success is just showing up." Well, the reason that so many companies get so little PR is that they don't show up. Opportunities present themselves every day, yours for the taking. But most people never see them. In this chapter, I show you how to condition yourself to spot PR opportunities as well as act to take advantage of them.

Remembering the Importance of Timing

I already said that part of getting a feel for PR is to consume media from the point of view of the PR professional, not the general public. Doing so is especially important in learning to identify and exploit PR opportunities. When you read the papers and watch the evening news with an eye toward spotting PR opportunities, you notice patterns emerging that you never really paid attention to before. For example:

✔ On April 15, the evening news always does a feature story about the last-minute taxpayers — every year.

✔ On the last day of public school, the media run stories on preparing for the summer and finding activities to keep kids busy and entertained.

✔ Stories on how to give flowers, buy flowers, or arrange flowers always run around Mother's Day.

The fact is, the media are always going to do "built-in" stories. And because they're always looking for a fresh angle to an old story, that's where you come in. If you can provide that fresh angle in a way that promotes your product, company, or cause, you can ride on the coat-tails of the story they were already planning.

An example is "Petting Day at the Post Office," a campaign we did for a pet manufacturers association. The objective was to promote pet ownership as healthy by demonstrating that pets help relieve people's stress.

We know that TV always sends cameras to the post office the evening of April 15 to do a short feature piece on last-minute taxpayers standing in line to file returns. We put a petting zoo in the post office and invited frazzled taxpayers to pet a cuddly puppy or kitten after finally getting their returns in the mail.

Naturally, the cameras turned to the petting zoo, showing the once-nervous taxpayers now relaxed and smiling as they petted the animals. The reason the campaign succeeded: timing.

The quintessential light campaign? To be sure, it's a little fluffy (pun intentional). But actually, it demonstrates an important message — the need to reduce stress — in a visual (and highly memorable) way. Sure, the campaign is cute. But it's also on target with the client's strategy.

Few things are as stressful as preparing your tax returns, and April 15 is the only day of the year when the broadcast media universally focuses on taxes. If we had put up a petting zoo anywhere else at any other time of the year, I am convinced that Petting Day would not have received nearly as much coverage as it did.

Reacting to Current News and Events

Opportunities can be keyed to one-time events as well as recurring events. For a decade, Seinfeld was the leading comedy on TV, so the ending of the show was big news. Now, Seinfeld said many times that it was a show about nothing. So for one client we devised a campaign we called "Thanks for Nothing Seinfeld."

The objectives were to reach a particular target audience — the demographics of which just happened to match the same audience Seinfeld reached — and get 100,000 consumers in this audience to sample a bag of potato chips.

Since Seinfeld was about nothing, nothing was what you had to do to get a free bag of these chips. Any consumer who sent in a bag or envelope containing nothing would get a free bag of chips. This campaign received enormous media coverage and won several PR awards. In fact, the Seinfeld people asked to use the story in their own promotions for the last Seinfeld episode.

Taking Advantage of Changing Conditions

Chopping down Christmas trees is a centuries-old tradition, but many people in our modern society find it wasteful, not to mention detrimental to the environment. IKEA Home Furnishings has an annual promotion called "Rent-a-Tree" that's perfect for today's environmentally-conscious times. Instead of buying a Christmas tree, you can rent one cheaply at IKEA. When you bring it back, you get the return of your deposit. In addition, IKEA will mulch the tree, eliminating the waste of throwing out a tree.

Or consider the once-fearsome corporate CEO. Today, with New Age male sensitivity, the rise of female CEOs, and the new Generation X CEOs of the dot-com world, CEOs no longer posture as granite men. We did a campaign for Calyx & Corolla, a direct marketer of flowers, showing that more and more CEOs liked getting flowers — and that those who did were more caring and generous than those who didn't. It worked like a charm.

Looking for an Opening

Do you have a marketing problem that PR can solve, but can't think of an angle that would appeal to the media? If you think creatively, chances are you can find some way to tie it in to current events or news.

Planting "evergreens"

Some promotions are known as "evergreens," because they can be used time after time, and doing a PR campaign based on changes — in politics, the economy, technology, society, culture — is a prime example of an evergreen. And the reason is that change itself is a constant in our society: It's always happening. One way to learn about changing trends that can possibly serve as sources of inspiration for PR campaigns is to watch the evening news and read a daily newspaper. Another good resource for tracking trends is American Demographics, a market research magazine (listed on the CD at the back of this book).

Astor Chocolate is a fine chocolate maker with a brand awareness problem: Nobody knows who they are. Yet when you stay at a fine hotel, the chances are 70 percent that the chocolate left on your pillow at bedtime is an Astor.

How to tie this in with anything? After some brain-stretching, we came up with "The 'Square One' Academy Awards Wake-Up Call." Every year, the Academy Awards show runs longer and longer, forcing people who want to watch until the end to stay up later and later. In this campaign, we promised that if you contacted us, you could stay up as late as you wanted and not oversleep, because we would give you a wake-up call along with free chocolates for your pillow.

To maximize your PR coverage, strive to go where the cameras already are. Now, where are the cameras on the Fourth of July? At the fireworks. How about on Labor Day? At the lake and shore, filming the bathers and boaters.

Another of our clients, Progressive Boat Insurance, wanted to show that it cared about the safety of the boat owners it insured. We came up with "Keys, Please," which was a variation of the liquor campaigns encouraging people who become inebriated at bars to give their keys to a friend who can drive them home: We offered, during the Labor Day weekend, a free towing service for boat owners who got too drunk to drive their boats safely (see Figure 18-1 — and view the video on the CD).

Note that promoting safe boating is not only good for Progressive Boat Insurance's image, but it also literally goes right to the bottom line: The fewer boating accidents its policyholders have, the lower the dollar amounts of policy payouts.

Figure 18-1:
Progressive
Boat
Insurance
"Keys
Please"
press
release.

For Immediate Release

Contact: Tim Schramm
Jericho Communications
212/645-6900

PROGRESSIVE LAUNCHES *FIRST-OF-ITS-KIND* PILOT PROGRAM FOR BOATERS THIS LABOR DAY

*"Keys... Please" Program Urges Boaters
To Have Fun, Safely*

Cleveland, OH, August 30, 1999--- It's Labor Day... a time for everyone to get outside and enjoy the last rays of summer. With the waterways jammed with summer-end revelers taking their boats out for one last spin, it's important to realize that safety on the waterways is equally as important as safety on the roadways.

That's why Progressive Watercraft Insurance is launching *"Keys... Please,"* a new pilot program to help provide boaters with a safe and fun holiday weekend. The program is providing a free towing service for those boaters who have had too much to drink and are concerned about operating their boat safely. As an added safety feature, for people who find out at the last minute that they have more guests than life jackets, Progressive is also loaning out adult and child-size life jackets throughout the entire weekend.

This unique program will be offered throughout the weekend for all boaters on Lake Erie (the "Flats"). Throughout the day beginning Friday, September 3 through Monday, September 6, Progressive will be patrolling the area in a specially marked boat....

"Our number one concern is that people have fun but also act responsibly this Labor Day weekend," comments Jeanette Hisek, Product Manager, Progressive Watercraft Insurance. "We developed this program because it exemplifies everything Progressive stands for – serving people the best that we can, reducing risks, and responding fully to their needs and concerns. We want everyone to have fun this Labor Day and to do so in the safest way possible"....

Getting Messages Noticed Quickly

Lots of midsize and large PR firms tell their clients that public relations is a strategic process and that they should be patient for results. And doing the strategic planning, as outlined in Chapter 3, takes time.

But almost no client is patient for results. If I don't get lots of press for my clients and fast, they'll be unhappy and restless. So how do you get the campaign off to a quick start once the strategy is approved?

The surest and quickest way to get PR is to go where the press already is and grab your share of the existing media spotlight. Doing so is a lot easier and more effective than trying to get them to haul out that spotlight and bring it just for you.

Seasonal or holiday tie-ins are perennial favorites. Linking your message to current events requires faster thinking and action, but it can work wonders when you pull it off. When there is a hot news story and you come up with an idea to piggyback on it, your window of opportunity is extremely short — typically a week and rarely more than two weeks (O.J. Simpson and Monica Lewinsky had unusual longevity). After that, it's old news and the campaign won't work.

Chapter 19

Knowing What to Do in a Crisis

. . . .

. . . .

I learned there are troubles

Of more than one kind.

Some come from ahead

And some come from behind.

—Dr. Seuss

According to a 1997 EPA report, between 1987 and 1996 there were more than 600,000 accidental releases of toxic chemicals in the U.S. that together killed 2,565 people and caused 22,949 injuries. A few years earlier, in 1984, the world experienced perhaps the worst industrial accident in its history. A chemical plant in Bhopal, India, spewed out toxic gas, killing more than 6,000 people. Investigators found 65 management errors, 12 operator errors, 21 equipment failures, and 28 regulatory breaches.

To be sure, these are terrible disasters — for both the victims as well as for the companies involved. But there are many levels of crises. Even a spilled cup of hot coffee turned into a crisis for McDonald's that involved a PR nightmare and a multi-million-dollar lawsuit.

I define a crisis as an event, rumor, or story that has the potential to affect your reputation, image, or credibility in a negative way. Examples include everything from product tampering (remember Tylenol?) and contamination to alleged discrimination or lawsuits (Microsoft is a recent example of the latter). The stock market once dipped on a false rumor that Federal Reserve Chairman Alan Greenspan had been killed in a car accident.

Most small businesses think that "crisis PR" is the concern of only Fortune 500 companies. But a crisis can strike any organization at any time. For your business, potential crisis situations may include the following:

- Public health (for example, a toxic spill or a cancer-causing product)
- Safety and security issues
- Financial and business issues
- Environmental issues
- Disasters (product tampering, service outages)
- Business practices and ethics
- Worker misconduct
- Legal issues
- Accidents and disasters (driver accidents, crashes, fires, building collapses)
- False advertising
- Customer complaints
- Out-of-stock products

If you think that your tiny business, out of the public eye, is invulnerable to a crisis, you're wrong. Smaller businesses, which often rely on one or two key customers, can lose that business at the drop of a hat. For this reason, I advocate planning for any possible crisis that could occur.

The more prepared you are, the better the chances that you can survive a crisis — however long the odds are of its occurrence — if it comes. If you're skeptical of the need for crisis planning, keep this fact in mind: Many companies never have more than one crisis, because the first crisis they have puts them out of business. I wrote this chapter to help make sure that this doesn't happen to you.

Remembering the Rules in a Crisis

In the movie *Twins,* Arnold Schwarzenneger repeatedly recites to Danny DeVito his "rules in a crisis." Well, when it comes to public relations crises, I have a few of my own. The first rule is this: Facilitate information in a quick and timely manner. How quickly you communicate the facts to the victims, press, investors, shareholders, and other audiences determines, in large part, how you emerge from the situation.

Here are some other critical rules for acting in a PR crisis:

- ✔ Always tell the truth.

- ✔ Be as forthright as you can. Do not be misleading or dishonest.

- ✔ Be prepared. Have a communications plan in place before disaster strikes. Don't wait until it happens to start thinking, "What do we do?"

- ✔ Act like you care. Demonstrate compassion.

- ✔ Move quickly. Don't stand there stunned.

- ✔ Make fast decisions and swift adjustments. If you're faced with having to spend money to clean up the situation, do it now while it seems like your choice, rather than later when it seems like you're acting only because of pressure.

- ✔ Never say, "No comment." If you don't have an answer, say so and then get it.

- ✔ Return all calls from the press promptly. Every day you do not respond to an accusation, the bad press it generates gets exponentially worse.

- ✔ Don't avoid the press. Actively seek opportunities to get in front of the cameras and tell your story.

- ✔ Admit when you messed up, apologize, explain how you're going to fix it, and then do what you promised.

Demonstrating Care, Compassion, and Commitment

I say throughout this book that PR is an art of demonstration — showing rather than stating your message — and crisis management is no exception. When you say that you care and are sorry, people are cynical. When you demonstrate compassion and caring in a dramatic and distinctive way, people not only believe your message but also pay attention to and remember it.

For example, years ago I was handling PR for an off-Broadway play. Well, the play got a terrible review in *The New York Times,* which usually spells death for such a production. We felt that the *Times* critic had made a mistake and wanted to get this message across without sounding like sour grapes. We sent out a press release saying, "Even *The New York Times* Makes Mistakes!" The gimmick: If people found a typo in *The New York Times,* they could send it in to us and we would mail them a free ticket to the show. The campaign generated a lot of press and demonstrated the point — that reviews do not have the final word on a piece of art or entertainment, but are just one person's opinion — in a fresh, credible, and nondefensive manner.

Another client, a retailer of home furnishings and accessories, published the wrong phone number in its catalog, and suddenly some poor guy was getting hundreds of phone calls every day. Our solution? Not only did we pay for a new phone number for him, but we also refurnished his home with our client's furniture absolutely free. He was delighted, and the press loved the story.

Customer service surveys show that, if a customer has a problem but you resolve it quickly and correctly, the customer actually becomes more loyal to you than before the problem occurred. It's the same with a PR crisis: If you resolve the crisis quickly and get your story out to the media, the event can actually strengthen your brand image.

That's why I see most crisis management as an opportunity rather than a threat. Properly handled, response to crisis is a showcase for great leadership. It can increase corporate visibility in a positive way, showcasing character and competence.

For example, when a food delivery client of mine was being widely viewed as promoting unsafe driver safety on "rushed" deliveries, we had to demonstrate a different example. My client was getting blamed because its advertising stressed fast delivery. The truth, however, was that the company could deliver faster because it had a more efficient cooking operation than its competitors.

To demonstrate this message — that our fast delivery was due to faster cooking, not reckless driving — we held a contest among company employees nationwide. The winning cook was the subject of a full-page profile in *People* magazine and appeared as a guest on both *Late Night with David Letterman* and *Good Morning America*.

Another client, a clothing company, called to tell me it would be several weeks late in delivering initial shipments of a much-promoted new clothing line. We immediately sent out a release on the theme "Caught with Our Pants Down," saying that we had screwed up and would be two weeks late. To dramatize the message, we said that for the first 1,000 people to send their pants to us (actually, a pair of underwear), we would make a donation to the homeless in their name and send them a free pair of our product.

Thinking of Every Crisis as a Red Alert

When the threat got really serious in the old *Star Trek* series — like when the Romulans were about to attack — Captain Kirk invariably upgraded the ship's status from yellow alert to red alert. I advise my clients to treat any PR crisis as a red alert. The keys to doing so are to

- ✔ Make the situation a management priority.

- ✔ Have plans in place before crises happen; if you wait until they happen before creating a plan, you're too late.

- ✔ Respond with same-day speed — "tomorrow" isn't good enough.

In crisis plans for large corporate clients, we say that every one of the top management people is always "on call." If a crisis occurs, every key decision maker must be available within a few hours — by phone if that's the best they can do, but preferably gathered in the same room. Once they're in the room (or connected with the people in the room via speaker phone), no one leaves until consensus is reached on what's to be done. The person managing crisis communications should have the home phone numbers of all executives in the group and shouldn't hesitate to call them at any time of the day or night.

Not having the team together slows decision making, which can be devastating for PR purposes — the media's job is to investigate and get at the truth, and their deadline for doing so is tomorrow (for print) or tonight (for broadcast) or even now (for the Web). For example, one American shoe manufacturer was faced with a rumor that a street gang wore its sneakers. They responded like a snail instead of in a flash, and the brand was destroyed.

More Tips for Successful Crisis Management

Remember Dorothy's famous line to her dog Toto in the film *The Wizard of Oz* — "Somehow I don't think we're in Kansas anymore"? The next time you get that queasy "We have a problem" feeling in your business, and your concern has to do with media exposure that threatens to damage corporate reputation, take a deep breath, get calm, and then put the following tactics into practice:

- ✔ Make every effort to gather the pertinent facts, quickly assess the situation, and respond to key audiences in an open and honest manner.

- ✔ Enact the necessary measures to swiftly resolve the situation without jeopardizing the integrity and safety of your company, your coworkers, and your customers.

- ✔ Appoint executives to a standing crisis communications team who will be called on in times of crisis to make decisions and determine policy. Members should include the CEO, COO, CFO, PR manager, marketing manager, and customer service manager at the very least. Appoint one member of the team — typically the PR manager — as the primary contact between the team and the public. Also appoint a deputy crisis administrator to serve as the backup for the primary administrator.

✔ Educate employees, especially top and middle managers, about your crisis procedures.

✔ Establish communication strategies to address crisis situations. Select the appropriate spokesperson. Create press materials. Communicate your crisis response to all key audiences: employees, government agencies, vendors, consumers, and the media.

✔ Continually monitor the media for signs of escalation. If signs are apparent, adjustments may be required. Remain objective and be willing to make the necessary adjustments. Remember that changing your strategy is okay if your original plan isn't working as well as you thought it would.

✔ At all times, take pains not to create the perception that your organization doesn't care or lacks integrity.

✔ Be as objective as possible when evaluating data, analyzing consumer and media reactions, and making judgments about the effectiveness of your crisis communication program. Is the media coverage positive or negative? What key message points are being made in media stories about the crisis? If they don't reflect your key message points, perhaps you could communicate them more clearly, credibly, or dramatically.

✔ After the crisis has passed, put together a post-crisis summary report. It should include the cause of the crisis, extent and tone of media coverage, suggested improvements in the crisis response process, ways to implement those changes, and possible alterations to company policy and procedures.

✔ After you have overcome the short-term threat, work to rebuild the goodwill from each of your key audiences over the long term.

Chapter 20

Evaluating PR Results

· ·

· ·

*W*ant to see a PR professional's expression change dramatically with amazing speed? Watch him go through a great pitch where the prospective client loves his presentation, hangs on every word of his creative strategy, and eagerly listens to everything he has to say. Then the potential client asks, "How are we to measure your success?"

Like a solar eclipse, the sunny PR person's confident smile sags to a frown. Those crisp words that moments before came out like Henry Higgins explaining how "the rain in Spain falls mainly on the plain" develops a slight stutter — much like Jackie Gleason's famous character Ralph Kramden trying to explain away his latest mess-up, and all that comes out of his mouth is *humm-a-na, humm-a-na.*"

The public relations industry has tried to take on the measurement issue for years and develop a system to give empirical value to PR results. So far, the industry's efforts have left us with a good news/bad news situation.

Measuring by "Advertising Equivalency"

The good news is that the PR industry has developed a number of different formulas to calculate results, most notably *advertising equivalency* (AE) and *media impressions* (MI). The bad news is that both of these formulas are flawed, are limited in their use, and leave you with comparative value, not empirical value. Let me show you what I mean.

The way AE works is to simply look at the media outlet in which a PR placement runs, how long it is, and its position within the medium (for example, front page versus back of the magazine). You then compute what placing an advertisement of the same size and in the same location would cost. For instance, if you secured an article in *The New York Times* on the third page of the Metro section, and the article ran a quarter-page, how much would it cost to run an ad in that spot? Or for TV, if you place a spokesperson on *Good Morning America* at 7:55 a.m., how much would it cost to run a commercial there? You then take all your placements, compute their values, and add them together, and you have your AE for that PR campaign.

I've said that PR achieves marketing objectives at a small fraction of the cost of advertising, and the AE clearly shows why this is true. If you're a do-it-yourselfer, your out-of-pocket costs for mailing a press release to a few hundred media outlets is only a few hundred dollars. When you add up the equivalent ad space cost for the pick-ups of that release, you often find that to pay for the space would have cost thousands or even tens of thousands of dollars or more.

A major flaw of the AE formula: It is, in a sense, unfair to your PR program, because a press pick-up is often more effective as an influencer of the consumer's mind than a paid ad of equivalent size. Consumers view advertising skeptically, precisely because they know that it's a sales effort from a paid sponsor. But consumers view PR as objective because the source is a neutral reporter or journalist, not a paid promoter. In fact, many consumers are unaware that much of what they read, see, and hear in the media originates from PR agencies rather than the investigative work of journalists. So the key assumption of the AE formula — that an ad of a certain size, space, and location, has equal value to a PR placement of like size, space, and location — is wrong.

For example, I once worked with a best-selling author, Matthew Lesko. Lesko has a very successful business in which he self-publishes books on how to get government grants and loans for everything from buying a house to learning how to play the piano. I did not only Lesko's PR but also his 800-number direct-response TV commercials at one time. I would book Matthew on press interviews, he would talk and then give the 800 number, and people would order the book like mad. After going on *Larry King Live,* we sold about 30,000 books in the first half-hour after the show via phone orders.

One day, we booked Matthew on the *Oprah* show as part of a panel. Although this was before the Oprah book club came into existence, it was still considered the best spot on television for promoting a book. (To give you some idea how effective TV PR is on the top talk shows, I once booked a chef on the *Phil Donahue Show,* which had a much smaller audience, a week before Thanksgiving. That one appearance drove his book to the number-one spot on the *Times* bestseller list.) The *Oprah* booking for Matthew did not have quite the same results, but orders still skyrocketed. So I figured: If an interview on the show worked, why not run our direct response ad during the show? If there is ad equivalency, then by definition we should have similar results.

Well, we didn't. Not even close. In fact, the commercial generated almost no orders at all.

Making "Media Impressions"

Media impressions (MI) measure how many people see your message. For instance, say that your press release is picked up in a women's magazine with a circulation of 200,000 readers. You have made 200,000 media impressions. To calculate the media impressions for print media, you take the circulation figure and multiply it by 2.5. Therefore, the 200,000 circulation times 2.5 gives you 500,000 total media impressions.

The reason you multiply the print circulation by 2.5 is that it's assumed that a newspaper or magazine, while purchased by one person, is passed on and read by others. In the publishing industry, this is known as "pass-along circulation."

For television and radio, media impressions are simply the audience that watches or listens to the show as computed by a national rating agency such as Neilson or Arbitron. If you're a guest on a radio talk show reaching an audience of one million, you have made one million media impressions.

Now, the problem with media impressions is that they base specific distinctions on general assumptions. Take the 2.5 factor by which you multiply readership. To start with, that number is not consistently used throughout the industry. I use 2.5 as my multiplier to be conservative. But whatever factor you choose, how do you know that a newspaper or magazine has actually been passed on to other people?

The 2.5 multiplier has been used for years. If it was accurate back then, then logically it should be reduced today. Why? People don't have the same relationship to print that they once had. During the Depression, it was considered good manners to leave your newspaper on the train so that someone else could read it. Today, we don't share nearly as much. And numbers show that younger people don't read like they used to, so the theory that the daily paper is passed around the family needs revising. Recycling also must be affecting that pass-along habit: Many of us now feel guilty if we don't get that paper in the right blue bin as soon as we're done. Once it's recycled, it can't be passed around.

The awful truth about measuring ad and PR results

Don't think that PR is any different from other forms of marketing. Here's a big secret: There is no way to really see the effect of advertising either — none at all. Studies to prove ad effectiveness sometimes appear biased toward selling the advertiser on more advertising, and bottom-line results from ad campaigns to sales are extremely difficult to prove, with the exception of direct-response advertising (direct mail, telemarketing, infomercials, and so on).

Increased "vertical" publishing (creating narrow-interest magazines catering to specific market niches) may also affect pass-along circulation. When there was one *People* magazine, everyone who liked *People* wanted to read it. Now there is *Teen People* and *Latino People* and *On-line People*. The parent getting regular *People* isn't going to want to read a pass-along copy of *Teen People* from her teenager. Publications are increasingly being targeted just for you, indicating that the multiplier should be lower.

And other problems exist with MI. Using viewership numbers as calculations can be misleading. Just because the evening news has a 350,000 viewership on an average night doesn't mean that anywhere near that number of people are watching your story. Just because a newspaper has 200,000 readers doesn't mean that many people are reading the section, column, or article that you're in.

And then there's the same issue as with ad equivalency. MI assumes an equal relationship of attention between an ad and editorial content — a mistaken assumption that often penalizes PR.

Although neither AE nor MI has real empirical value, they do have some value. Both measures are useful in comparing one PR campaign or initiative to another. They can show whether your PR efforts are working better or worse than they were previously, or whether one tactic has outperformed another. But that's about as far as they go.

Using "Key Message Points"

A somewhat more valuable — albeit more difficult to compile — measure of PR performance is *key message points*. You begin by identifying, in the planning stage of your PR campaign, the key message points you want to convey. A potato chip company, for example, may have as a key message point: "Our potato chips taste lighter." Another may be that the chips are less oily.

You deliberately work key message points into all your PR campaigns and materials. When you get media coverage, you analyze the stories and count the key message points. You then add up all the times key message points are mentioned to get a total count. If your key message point is "fewer calories" and three articles mention your lower calorie count two times each, you get six key message points.

A common mistake that amateurs make is to seek, get, and be thrilled about publicity that is devoid of their key message points. People love to see their names in the paper or tell their relatives and friends, "Watch the news — I'm on TV tonight." But if you don't communicate a key message point during the exposure, what good is it? How has it helped your business? Publicity that doesn't contain your key message points is a waste of your time and money.

Zooming In on Market Research

Ad people use focus groups to test their ads. They have used focus groups for decades, but focus groups don't always give accurate results. If focus groups worked all the time, you would never see a bad ad. Well, here's a shocker: There are lots of bad ads.

The problem with focus groups, aside from not being a statistically valid sampling, is pretty simple. Say you and I are in a focus group together. The group leader shows a slide of a beautiful luxury car, explains that the price is $85,000, and then goes around the room asking each one of us whether we would consider buying it.

The first two people answer yes. But the third person, who can't afford such a car, also answers yes. So does the fourth person, who can afford the car but would never spend money on such a frill. The third and fourth people answered yes because they didn't want the first two to think less of them. So their answer was swayed by the need to impress other group members, as is frequently the case.

Suppose that a focus group leader shows an ad and asks the participants whether the ad would sway them to buy the product. People read advertising as critics very differently than they do as consumers. In focus groups, they enjoy showing off and saying how much more brilliantly they could have designed the ad. But this is no indication of whether they would actually buy the product if they saw it on TV. Too much one-upmanship occurs in focus groups to consider them wholly accurate.

Ad people also use impact studies to test awareness of product, image, and likelihood to purchase. They do the studies before and after an ad runs in a certain area. Then they tell their clients, "People remember our commercials," or, "Sales went up after we started our campaign."

The cry from everyone hiring a PR or advertising firm is *accountability*. "We want to see direct sales from every dollar we spend!" clients shout. Business owners and managers are hoping for the day when every ad or PR campaign drives an immediate sale. Certainly, the rise of e-commerce — the ability to buy products over the Web — provides a new electronic link between marketing communication and purchasing. It's a nice idea, but for many categories of products and services, it's not a reality. People don't make most of their purchases or become loyal customers in a split second. It takes time.

Companies like loyal customers because convincing the loyal ones to buy more costs far less money than converting someone to switch to your brand for the first time. By striving to make every aspect of your marketing mix generate an immediate sale, you risk taking the focus off building a personality for your brand — an image that a customer can relate to and be loyal to.

A good example is IKEA Home Furnishings. When IKEA opens a new store in a city, just by reputation they get enormous sales volume in the first two days they're open. How much more money would they have to spend to reach out and convince that many people to come to the store if no one felt a relationship with the IKEA image?

Of course, some ads or PR campaigns turn a company around in such a way that there is an immediate lift in sales. I think the Pepsi challenge of a couple of decades ago had that effect. It happens in PR, too. A mention by Dan Rather of one of my clients, Ken Hakuta — who was selling the Wacky Wall Walker toy — started a nationwide fad.

Measuring Inquiries and Sales

If your goal is to generate inquiries or orders rather than to build brand awareness or positioning, you may find it easier to show a direct relationship between PR and sales. This type of public relations is sometimes called *direct-response PR* because — like an infomercial, direct-mail package, or mail-order ad — it has as its goal direct response (an inquiry or order) rather than image-building.

The marketing objectives in direct-response PR are as follows:

✔ Get not only the client's name in the media but also the address, phone number, and Web site so that the client can be reached easily by potential customers interested in learning more about the product or service.

✔ Generate inquiries directly from PR items as they're published or broadcast.

✔ Increase both the quantity and the quality of sales leads generated by PR — that is, get the greatest number of qualified prospects to inquire about the client's product or service as a direct result of the PR coverage.

✔ If it's feasible, generate direct sales or walk-in trade or traffic from PR items.

In your press releases, include the toll-free number you use in commercials, ads, and direct mail for taking orders. If you sell on the Internet, include your Web site URL as well.

Marketers traditionally think of public relations as an image-building, rather than a direct-selling, activity, yet PR is one of the most cost-effective and successful methods for generating large volumes of direct inquiries and sales. One of my former clients, Trillium Health Products, used a toll-free 800 number in infomercials selling juice machines. We got the company's juicing expert to do a 20-minute segment on a radio talk show on WBZ in Boston. The callers were invited to phone for a free information booklet on juicing, which contained juicing information but also was a promotional piece for the machine.

Approximately 50,000 listeners called for the free juicing information. Of those, 10 percent bought a $350 juicing machine. That comes out to gross sales of $1.75 million for a single radio placement.

If you do direct-response PR, make sure that the producer or editor will allow you to feature your phone number or Web site address. Without this contact information, you will not get direct orders.

One author who self-published a how-to book went on *Oprah* without checking whether the show would give her toll-free number for orders. It wouldn't and didn't, and her book was not in bookstores. She sold only a handful of books.

Another example: Adrienne Zoble, a marketing consultant and author of the book *The Do-Able Marketing Plan,* did some PR for her book and got a small (approximately one-sixth of a page) article about the book published in *Inc.* magazine. This tiny article, which gave the price of the book and a phone number for placing orders (no address), generated 650 orders at $49.70 each, for a gross of $32,305 — proof that PR is effective at generating a measurable and substantial direct response.

Marketing professionals serving clients who seek to generate leads and sales via direct response traditionally recommend such vehicles as direct mail and advertising. Although I believe in direct mail and advertising and use both frequently, they are expensive. Consider direct mail. The cost per thousand for a direct-mail package might be $600, including printing, mailing, postage, and lists. If the response rate is 2 percent, you're getting 20 leads for every 1,000 pieces mailed, at a cost of $30 per lead.

By comparison, when my coauthor Bob Bly was the advertising manager at Koch Engineering, he paid his PR firm $1,000 to write, print, and distribute a press release on the firm's dry scrubber air pollution control device. Picked up in 18 publications, it generated 2,500 leads, at a cost per lead of about 40 *cents*.

The advantage of direct-response PR over direct mail (and direct-response advertising) is that it generates the same type of direct inquiry or order at a fraction of the cost per response. On the other hand, while you can roll out a direct-mail package that generates a certain percentage of responses to a large number of mailing lists and mail it again and again, you can use a given press release usually only once. (Of course, there are exceptions.)

Therefore, direct-response PR does not necessarily replace traditional direct-mail and print advertising as a response-generating tool, but its cost-effectiveness does suggest that you should almost always use a direct-response PR campaign to supplement or augment direct-mail and space advertising. Experience shows that an offer that works well in direct-mail and direct-response space ads usually works in a public relations campaign, too.

Taking the Long View of PR Success

The bottom line is this: If your PR is successful, it will increase your overall revenues and profits over a period of time. If you're getting a lot of media placements, your audiences are excited, your sales are growing, and the phone is ringing, chances are that you have a good PR program; if not, you probably don't.

In most cases, PR can be evaluated in comparison to what came before it, what came after it, and by anecdotal observation. How is your business doing now versus before you started the PR program? Two quick case studies illustrate this point.

Positioning a NY attorney as an expert

A successful New York matrimonial attorney was interested in enhancing his image and developing a strong profile as one of the nation's top authorities. The strategy was to position the attorney as an expert in all areas of family law. Because principals in major cases are inundated by requests for interviews from the media, an outside expert who can provide thoughtful and insightful commentary on legal issues of the day is a valuable commodity to a journalist or reporter.

The PR strategy? When the press covered a high-profile trial (the Trump divorce), pitch letters were prepared featuring the attorney's observations on that particular issue, suggesting that journalists use him as a source of "expert legal opinion" in stories they were preparing about the case.

This strategy resulted in a steady flow of publicity as the press became aware of his credentials and began to rely on his expert commentary. The placements ranged from ABC TV's *Primetime Live* to WNEW Radio's nationally syndicated *Larry King Live* to articles in *Harper's Bazaar* and *Manhattan Inc.* In addition, the attorney was booked by his PR agency as a regular lecturer for an adult seminar entitled "The Legality of Love." With this newfound publicity and notoriety, even a British journalist took note of all the media attention this attorney was receiving and featured him in a major story in the *London Daily Mail.*

This exposure became an invaluable addition to the attorney's business and following. Calls for consultations poured into his office and, over the course of a year, led to a substantial increase in his total client base. After a year of PR efforts, the attorney and his PR firm are now contacted daily by television producers, magazine editors, and radio commentators for ideas regarding upcoming feature stories and scheduled programs.

Courier service

At the time the PR program began, this company was a messenger service in the process of expansion via the acquisition of other messenger companies. The problem was that the industry was suffering from the rapidly increasing popularity of fax machines. In the past, a time-sensitive document would have required expeditious hand delivery. Now, due to fax machines, e-mail, and almost instant transmission, they can be sent and received at a fraction of the cost of using a messenger.

Realizing that the messenger industry would never return to its pre-fax status, the company wanted to publicize a new service, "facilities management," which is the business of taking over a major corporation's entire support center (mailrooms, messenger services, and in-house copy centers) as a way to reduce staff and overhead and thereby lower operating costs. The PR campaign focused on facilities management as being the wave of the future as corporate America seeks leaner, highly cost-effective methods to maintain operations.

The courier company's role in this new management strategy was highlighted in numerous pitch letters and press releases directed to media outlets catering to the target market: chief executive officers and upper management. Media materials also included several articles about facilities management with the client's name featured in the byline.

Leader's magazine, a publication whose controlled circulation is composed exclusively of CEOs of top corporations, was one of many publications that accepted the articles. The PR effort also got the client (the CEO of the courier company) on Financial News Network as well as *Business News Network,* a well-received syndicated radio program. In addition, several business publications, including *Fortune* and *Forbes,* ran stories on facilities management in which the client was prominently featured and quoted.

Part VI
The Part of Tens

In this part . . .

Every media maven worth his or her salt knows David Letterman's Top Ten lists. Well, here are some of our own top ten lists for PR. Chapter 21 presents ten of the most successful and creative public relations campaigns of all time. Chapter 22 outlines ten situations where PR can be an extremely effective solution to your marketing problem. In Chapter 23, I make you look good by showing you ten ways to come off as a PR pro, even if you're a newcomer to the field. Chapter 24 helps you avoid no-no's with ten things you should never, ever do in PR. And Chapter 25 gives you guidelines for making your PR writing as focused as a laser and as clear as crystal.

Chapter 21

The Ten Greatest PR Coups of All Time

*W*hat makes a PR campaign great? Two things. First, it has to achieve and surpass its objectives, achieving results beyond what anyone had a right to expect. Second, it has to be memorable — the kind of campaign people will remember 10 years or even 100 years later. If the campaign also pioneers or improves on an innovative idea, practice, or technique, that's icing on the cake.

In this chapter are, in my opinion, the top ten PR coups of all time — stellar examples of using public relations to achieve difficult marketing objectives. I hope that this list inspires your thinking (and mine) to similar heights.

Lucky Strike

Edward Bernays is widely known as the "father of public relations" for his groundbreaking work in the field. One of his most famous campaigns from the early 1900s was to position Lucky Strike, one of many brands, as the premier cigarette for women. (Keep in mind that this was well before tobacco use was linked to cancer.)

Lucky Strike was founded by R.A. Patterson in Richmond, Virginia, in 1871. The name refers to what miners made when they found gold during the Gold Rush — a "lucky strike." Bernays realized that most cigarette marketing at the time was either generic or male-oriented. By positioning Lucky Strike as a woman's cigarette, he hoped to capture a dominant share of half of the total market.

In those days, it was acceptable for women to smoke only at home, if at all — and certainly not in public places. A research study commissioned by Bernays on behalf of Lucky Strike showed that women perceived smoking in public as a sign of freedom. In his PR campaign, Bernays positioned Lucky Strike as the "Torches of Freedom" for American women.

John D. Rockefeller

John D. Rockefeller Sr. (1839–1937), America's first billionaire, had a reputation as being a ruthless businessman. The public saw him as cold, calculating, controlling, and greedy. And there was some truth to this image: Rockefeller once gave his groundskeeper only $5 as a Christmas bonus, only to dock him the same amount of pay for taking Christmas off as a holiday.

What the public did not know was that Rockefeller was an active philanthropist. He had tithed 10 percent of his income since he was a child, and by the time he reached his 66th birthday, that amount approached $100 million.

Bothered by the bad press he received, Rockefeller hired consultant Ivy Lee to change his image. Lee had once been paid $25,000 — a huge sum in those days — for a single's day work with Charles Schwab, CEO of Bethlehem Steel. Lee had simply shown Schwab how to be more efficient and get more done by making a simple to-do list each day.

Lee immediately began publicizing Rockefeller's generosity and charitable activities, which were not common at the time. One of Lee's ideas was to have Rockefeller carry a roll of shiny dimes and give them away to children in public, with a photographer always present to capture the photo opportunity. Rockefeller gave away more than 30,000 dimes during his lifetime.

Tylenol

Tylenol is a classic case of good crisis planning and execution. In 1982, seven deaths resulted from poisoned Tylenol pills. When reports that someone had tampered with Tylenol and people had died as a result hit the evening news and front pages, Johnson & Johnson responded by immediately pulling $100 million worth of the product off the shelves in a single day.

The PR was simple but powerful: Johnson & Johnson did the right thing. It didn't harm anyone deliberately or even through a mistake or accident; someone tampered with its product. It could have happened to any manufacturer that sells its products in pharmacies and grocery stores. But instead of pointing out this fact in its defense, J&J focused on solving the problem rather than laying blame somewhere else.

The company was available to the media throughout the crisis to answer questions and provide information. It used daily opinion polls to accurately gauge public reaction and adjust its communications strategy accordingly.

J&J did not ship Tylenol again until a tamper-proof bottle had been designed. When the improved container was ready, J&J reintroduced Tylenol with a major media campaign that included a 30-city teleconference. Within a year, Tylenol had regained its 70 percent market share.

Bill Clinton's 1992 Presidential Campaign

Although history will determine Bill Clinton's place in the rankings of presidents and of men, few dispute that he ran a masterful campaign to beat incumbent George Bush in the 1992 presidential race. Clinton's campaign manager deliberately steered him away from the traditional hard news venues and towards TV programming targeting a younger audience.

A turning point was Clinton's appearance on *The Arsenio Hall Show,* during which he played his saxophone on national television. Stunts like this humanized him as a candidate and highlighted his relative youth compared to his opponent.

A series of TV roundtables, including one on MTV, showed Clinton as able to answer tough questions. Actually, most of the attendants for these roundtables were idealistic college students who asked big-issue questions (for example, whether Clinton is pro-choice) that made for good television. At the same time, the audience's lack of in-depth political and foreign affairs knowledge — compared with, say, a Sam Donaldson or other professional journalists — allowed Clinton to avoid complex issues and tough-to-answer questions.

Even back then, rumors of Clinton's marital infidelity were circulating. He immediately went on *60 Minutes* and vigorously denied these accusations, cutting them off before they mushroomed.

The New VW Beetle

When the original VW Beetle was introduced in the 1960s, its low price and odd bug-shaped appearance made it a popular economy car. But when the New Beetle was introduced in 1998, the price was no longer rock-bottom.

What made the New Beetle so popular? In part, a promotional campaign that exploited the nostalgic appeal of the Beetle — people bought because they remembered it fondly from their youth. According to a Volkswagen press release, the New Beetle "instantly rekindled the magic of its legendary namesake."

A number of creative public relations initiatives helped make the introduction of the New Beetle a success. In March 2000, Volkswagen sponsored a "New Beetle Cup Race" in conjunction with the Atlanta Auto Show, with half a million deutsche marks as prize money. Volkswagen also did an innovative Internet promotion, selling special color editions of the New Beetle only over its Web site. To appeal to die-hard Beetle enthusiasts, VW also introduced New Beetle collectible trading cards. The cards were issued only to people who purchased the car or visited the VW Web site.

Traditionally, car manufacturers publicize their new models by offering test drives to editors of specialized car and consumer magazines, like *Road and Track* and *Consumer Reports*. Breaking with that tradition, VW offered test drives of the New Beetle to editors and producers of more general media outlets such as *USA Today* and *Family Circle*.

Driving the New Beetle brought back fond memories of their teen years to these people, generating massive media exposure for the car. By turning to consumer media instead of the usual automobile publications, VW immediately moved the campaign to a new playing field on which no other car was competing for attention. Tremendous media coverage followed.

Cabbage Patch Kids

PR can start trends or work to accelerate them. Such is the case with the Cabbage Patch Kids, a line of odd-looking dolls launched by Mattel in the early 1980s.

From the beginning, Cabbage Patch Kids were not positioned as ordinary toys; children were urged to "adopt" Cabbage Patch Kids as if they were their babies. Each doll came with an "adoption form" — blue for boys, pink for girls — imprinted with the doll's name.

Children were encouraged to write their names on the adoption certificates as the parents and take good care of their Kids. By mailing in the forms, they enrolled in the Cabbage Patch Kids Parents' Association and received congratulatory notes in the mail. A year later, the adopted Kids received birthday cards from their maker. This campaign transformed Cabbage Patch from just another plaything to a companion. Many children began collecting multiple Cabbage Patch Kids and forming families.

At holiday time, stories appeared in the press saying that stores had a shortage of the dolls. Parents stampeded to get Cabbage Patch Kid dolls for their kids. I don't know whether there was really a shortage or if it was just a rumor started by the toy company to stimulate sales.

More recently, Mattel created a Web site at www.cabbagepatchkids.com serving as an online community for these doll owners and their parents.

Domino's Pizza Meter

I discuss in detail in this book the various campaigns my PR agency did for Domino's Pizza when it was my client, and my favorite of those is the Pizza Meter. My agency measured the number of pizza deliveries to the White House, Pentagon, and CIA, and found that whenever there was a national crisis, the number of deliveries went up to feed government officials at late-night office meetings. We sent a press release about this occurrence, generating huge media exposure for Domino's.

The reason I include the campaign here is that it had an unusually long life. Once we did the campaign, we realized that the Pizza Meter didn't have to be a one-time PR initiative — the pizza delivery could be monitored continuously throughout the year.

My agency did this monitoring, and at the end of every year, we did the Pizza Meter campaign again, showing the big events of the year and how accurately the Meter predicted them based on pizza deliveries. There was no end to how many times we could get a whole new wave of media exposure by recycling this idea annually. We didn't even need a new twist; the news angle was the major events that spurred the increase in pizza deliveries. We eventually did 41 different pizza meter campaigns over a 12-year period.

IBM Big Blue versus Gary Kasparov

In 1997, IBM conducted one of the most brilliant PR campaigns ever: It challenged world chess champion Gary Kasparov to play an IBM computer specifically programmed to be good at chess. The computer, Big Blue, contained a special-purpose chip capable of evaluating 2.5 million chess positions per second.

In our technological age, one of the most dramatic and emotional issues is man versus machine: Elevator operators are unemployed because elevators are automatic. Graphic artists must learn to use a Macintosh instead of an Exacto knife or they are out of a job. Pitting IBM against the world chess champion was the ultimate man-machine challenge.

The campaign was a no-lose proposition for IBM. If Big Blue won, it would dramatically demonstrate the superiority of IBM computing technology. If Big Blue lost, people would still be impressed that a computer could play competitive chess with a grandmaster at all.

Big Blue won, and Kasparov lost, shocking many in the chess world. But the event was actually good for the world of chess — not since Bobby Fisher has chess received such media attention.

Gillette Sensor Razor

The PR campaign for the introduction of the Gillette Sensor was a first and maybe a last: The new razor made *Fortune* magazine's list of the top ten new product introductions of 1989 — but the product wasn't available until 1990.

The name Sensor implied high technology, and the SensorExcel for Women looked more like a Star Trek phaser than a razor. Advertising touted a unique rubber grip on the handle that gave the shaver more control for a closer and safer shave. Because of the rubber grip, your hand won't slip even if the handle is wet, so you won't get cut.

The incredible PR campaign for Sensor achieved more than 800 media placements worldwide in 19 countries. Media running stories included *Good Morning America, CBS Evening News, Newsweek, Forbes, The Wall Street Journal, The New York Times,* and Associated Press.

Jack in the Box

Jack in the Box is another example of stellar crisis planning and management in action. In January 1993, four children died and hundreds of people got sick after eating hamburgers tainted with the bacteria *E. coli* at Jack in the Box restaurants in the Pacific Northwest. In response, Jack in the Box immediately established a comprehensive food-safety system, patterned after NASA's food safety program for astronauts. It also worked with federal and state regulators, health officials, and consumer advocacy groups to bring about new laws and regulations.

Following the incident, Jack in the Box posted strong earnings, and the communications team aggressively placed these positive business stories in the press, helping re-establish credibility as a viable company. Its parent company later reached a $58.5 million settlement with nine beef suppliers over the tainted burgers. The chain also made amends with victims' families.

In 1997, Hudson Foods recalled 25 million pounds of hamburger meat, and the earlier Jack in the Box incident was again referenced in the media. At this point, the steps the restaurant had taken in 1993 helped it when the press started calling again.

Jack in the Box's parent company, Foodmaker, positioned Dr. David Theno, the company's vice president of quality assurance, as an expert on *E. coli.* The PR team developed press kits explaining that *E. coli* is a food-chain problem, not just a Jack in the Box problem. Because of this education program, the media in 1997 stated how far Jack in the Box had come, how much it had improved, and how much it had recovered from the difficult situation in 1993.

This case is an example of a company's seeing a problem, taking steps to correct it (possibly above and beyond what other companies would do), and — because of these steps — being able to distance itself when more outbreaks occurred and turn a bad situation into a positive one for the company.

Chapter 22

Ten Reasons to Do PR

*E*ngineers have a saying: "An engineer can do with $1 what any dummy can do with $10." In a similar vein, I tell clients that PR can achieve with $1 more media exposure than you can buy with $10 worth of advertising.

Actually, I think the cost-effectiveness of PR beats advertising more along the lines of 100:1, not 10:1. If that alone isn't enough reason for you to start using PR, here are ten more.

You're a Little Fish in a Big Pond

Your competitors may be bigger and more well-established and have more money. They probably spent more on that giant booth at the industry trade show last week, or on that full-page magazine ad last month, than you can afford in a year.

Beating someone else's ad campaign with your own paid advertising can be difficult if your competitor can afford to outspend you 10:1. But PR levels the playing field. In advertising, money buys you more media space and airtime. In PR, creative thinking wins you media space and airtime. The big companies don't have an advantage here. If anything, their bureaucratic structures sometimes hamstring them from moving quickly on creative public relations ideas, while smaller firms can move right away.

Some of the public relations techniques described in this book, such as events, can be expensive. But most can be done on a shoestring budget.

Running your TV spot during the Super Bowl costs a million dollars, not to mention the $100,000 or more for producing the commercial. But sending a press release that gets you booked as a guest on Oprah Winfrey's show costs only the first-class postage.

Your Product or Service Is the Best — and Nobody Knows about It

Advertising can, surprisingly, sometimes be very ineffective at getting consumers to buy your product because of a real advantage inherent in your product over another. You can write an ad that clearly communicates the advantage, but consumers are skeptical about advertising. It's precisely because you, the advertiser, are stating the advantage of your product that the reader is inclined not to believe you.

Consumers know that an ad is an ad. So when you start talking to them in an ad, their defense subconsciously goes up, and only a really great ad can penetrate that defense. PR, with its elevated credibility, never raises those defensive shields in the first place: When people read an article about you, they tend to believe that it's true.

In public relations, you can't merely state a product or service claim, because the media is not interested in advertising your product for free for you. To get media exposure, you have to demonstrate your claim in an interesting and entertaining way. For instance, when my agency represented Domino's Pizza, we worked on a "World's Fastest Pizza Maker" contest among Domino's employees. This event dramatized that Domino's could deliver faster because it made pizza faster, not because its drivers drove too fast.

PR has two advantages over paid advertising. First, you're forced to tell your product story in a more engaging manner. Second, the consumer, reading your message in an article or seeing it on a TV show, is more inclined to believe it, because it is, in a way, "endorsed" by the media.

Your Product or Service Isn't Better than Anyone Else's

Winston March, an Australian business consultant, says that to succeed today, "It's more important to be a good marketer of what you do than a good doer of what you do." You may have cringed when you read that sentence, but the fact is that the most successful people and organizations are often the best self-promoters, not the best at making widgets or whatever it is they do. Can you cook a better hamburger than McDonald's? Of course you can. Then why does McDonald's make more money than you? Marketing plays a big part in it.

The more PR you do, the more you, rather than your competitors, become established as the leader in your field. Read the brief case history of the matrimonial attorney in Chapter 20, if you haven't done so already. Is he necessarily a better lawyer than his competitors? It doesn't matter. As long as he keeps sending editors useful material that they will publish, people will read his articles and consider him a knowledgeable authority.

In Chapter 11, we discuss the strategy of becoming the "go-to guy" — establishing yourself as the source the media people call on when they need an interview for a story on your particular subject of expertise. You may have said to yourself in disgust concerning a competitor, "Why is he always quoted in the media? He doesn't know anything about widget technology? That reporter should be interviewing *me!*"

The reason he's quoted so much is because he deliberately pursued the media for the exposure, and they came to rely on him as a good source for stories. Even if he's not as knowledgeable as you are, journalists find him clear and credible. And just as important, he's always available when they're on a deadline, any time of the day or night.

Believe me, these go-to people never have to go out and cold call to get new business. Prospects come to them in droves, cash in hand, ready to pay their rather hefty fees for advice, service, expertise, and product — simply because they used the media to make themselves stand out from the pack.

Management Cuts Your Marketing Communications Budget

Marketing costs go up every year. Ad space costs more, printing costs rise, hourly rates of graphic design studios increase, and photographers up their day rates. Yet marketing budgets often stay flat, even though management is adding products, divisions, services, and new markets.

Public relations is arguably the most cost-effective marketing on the planet. It can achieve equal or better results than paid advertising at as little as 1/100th of the cost. When your ad budget is slashed and you can't run as many ad insertions as you used to, step up your public relations efforts. PR can continue your presence in those media outlets that are important to you but in which you can no longer afford to advertise as frequently as in the past.

Management Demands Tangible Results from Marketing Expenditures

Twenty years ago, if managers liked the way your ads looked, or if they got compliments on the advertising from their friends and neighbors, they were happy.

But for the past couple of decades, pretty pictures haven't been enough. "What results are we getting from our marketing dollars?" management demands. "Show me the numbers."

In Chapter 20, I discuss the pros and cons of different systems used to measure PR effectiveness. If your management is numbers-oriented, use these systems freely. Also do more direct-response PR designed to generate inquiries (refer to the "recession booklet" press release in Chapter 14 as an example). Submit reports showing how many leads PR generated and the low cost per lead.

Traditional Marketing Isn't Working as Well as It Used To

Many marketers find that current tactics decline in effectiveness over time. Sometimes the specific promotion isn't working: Response to an ad drops off after several insertions. Other times, the nature of the media itself may be the problem: Direct-mail response rates have declined in recent years, while postage and printing costs have been rising, making it more difficult for direct mail to generate a profit.

When current tactics are underperforming, try new promotions. And make PR one of them. PR can generate significant return on your marketing dollars alone or in tandem with other marketing communications.

Show, don't tell

Consider assembling all your press clippings into a quarterly newsletter and distributing it to management and customers. Doing so will visibly demonstrate to management that your PR is working and give your customers and prospects a second exposure to your media coverage.

Desperately seeking synergy

Make sure that the objectives and messages for all your marketing communications — PR, print advertising, direct mail, trade shows, the Internet — are in synch. You don't want to negate the impact of a successful PR campaign by promoting a completely different message in your print advertising.

Your Competitors Get All the Good Press

One of the most dreaded phone calls for any PR professional to receive from a client or boss is, "Big Magazine just did an industry round-up, and we were not listed. Why not?" The boss, understandably, is upset that journalists are so unaware of his company or product that they didn't even mention it in an industry overview.

The way to minimize such an unpleasant incident is through diligent, vigilant PR. Motivational speaker Rob Gilbert says, "The way to be there when people are looking for you is to be there all the time." You can't afford to be there with a paid ad all the time. But by conducting an ongoing PR program, you dramatically increase the likelihood that editors will think of you — and not just your competitors — when they're writing about your industry or product category.

I often hear people say, "We got lucky today," when a big story about them is published in the newspaper or the TV crews cover their event. But if they've been doing PR, it's really not luck — it's effort meeting with opportunity. Or as Pasteur observed, chance favors the prepared mind.

You Need Venture Capital or Are Planning an IPO — and Nobody Knows Your Name

In the dot-com era — and I handle PR for a growing number of dot-coms — entrepreneurs are focused on getting venture capital to start their ventures and doing an IPO (initial public offering) — the first opportunity to buy stock in a company when it goes public — to get rich from their ventures early.

Public relations can go a long way to helping you achieve both milestones. A few pages of press clippings in prominent publications, appended to your business plan, make an impression on venture capitalists that your carefully conceived projections do not: If you're already in *Wired* magazine, you must be a serious player.

As for IPOs, stock prices are affected, to a large degree, by the media. A positive article in a major magazine can send share prices soaring, especially in the dot-com market. If investment bankers see proof that you can generate positive press, they'll be more confident about taking your company public.

You Are Media-Genic

Almost any product or service can be promoted via PR, but some are naturally more promotable than others. If you have a product or service with an inherent element of fun in it, for example — such as a trend like the Wacky Wallwalker of the 1980s — you're well positioned to gain tons of media exposure. You may as well take advantage of it.

Similarly, some people are just more "media-genic" than others. Colorful and eccentric characters have the edge, so if you're colorful or flamboyant, don't be shy. Use your natural charisma to your advantage in charming the public and the press.

You Really Enjoy Working with the Media

I never engage in PR for PR's sake: getting my name in the paper just to see my name in the paper. I value my time too much. When I contact the media to place a story, it's because the story will help me achieve a specific business goal.

That said, if you enjoy media attention, put your natural enthusiasm to work — in a PR campaign that generates results for your company and your product. After all, we tend to do more of the things we enjoy most, and better. So if being in the spotlight is your thing, go for it. Just don't lose sight of your business objectives — the end result of all this PR should be more money in your pocket. Getting your picture in the paper is only a side benefit, not the main event.

Conversely, if being in the spotlight makes you sweat, cringe, and blink, let it shine on your company or product, but not you personally. Or hire a spokesperson to stand under the spotlight for you.

More Benefits of Doing PR

Here are some other advantages PR can offer your business:

✔ News is the primary public relations weapon — therefore, it is a strong tool in creating and reinforcing brand images.

✔ Because a third party delivers the message and the audience doesn't realize that they are being sold, public relations is effective in its ability to motivate desired behavior.

✔ Unlike advertising and direct mail, public relations can be a cost-efficient way to get exposure. (Please note that public relations works well with other marketing tactics, but can be used alone.)

✔ Public relations can set you apart from your competitors and give you an advantage.

✔ Public relations can generate traffic, boost revenue, and improve your bottom line.

✔ Public relations can pre-sell your potential customers and increase the loyalty of existing customers.

✔ In an extremely cluttered environment (the Internet, direct mail, television, radio, billboards, newspapers, magazines, in-store displays, coupons), public relations can help break through the clutter.

✔ Public relations can work for any and every industry, business, or person with a message to deliver or goal to achieve: consumer products, stores, doctors, lawyers, entertainers, authors, nonprofit organizations, Web sites, politicians, restaurants, associations, service business, companies, and entertainers.

✔ Public relations can help you deal with a problem, bad image, or crisis.

✔ Public relations can be multitiered and can be targeted to specific audiences individually or to your whole audience at once. You can conduct grassroots activities; local, regional, and national outreach; and outreach to specific trade or consumer media by different aspects of your potential audience's lifestyle (parents, sports fans, food enthusiasts, business, men, women, teenagers, kids, health, business owners, managers, supervisors, technicians) for a minimal cost.

Chapter 23

Ten Tips for Coming Off as a PR Pro

In This Chapter

▶ Staying up on current events, trends, and fads

▶ Understanding your industry

▶ Becoming well known in your field

▶ Remaining positive

*T*he old saying "If a thing is worth doing, it is worth doing well" certainly applies to PR. By going the extra mile in your efforts, you can often stretch your results 10, 20, or 100 miles or more.

Unlike advertising, where media exposure can be bought with dollars, in PR you generate media exposure with time and thought. Here are ten suggestions for helping you be the best PR person you can for your business. They can help whether you're a full-time PR professional or an executive or entrepreneur who has taken on your company's PR as yet another of the zillion hats you already wear.

Become a Media Maven

Scan the news. A PR person who knows what's going on in the world always looks smart. And don't feel the need to read everything; even simply scanning the headlines can get you up to speed.

Read at least one daily newspaper, *Time* or *Newsweek,* and the key trade publications in your industry. Sample new magazines as you come across them on newsstands or through direct-mail subscription offers. If you decide after reading an issue that the magazine is not for you, most subscription offers allow you to cancel with no penalty after your first issue.

Through constant reading, watching, and listening, you constantly expand your knowledge. The fact that almost any knowledge you acquire, general or specific, can be used somehow in your PR efforts is both a blessing and a curse. Learning new things is fun. But because you never know where the next great idea may come from, you're constantly on the lookout for new information and data.

Get in the clipping habit

As you read print media, you will spot articles of interest to your friends, colleagues, coworkers, prospects, and customers. Clip these articles and mail them to the appropriate people with a brief handwritten note that simply says, "FYI. Thought you should see this." It's a great way to let people know you're thinking of them and to remind them of your existence.

According to an article in *Better Life Journal* (Issue 13, page 7), Sir Joshua Reynolds said, "It is indisputably evident that a great part of every person's life must be employed in collecting materials for the exercise of genius. Invention, strictly speaking, is little more than a new combination of those images which have been previously gathered and deposited in the memory; nothing can come of nothing. He who has laid up no materials can produce no combinations."

Successful PR people devour media and information as if it were steak or caviar — and so should you. Attend seminars, listen to tapes, read books, clip articles from periodicals, tap into online databases, explore the Internet, surf Web sites, and ruthlessly mine information sources to find nuggets of knowledge that help you serve your clients better. It's fun but tiring — and absolutely necessary.

Keep Current with Trends and Fads

I have to assume that if you don't know what a Pokemon is, you recently awakened from a coma. As for tomorrow's trends, who knows what they will be?

Be aware of the current trends. Keep abreast of what's popular in TV, music, fashion, and movies. Skim publications like *Entertainment Weekly, Spin,* and *Vogue.* Watch and talk to kids. They're usually at the leading-edge of any new trend or fad. Visit malls once in a while — especially toy and gadget stores. In the adult world, keep your eye on Generation Xers for the same reason. They're usually early adopters of technology and trends. Go to consumer electronics shows to see the new gadgets.

Surf the Internet, too. If a hot new trend is brewing, buzz often travels first on the World Wide Web and moves a lot faster there than in the print or even the broadcast world.

Know Who Covers What

Know who covers what. Who covers health issues at *USA Today?* Who's the advertising reporter for *The New York Times?* You'll be surprised how many times this comes up with a client. At the very least, find out who covers your industry at the major media (national TV, national newspapers, online journalists) as well as your industry's local media.

Blanket Your Industry

Know the industry you're publicizing. Every industry has trade publications. Subscribe to them so you know the industry inside out, whether it's fast food or agribusiness. The PR industry has very useful and informative trade publications as well (refer to the CD enclosed with this book).

Join the industry trade associations. Go to the annual national conference of the largest association. Attend at least two or three local chapter meetings a year. Network with other members. Find out what their problems are, how they're positioning their companies, and which marketing campaigns are working best for them. The atmosphere at many local chapter meetings is quite congenial, with members willing to share secrets among themselves.

Listen

Listening is one of the hardest traits to master but one of the most valuable skills in PR or any other pursuit. The success of many business activities depends on how well you listen. Studies show that people spend about 80 percent of their waking hours communicating and at least 45 percent of that time listening.

But although listening is so critical in our daily lives, it is taught and studied far less than the other three basic communications skills: reading, writing, and speaking. Poor listening skills are the cause of much of the trouble we have communicating with others.

Most people are not good listeners. Years ago, the Sperry Company, a technology company that built its corporate identity around the theme of good listening, found that 85 percent of people questioned rated themselves average or less in listening ability. Fewer than 5 percent rated themselves either superior or excellent. (Sperry has since merged with Burroughs, another computer company, to form UniSys.)

The good news is that you can improve listening efficiency by understanding the steps involved in the listening process and by following some basic guidelines.

You can come up with a pretty good idea of how you rate as a listener by thinking about your relationships with the people in your life: your boss, colleagues, subordinates, best friend, spouse. If asked, what would they say about how well you listen? Do you often misunderstand assignments or only vaguely remember what people have said to you? If so, you may need to improve your listening skills.

Hearing is the first step in the process. At this stage, you simply pay attention to make sure that you have heard the message. If your boss says, "Zais, I need the report on last month's sales," and you can repeat the sentence, then you have heard her.

The second step is interpretation. Failure to interpret the speaker's words correctly frequently leads to misunderstanding. People sometimes interpret words differently because of varying experience, knowledge, vocabulary, culture, background, and attitudes.

A good speaker uses a tone of voice, facial expressions, and mannerisms to help make the message clear to the listener. For instance, if your boss speaks loudly, frowns, and puts her hands on her hips, you know that she's probably upset and angry.

During the third step, evaluation, you decide what to do with the information you have received. For example, when listening to a sales pitch, you have two options: You choose either to believe or to disbelieve the salesperson. The judgments you make in the evaluation stage are a crucial part of the listening process.

The final step is to respond to what you've heard. This is a verbal or visual response that lets the speaker knew whether you got the message and what your reaction is. When you tell the salesperson that you want to place an order, you show that you have heard and believe his message.

Impress the CEO

This tip is for readers who work for PR firms, in PR departments, or as PR freelancers.

Before a big client meeting with a CEO or other executive with whom you're going to work, try to find out her interests (you can usually find it in a resume or bio on the company Web site), where she went to college, or some other interesting fact. If you can drop in a line or two about something that personally interests her, it'll help you make an impression.

Join a PR Club

Industry groups like the Public Relations Society of America (PRSA) or your local PR club help you stay on top of what's going on in the PR industry. These groups are also good networking tools.

PRSA (refer to the CD in this book) has a wealth of publications, surveys, studies, and other information you can take advantage of. Also look into marketing and advertising clubs or associations. Although they're not dedicated solely to PR, they often have a group, division, seminar, or publication that covers PR in depth.

If you're a newcomer to PR, these groups can be a gold mine. Don't let the fact that many members are more experienced than you intimidate you in any way. People love showing off their knowledge and helping others, especially beginners; doing so makes them feel smart, and they're flattered that you ask. Networking at meetings can get you PR advice that would otherwise cost thousands of dollars.

Blow Your Own Horn

Publicize yourself, not just your client or your business. What better way to show potential clients or supervisors that you can get press for their business than by getting it about yourself? You'll have a big advantage when a potential client recognizes you from seeing or reading about you in the media.

Speak Up for Yourself and Your Business

As I outline in Chapter 11, what better way to gain fame fast than to become a public speaker? Start talking, and people will listen and get to know your name.

Speakers bureaus are always looking for knowledgeable sources on a variety of topics, and they can put you in front of many different groups and industries. These speaking engagements are another great networking opportunity. Speak to enough people at enough events, and you may even become famous in your field.

Have a Positive Attitude

Believe in yourself. In your PR career, you will meet a lot of people — clients, coworkers, and supervisors — who will tell you what can't be done. If you let self-doubt get in the way of your instincts, you will have a short or, at the very least, unfulfilled career.

Don't let the opinions of other people decide for you whether you're successful. When you have what you want and come by it honestly without hurting others, you are successful.

Success and failure are temporary rather than permanent conditions. There is an ebb and flow in business. Just as you lose a client because your contact at the company was laid off, a bigger competitor may hire you at a higher fee. Do not become too elated if your clients say you're the best PR person they ever hired; likewise, don't become too depressed if another client dislikes you and your work. Sir Winston Churchill once said, "Success is the ability to go from failure to failure without losing your enthusiasm."

Bob Kalian, a successful author and entrepreneur, comments, "I've discovered that the one secret that determines success is you cannot fail unless you quit. It's honestly just that simple." Come up with your own definition of success. Mine is "Doing what I want to do, when and where I want to do it, and being paid well for it — sometimes very, very well."

When you achieve your first (or your next) major PR coup, keep your head about you and stay humble. Don't think that one big placement or one note-worthy campaign makes you a master. You still have much to learn, and you always will. School is never out for the pro.

Some PR professionals grow big egos. I advise against this. It's better to be humble than arrogant. You know many things, but not most things; there's just so much information for any one person to absorb that no one can know more than a small fraction of the total. You're smart, but many times your advice will not work, and your client will be disappointed with the results. Thomas Edison once said, "We don't know one-millionth of one percent about anything." Keep this in mind if your head ever starts to swell.

Chapter 24

Ten Things You Should Never Do in the Name of PR

Throughout this book, I give you a lot of the do's of public relations. In this chapter, you get the don'ts — ten things you should never do as you pursue PR for yourself, your business, or your clients.

Lie or Mislead

Rule number one: Never lie to or mislead a reporter. If a reporter catches you in a lie, she will never trust you again. The reporter will also tell colleagues, and your reputation as an untrustworthy source will spread. This will severely compromise your ongoing ability to work with the media, even when you're telling the truth.

Stonewall

Rule number two: Never say "no comment" to a reporter. "No comment" is very similar to "I plead the Fifth Amendment." In both cases, the other party automatically assumes that you're guilty.

When a reporter asks you a question to which you don't know the answer or don't want to respond to on the spot, the correct answer goes something like this: "Joan, you know we are always responsive to the media, but I am not the right person to give you that information. I will contact the right person and get back to you before your deadline today."

Procrastinate

As far as deadlines and commitments go, treat journalists like you treat customers. Always do what you say you're going to do, when you say you're going to do it. Journalists have deadlines that are not flexible. If you promise information and fail to deliver it on time, you will tick them off considerably at best. At worst, the story will run without your having a chance to defend yourself, possibly resulting in a negative portrayal of you in tomorrow's paper.

Be Inaccessible

I advise executives at my clients' companies, including the CEOs, to treat any call from a journalist as the most important thing they have to do that moment. Once, I was at a press conference where NBA rookie of the year Derek Coleman was supposed to appear. Top sportswriters eagerly awaited the young superstar's arrival. When he didn't show, they waited about 40 minutes and then left.

If sportswriters give the NBA rookie of the year only 40 minutes, you'll be lucky if the media gives you 10 minutes. When the press calls, you're of interest to them only at the moment. Tomorrow, the story will have already been filed, and they won't even take your return call.

Striking while the iron is hot is the only way to get a steady stream of regular media exposure. I make it a point to be available to the media 24 hours a day, 7 days a week — whether it's on Thanksgiving Day during turkey or in the middle of the night. Most successful PR professionals I know have a similar policy of being totally accessible to the media.

Offer a Bribe

Never tell an editor or reporter, "Run my press release, and I will advertise in your publication." Conversely, don't call an editor at a publication in which you already advertise and attempt to bully him with, "Run my press release, or I will pull my advertising." Most print publications have three departments: editorial, advertising, and circulation. These are separate departments, and the PR professional who pits one against the other is making an error.

As a general rule, the top media outlets never let advertising influence editorial situations. As I am fond of telling my PR clients, no one gets favors from *The New York Times.*

At trade journals covering specialized industries or smaller regional or local publications, publishers sometimes do favor advertisers with editorial coverage. But you should never be the one to bring up this idea with the editor.

If a space rep (a person selling ad space in the publication) approaches you with an offer of special editorial treatment in exchange for placing an ad, that's perfectly acceptable. But leave that between the space rep, the publisher, and the editor. Don't approach an editor about such a favor directly on your own.

Turn Up Your Nose

Advertising, PR, and promotion are increasingly becoming acceptable and even desirable in many industries that, a decade or so ago, would thumb their noses at it. The obvious example is the increase in advertising by professionals such as lawyers and doctors.

If you think advertising is beneath you and unprofessional, PR offers a marketing alternative that enables you to promote yourself, your practice, or your business in a more dignified and professional manner. Maybe you don't want to run commercials on late-night television or have full-page ads in the Sunday paper.

But how about a weekly column by you on your specialty in the local paper? Or a speech by you on that same topic at the library, YMCA, or Rotary Club? Even for people who don't like marketing, PR offers plenty of low-key, soft-sell marketing opportunities you can like and feel comfortable with.

Bore People

David Ogilvy said, "You cannot bore someone into buying your product." Around our agency, the greatest sin is to be boring. Not because we love creativity for creativity's sake. But because in PR, boring simply doesn't work.

The most boring thing is to do the same PR, the same marketing, that everybody else does. If everyone's press releases and brochures look and read the same, how will one stand out from the other and get noticed? In PR, "same old same old" is the kiss of death.

We are bombarded by information and media messages today, and most of it, frankly, is incredibly dull. Successful PR finds or creates an element of fun in a product, service, organization, or event — one that can gain media attention while communicating a key message in an interesting, memorable fashion.

Joseph Kelley, speechwriter for President Dwight Eisenhower, once said, "Everything God created has a kernel of excitement in it, as has everything civilization invented or discovered." Saying that your product is boring because it is technical or a commodity is no excuse. What makes it exciting to the potential customer? Something, obviously, or people wouldn't buy. Your job is to find that excitement and build a PR campaign around it. There's no excuse for being a bore — at least not in PR.

Be a "No" Man

People love to kill ideas. They seem oddly eager to say no or explain why something won't work or can't be done. Saying no whenever someone proposes an idea is a cop-out. Such a response is too easy. Critics are a dime a dozen. But in PR, creators and doers earn annual salaries of $100,000 or more.

A lot of great PR campaigns are killed out of fear. Someone suggests a breakthrough idea that's different — *not* the same old same old — and top management says, "Why take the risk?" Because the greater the risk, the greater the potential pay-off. That's true in many fields, whether it's business, PR, or investing.

I have no patience for critics. At our PR firm, I tell my employees that it's okay to have a brilliant idea or opinion I disagree with; what's not okay is *not* to have an idea or opinion. Don't just say, "I don't like it." Say what you would do instead.

In her book *The 7th Sense* (William Morrow and Company), Doris Wild Helmering presents criteria to distinguish constructive (that is, helpful and useful) criticism from nonconstructive (that is, petty, denigrating, and useless) criticism. Her criteria are meant for general criticism of creative work, but they certainly apply to creation and evaluation of PR campaigns.

According to Helmering, constructive criticism has three components. To be constructive, your criticism must have all three components present:

- There is a contract between the people involved. The person who is making the critical comment is involved with the project, has some authority, and has been invited to do so.

- The negative feedback addresses a specific issue (for example, "This article ignores the current slump in tech stocks" versus "This stinks").

- There is direction for change (for example, "Why not talk about why now is a time to pick up good stocks at bargain prices before the market picks up again?").

Inappropriate criticism, on the other hand, has one or more of the following characteristics:

- It is uninvited. There is no contract. It is unsolicited.

- The feedback is nonspecific or broad-based.

- The commentary is without direction for change.

When giving negative criticism, say what you *like* about the work before you say what you don't like. This approach preserves the recipient's ego, softens the blow, and ensures a positive working environment.

In a presentation skills course at Westinghouse, the instructor taught the following method for criticizing creative work. First say, "Here's what I liked," and recap at least three positive points. (If you look hard enough, it's impossible not to find at least three good things to say about almost anything.)

Then say, "Now, if it were mine to do. . . ." and proceed with your list of specific criticisms. This phrase implies that what you're telling the recipient is your opinion, and not an accusation of incompetence or shoddy work on his part.

If someone gives you inappropriate criticism, especially comments that attack you as a person or demean you as a professional, say to that person, "Is there a purpose for your saying this to me?" This response alerts the person that you're aware of the demeaning tone and you want it to cease.

Sacrifice Long-Term Relationships for Short-Term Results

Many times clients have pressured me, "You've got to get this press release on the front page of *The Wall Street Journal.* Call your contacts there and put on the pressure."

What the critics killed

People often ask me, "What really good PR ideas did you come up with that clients didn't let you run?" Here are four of my favorites that never saw the light of day:

✔ "Now that's a Mother's Day Campaign." We proposed that Palmer Video give a free video on Mother's Day to any customer who brought in a positive home pregnancy test.

✔ "Call your grandma." For a long-distance discount phone company, we proposed a campaign for Grandparents Day. Grandparents would write us a letter saying

they loved their grandchildren, but the kids or their parents were too cheap to call. We would arrange to have the grandchildren call the grandparents on Grandparents Day for free.

✔ "Guns for shoes." For British Knights sneakers, we proposed a campaign based on the idea of making the streets of New York City safer. If you turned in an illegal handgun, you would get a free pair of BK sneakers.

I advise against strong-arm tactics in dealing with the press. The idea that any one story is important enough to jeopardize your relationship with an editor or producer is a mistake. You plan on being in business for many years. Well, guess what? That editor or producer plans on being in the industry for just as many years, too. And so will *The Wall Street Journal* and CNBC and your local TV news.

In the last several decades, businesses have learned the concept of lifetime customer value and customer relationship management — that keeping a customer satisfied for the long term is more important than the immediate sale or the profits from it.

Treat the press as you would a customer. Don't place today's story above the long-term relationship. If the editor or producer says no and you've tried every conceivable angle to convince them otherwise, let it go. You will want to place other stories tomorrow. Preserve the relationship so that the editor or producer will continue to be friendly and receptive when you call with your next idea.

Behave Unethically

You'll live a happier and better life when you do not violate your personal code of ethics for PR or any other business pursuit. In PR, you will also be more successful, because editors and reporters seem to be better able to spot unethical behavior than other people. If you try to pull a fast one on the media and they spot it, it'll backfire terribly.

Other than media sensitivity, why behave ethically in business overall? For several reasons.

First, if you've ever been treated unethically, you know it was an unpleasant experience. People give as good as they get. Therefore, if you want people to behave ethically when dealing with you, you should behave ethically when dealing with them.

Second, your organization's reputation is one of its most important assets. Good business ethics maintain your reputation and enhance this asset. People who trust you are more likely to do business with you. Consultant Paul C. Ritchie notes that, according to a 1995 survey by the Walker group, when quality, service, and price were equal among competitors, 90 percent of consumers were more likely to buy from the company with the best reputation for social responsibility.

Unethical behavior, on the other hand, can result in ill will and negative publicity that mar your organization's reputation. This behavior can cost you customers, sales, and revenues and make it more difficult to acquire the products and services you need from good vendors at favorable prices and terms. Ritchie cites a 1996 *Business Week*/Harris poll in which 71 percent of those surveyed said business has too much power and is morally responsible for the country's woes.

"One transgression by one employee can have an enormous impact — whether it is the liability incurred by not coping properly with an environmental problem or the financial penalty resulting from an engineering failure," writes Norm Augustine, chairman, Lockheed Martin Corporation. "Even more daunting is trying to restore one's collective reputation once it is tarnished."

Another reason to adhere to ethical business practices is to do so simply because it's *right*. For many of us, doing the right thing is important to our fundamental make-up as human beings, and so we strive to do right — although on many occasions we may be tempted to stray. Scientist Charles Darwin said, "The moral sense of conscience is the most noble of all the attributes of man."

If you don't feel a compulsion or obligation to do right, the other two factors — encouraging decent treatment from others and protecting your organization's reputation and good name — will have to provide sufficient motivation for you to adhere to ethical business practices.

And often, it isn't. Research shows that many workers these days feel tempted to do things that border on the illegal or the unethical:

> ✔ In one poll, 57 percent of workers surveyed felt more pressured now than five years ago to consider acting unethically or illegally on the job, and 40 percent said that pressure has increased over the last 12 months.

✔ According to a 1997 study sponsored by the Ethics Officer Association, 48 percent of employees admitted to illegal or unethical actions in 1996. In 1997, half of U.S. workers surveyed by the Ethics Officer Association said they used technology unethically on the job during the year, including copying company software for home use and wrongly blaming a personal error on a technology glitch.

✔ In a Gallup poll, half of those interviewed said business values were declining.

✔ In an April 1997 survey of top executives, honesty and integrity were found to be the most important qualities interviewers look for in prospective employees.

In response, more and more organizations are training employees in ethics and establishing ethical guidelines for employees to follow. According to Harvard Business School Professor Joseph L. Badaracco Jr., one of three American firms has ethics training programs, and more than 500 have ethics officers. Six of ten firms have ethical codes that employees are supposed to follow. Lockheed Martin even has a toll-free "ethics hotline" that its employees and suppliers can call to get advice on business ethics issues. More than 500 ethics courses are offered at American business schools.

Chapter 25

Ten Steps to Better PR Writing

*Y*ou can hire a PR firm, a publicist, or a freelance writer to craft your press releases for you (refer to Chapter 9) — but, of course, you can do it yourself.

If you're a natural writer, writing press releases should be easy for you. If not, practice and you can improve. This section is a reminder to practice ten rules of good writing. Apply these rules to your drafts to achieve greater clarity and power in your prose.

1. Organize!

Poor organization is a major cause of foggy writing. If the reader believes the content has some importance to him, he can plow through a document even if it is dull or has lengthy sentences and big words. But if it's poorly organized, forget it. There's no way to make sense of what is written.

Poor organization stems from poor planning. Before you write, plan. Create a rough outline that spells out the contents and organization of your release or tip sheet. The outline need not be formal. A simple list, doodles, or rough notes will do. Use whatever form suits you.

By the time you finish writing, some content in the final draft might be different from the outline. That's okay. The outline is a tool to aid in organization, not a commandment cast in concrete. If you want to change it as you go along, no problem!

The outline helps you divide the writing project into many smaller, easy-to-handle pieces and parts. The organization of these parts depends on the type of document you're writing. If the format isn't strictly defined by the type of document you are writing, select the organizational scheme that best fits the material.

Some common writing formats include:

- ✔ **Order of location:** An article on the planets of the solar system might begin with Mercury (the planet nearest the sun) and end with Pluto (the planet farthest out).

- ✔ **Order of increasing difficulty:** Computer manuals often start with the easiest material and, as the user masters basic principles, move on to more complex operations.

- ✔ **Alphabetical order:** This is a logical way to arrange a booklet on vitamins (A, B-3, B-12, C, D, E, and so on) or a directory of company employees.

- ✔ **Chronological order:** In this format, you present the facts in the order in which they happened. History books are written this way. So are many case histories, feature stories, and corporate biographies.

- ✔ **Problem/solution:** Another format appropriate to case histories and many types of reports, the problem/solution organizational scheme begins with "Here's what the problem was" and ends with "Here's how we solved it."

- ✔ **Inverted pyramid:** This is the newspaper style of news reporting where the lead paragraph summarizes the story and the following paragraphs present the facts in order of decreasing importance. You can use this format in journal articles, letters, memos, and reports.

- ✔ **Deductive order:** You can start with a generalization, then support it with particulars. Scientists use this format in research papers that begin with the findings and then state the supporting evidence.

- ✔ **Inductive order:** Another approach is to begin with specific instances, and then lead the reader to the idea or general principles the instances suggest. This is an excellent way to approach trade journal feature stories.

- ✔ **List:** The article you're now reading is a list article because it describes, in list form, the most common problems in technical writing. A technical list article might be titled "Six Tips for Designing Wet Scrubbers" or "Seven Ways to Reduce Your Plant's Electric Bill."

2. Know Your Reader

With most marketing documents — articles, press releases, brochures — you are writing for many readers, not an individual. Even though you don't know the names of your readers, you need to develop a picture of who they are — their job title, education, industry, and interests. You can get a clear picture of your reader by studying some of the publications to which you are mailing your release.

Consider the following areas to help identify your key readers:

- ✔ **Job title:** Engineers are interested in your compressor's reliability and performance, while the purchasing agent is more concerned with cost. A person's job influences her perspective of your product, service, or idea. Are you writing for plant engineers? Office managers? CEOs? Machinists? Make the tone and content of your writing compatible with the professional interests of your readers.

- ✔ **Education:** Is your reader a Ph.D. or a high-school dropout? Is he a chemical engineer? Does he understand computer programming, thermodynamics, physical chemistry, and the calculus of variations? Write simply enough so that even the least technical of your readers can understand what you are saying.

- ✔ **Industry:** When engineers buy a reverse-osmosis water purification system for a chemical plant, they want to know every technical detail down to the last pipe, pump, fan, and filter. Marine buyers, on the other hand, have only two basic questions: "What does it cost?" and "How reliable is it?" Especially in promotional writing, know what features of your product appeal to the various markets.

- ✔ **Level of interest:** Is your reader interested or disinterested? Friendly or hostile? Receptive or resistant? Understanding her state of mind helps you tailor your message to meet her needs.

3. Shun "Corporatese"

Anyone who reads corporate documents knows the danger of "corporatese" — the pompous, overblown style that leaves your writing sounding as if it were written by a computer or a corporation instead of a human being.

Corporatese, by my definition, is language more complex than the concepts it serves to communicate. By loading up their writings with jargon, clichés, antiquated phrases, passive sentences, and an excess of adjectives, executives and bureaucrats hide behind a jumble of incomprehensible memos and reports.

To help you recognize corporatese (also known as *corporitis*), I've assembled a few samples from diverse sources. Note how the authors seem to be writing to impress rather than to express. All of these excerpts are real:

> *"Will you please advise me at your earliest convenience of the correct status of this product?*
>
> —Memo from an advertising manager

> *"All of the bonds in the above described account having been heretofore disposed of, we are this day terminating same. We accordingly enclose herein check in the amount of $30,050 same being your share realized therein, as per statement attached."*
>
> —Letter from a stockbroker

> *"This procedure enables users to document data fields described in master files that were parsed and analyzed by the program dictionary."*
>
> —Software user's manual

How do you eliminate corporatese from your writing? Start by avoiding jargon. Don't use a technical term unless it communicates your meaning precisely. For example, never write "mobile dentition" when "loose teeth" will do just as well. Legal scholar Tamar Frankel notes that when you avoid jargon, your writing can be read easily by novices and experienced professionals alike.

Use contractions. Avoid clichés and antiquated phrases. Write simply. Prefer the active voice. In the active voice, action is expressed directly: "John performed the experiment." In the passive voice, the action is indirect: "The experiment was performed by John."

When you use the active voice, your writing will be more direct and vigorous; your sentences, more concise. As you can see in the samples below, the passive voice seems puny and stiff by comparison:

Passive voice	*Active voice*
Control of the bearing-oil supply is provided by the shutoff valves.	Shutoff valves control the bearing-oil supply.
Leaking of the seals is prevented by the use of O-rings.	O-rings keep the seals from leaking.
Fuel-cost savings were realized through the installation of thermal insulation.	Installing thermal insulation cut fuel costs.

4. Avoid Long Sentences

Lengthy sentences tire the reader and make your writing hard to read. A survey by Harvard professor D.H. Menzel indicates that in scientific papers, the sentences become difficult to understand when they are longer than 34 words.

One measure of writing clarity, the Fog Index, takes into account sentence length *and* word length. Here's how it works:

1. **Determine the average sentence length in a short (100 to 200 words) writing sample.**

   To do this, divide the number of words in the sample by the number of sentences. If parts of a sentence are separated by a semicolon (;), count each part as a separate sentence.

2. **Calculate the number of big words (words with three or more syllables) per 100 words of sample.**

   Don't include capitalized words, combinations of short words (butterfly, moreover), or verbs that turn into three syllables by adding ed or es (accepted, responses).

3. **Add the average sentence length to the number of big words per hundred words and multiply by 0.4.**

   This result gives you the Fog Index for the sample.

The Fog Index corresponds to the years of schooling you need to read and understand the sample. A score of 8 or 9 indicates high-school level; 13, a college freshman; 17, a college graduate.

Popular magazines have Fog Indexes ranging from 8 to 13. Technical journals should rate no higher than 17. Obviously, the higher the Fog Index, the more difficult the writing is to read. Scientific writing contains some of the densest fog, as in this 79-word sentence:

> *In this book I have attempted an accurate but at the same time readable account of recent work on the subject of how gene controls operate, a large subject which is rapidly acquiring a central position in the biology of today and which will inevitably become even more prominent in the future, in the efforts of scientists of numerous different specialists to explain how a single organism can contain cells of many different kinds developed from a common origin.*

With 17 big words, this sample has a Fog Index of 40 — equivalent to a reading level of 28 years of college education! Obviously, this sentence is way too long. Here's a rewrite I came up with:

> *This book is about how gene controls operate — a subject of growing importance in modern biology.*

This rewrite gets the message across with a Fog Index of only 14.

Give your writing the Fog Index test. If you score in the upper teens or higher, it's time to trim sentence length. Go over your text, and break long sentences into two or more separate sentences. To further reduce average sentence length and add variety to your writing, you can occasionally use an extremely short sentence or sentence fragments of only three to four words or so. Like this one.

Short sentences are easier to grasp than long ones. A good guide for keeping sentence length under control is to write sentences that can be spoken aloud without losing your breath. (No cheating — don't take a deep breath before doing this test!)

5. Use Short, Simple Words

Business executives sometimes prefer to use big, important-sounding words instead of short, simple words. This is a mistake; fancy language just frustrates the reader. Write in plain, ordinary English, and your readers will love you for it.

The following table shows a few big words that occur frequently in technical literature. The column on the right shows shorter, and preferable, substitutions:

Big word	*Substitution*
Terminate	End
Utilize	Use
Incombustible	Fireproof
Substantiate	Prove
Eliminate	Get rid of

Use legitimate technical terms when they communicate your ideas precisely, but avoid using jargon just because the words sound impressive. Don't write that material is "gravimetrically conveyed" when it is simply "dumped."

In your writing, use the simplest word you can while still being accurate and specific. Don't be content to say something is good, bad, fast, or slow when you can say *how* good, *how* bad, *how* fast, or *how* slow. Be specific whenever possible.

General	*Specific*
A tall spray dryer	A 40-foot-tall spray dryer
Plant	Oil refinery
Unit	Evaporator
Unfavorable weather conditions	Rain
Structural degradation	A leaky roof
High performance	95% efficiency

The key to success in technical writing is to *keep it simple.* Write to express — not to impress. A relaxed, conversational style can add vigor and clarity to your work.

Formal style	*Informal conversational style*
The data provided by direct examination of samples under the lens of the microscope are insufficient for the purpose of making a proper identification of the components of the substance.	We can't tell what it is made of by looking at it under the microscope.
We have found during conversations with customers that even the most experienced of extruder specialists have a tendency to avoid the extrusion of silicone profiles or hoses.	Our customers tell us that experienced extruder specialists avoid extruding silicone profiles or hoses.
The corporation terminated the employment of Mr. Joseph Smith.	Joe was fired.

6. Sidestep "Writer's Block"

Writer's block isn't just for professional writers; it can afflict nonwriters, too. Writer's block is the inability to start putting words on paper or personal computer, and it stems from anxiety and fear of writing.

When people write, they're afraid to make mistakes, and so they edit themselves word by word, inhibiting the natural flow of ideas and sentences. But professional writers know that writing is a process consisting of numerous drafts, rewrites, deletions, and revisions. Rarely does a writer produce a perfect manuscript on the first try.

Follow these tips to help you overcome writer's block:

- **Break the writing up into short sections, and write one section at a time.** Tackling many little writing assignments seems less formidable a task than taking a large project all at once. This technique also benefits the reader. Writing is most readable when it deals with one simple idea rather than multiple complex ideas. Your entire paper can't be simple or restricted to one idea, but each section of it can.

- **Write the easy sections first.** Put in the page headers, section titles, cover page, and other boilerplate text. You'll feel an immediate sense of accomplishment, and the existence of a starting framework will make it easier for you to fill in the rest.

- **Avoid grammar-book rules that inhibit writers.** One such rule says every paragraph must begin with a topic sentence (a first sentence that states the central idea of the paragraph). By insisting on topic sentences, teachers and editors throw up a block that prevents people from putting their thoughts on paper. Professional writers don't worry about topic sentences (or sentence diagrams or ending a sentence with a preposition). Neither should you.

- **Sleep on it.** Put your manuscript away and come back to it the next morning — or even several days later. Refreshed, you'll be able to edit and rewrite effectively and easily.

7. Define the Topic

Effective writing begins with a clear definition of the specific topic you want to write about. The big mistake many people make is to tackle a topic that's too broad. For example, the title "Project Management" is too all encompassing for a trade journal article. You could write a whole book on the subject. But by narrowing the scope, say, with the title "Managing Chemical Plant Construction Projects With Budgets Under $500,000," you get a clearer definition and a more manageable topic.

Knowing the purpose of the document is also important. You may say, "That's easy; the purpose is to give technical information." But think again. Do you want the reader to buy a product? Change methods of working? Look for the hidden agenda beyond the mere transmission of facts.

8. Gather Lots of Information

Okay. You've defined your topic, audience, and purpose. The next step is to do some homework and to gather information on the topic at hand. Most managers and entrepreneurs I know don't do this. When they're writing a release, for example, their attitude is, "I'm the expert here. So I'll just rely on my own experience and know-how."

That approach is a mistake. Even though you're an expert, your knowledge may be limited, your viewpoint lopsided. Gathering information from other sources helps round out your knowledge or, at the very least, verify your own thinking. And there's another benefit: Backing up your claims with facts is a real credibility builder.

After you cram a file folder full of reprints and clippings, take notes on index cards or a PC. Not only does note-taking put the key facts at your fingertips in condensed form, but also reprocessing the research information through your fingers and brain puts you in closer touch with your material.

9. Write, then Rewrite, Rewrite

Once you gather facts and decide how to organize the piece, the next step is to sit down and write. When you do, keep in mind that the secret to successful writing is rewriting.

You don't have to get it right on the first draft. The pros rarely do. E. B. White, essayist and co-author of the writer's resource book *The Elements of Style,* was said to have rewritten every piece nine times.

Maybe you don't need nine drafts, but you probably need more than one. Use a simple, three-step procedure that I call SPP: Spit, Prune, and Polish:

> ✔ **When you sit down to write, just spit it out.** Don't worry about how the text sounds, or whether the grammar's right, or if it fits your outline. Just let the words flow. If you make a mistake, leave it. You can always go back and fix it later. Some non-keyboarding types find it helpful to talk into a tape recorder or dictate to an assistant. If you can type and have a personal computer, great. Some old-fashioned folks even use typewriters or pen and paper.

✔ **To prune, print out your first draft (double-spaced, for easy editing) and give it major surgery.** Take a red pen to the draft and slash out all unnecessary words and phrases. Rewrite any awkward passages to make them smoother, but if you get stuck, leave it and go on; come back to it later. Use the cut and paste feature in your word-processing program to cut the draft apart and reorganize to fit your outline, or to improve on that outline. Then print out a clean draft. Repeat the pruning step if necessary as many times as you want.

✔ **Polish your manuscript.** Check such points as equations, units of measure, references, grammar, spelling, and punctuation. Again, use the red pen and print out a fresh copy with corrections.

10. Be Consistent

"A foolish consistency," wrote Ralph Waldo Emerson, "is the hobgoblin of little minds." This may be so. But, on the other hand, inconsistencies in writing will confuse your readers and convince them that your products and company are as sloppy and unorganized as your prose. Good business writers strive for consistency in the use of numbers, hyphens, units of measure, punctuation, equations, grammar, symbols, capitalization, technical terms, and abbreviations.

Appendix

About the CD

*H*ere's some of what you can find on the *Public Relations Kit For Dummies* CD-ROM:

- ✔ Dozens of sample press releases, forms, contacts, and other public relations materials.
- ✔ Templates that you can use to create your own PR management tools.
- ✔ Adobe Acrobat Reader for Mac and Windows, a freeware version that allows you to read the PDF documents on this CD.

System Requirements

Make sure your computer meets the minimum system requirements listed below. If your computer doesn't match up to most of these requirements, you may have problems in using the contents of the CD.

- ✔ A PC with a Pentium or faster processor, or a Mac OS computer with a 68040 or faster processor.
- ✔ Microsoft Windows 95 or later, or Mac OS system software 7.5.5 or later.
- ✔ At least 16MB of total RAM installed on your computer. For best performance, we recommend at least 32MB of RAM installed.
- ✔ At least 50MB of hard drive space available to install all the software from this CD. (You'll need less space if you don't install every program.)
- ✔ A CD-ROM drive — double-speed (2x) or faster.
- ✔ A sound card for PCs. (Mac OS computers have built-in sound support.)
- ✔ A monitor capable of displaying at least 256 colors or grayscale.
- ✔ A modem with a speed of at least 14,400 bps.

If you need more information on the basics, check out *PCs For Dummies*, 7th Edition, by Dan Gookin; *Macs For Dummies,* 6th Edition, by David Pogue; *The iMac For Dummies,* by David Pogue; *Windows 95 For Dummies,* 2nd Edition, or *Windows 98 For Dummies,* both by Andy Rathbone (all published by IDG Books Worldwide, Inc.).

Using the CD with Microsoft Windows

1. **Insert the CD unto your computer's CD-ROM drive.**

   Give your computer a moment to take a look at the CD.

2. **Open your browser.**

   If you do not have a browser, we include Microsoft Internet Explorer on this CD.

   Select File⇨Open (Internet Explorer) or File⇨Open page (Netscape).

3. **Double-click the file called License.txt.**

   This file contains the end-user license that you agree to by using the CD. When you are done reading the license, close the program, most likely Notepad, that displayed the file.

4. **Double-click the file called Readme.txt.**

   This file contains instructions about installing the software from this CD. It might be helpful to leave this text file open while you are using the CD.

5. **In the dialog box that appears, type** D:\START.HTM **and click on OK.**

   Replace the letter D with the correct letter for your CD-ROM drive, if it is not D.

   This action will display the file that will walk you through the content of the CD.

6. **To navigate within the interface, simply click on any topic of interest to take you to an explanation of the files on the CD and how to use or install them.**

7. **To install the software from the CD, simply click on the software name.**

   You'll see two options — the option to run or open the file from the current location or the option to save the file to your hard drive. Choose to run or open the file from its current location, and the installation procedure will continue. After you are done with the interface, simply close your browser as usual.

To run some of the programs, you may need to keep the CD inside your CD-ROM drive. This is a Good Thing. Otherwise, the installed program would have required you to install a very large chunk of the program to your hard drive space, which would have kept you from installing other software.

Using the CD with Mac OS

To install the items from the CD to your hard drive, follow these steps.

1. **Insert the CD into your computer's CD-ROM drive.**

   In a moment, an icon representing the CD you just inserted appears on your Mac desktop. Chances are, the icon looks like a CD-ROM.

2. **Double-click the CD icon to show the CD's contents.**

3. **Double-click the Read Me First icon.**

   This text file contains information about the CD's programs and any last-minute instructions you need to know about installing the programs on the CD that we don't cover in this appendix.

4. **Open your browser.**

   If you don't have a browser, we include Microsoft Internet Explorer on the CD.

5. **Select File⇨Open and select the CD titled "Public Relations Kit." Double-click the Start.htm file to see an explanation of all files and folders included on the CD.**

6. **Some programs come with installer programs — with those you simply open the program's folder on the CD and double-click the icon with the words "Install" or "Installer."**

   After you have installed the programs that you want, you can eject the CD. Carefully place it back in the plastic jacket of the book for safekeeping.

What You'll Find on the CD

Shareware programs are fully functional, free trial versions of copyrighted programs. If you like particular programs, register with their authors for a nominal fee and receive licenses, enhanced versions, and technical support. Freeware programs are free, copyrighted games, applications, and utilities. You can copy them to as many PCs as you like — free — but they have no technical support. GNU software is governed by its own license, which is included inside the folder of the GNU software. There are no restrictions on distribution of this software. See the GNU license for more details. Trial, demo, or evaluation versions are usually limited either by time or functionality (such as being unable to save projects).

The CD-ROM contains business software as well as example files, templates, and forms that relate to specific chapters in the book.

Business software

What follows are descriptions of the software applications available on the CD:

Acrobat Reader
For Mac and Windows. Evaluation version. This program from AdobeSystems program lets you view and print Portable Document Format (PDF) files. You can get more information by visiting the Adobe Systems Web site at `www.adobe.com`.

Internet Explorer
For Windows and Mac. Commercial product. This browser from Microsoft enables you to view Web pages and perform a host of other Internet functions, including e-mail and newsgroups.

BBEdit Lite 4.6
For Mac and Windows. This is the freeware version of the popular HTML editor. We also include a demo version of the more full-featured BBEdit 5.1.1.

Start Right Marketing
For Windows. Trial version. Start Marketing Right is multimedia software that teaches you the fundamentals of marketing. This is a demonstration version of the program. Vendor: Do It Right Software; `www.doitright.com`.

Maximizer 5.5
For Windows. This a trial version of powerful contact manager software that allows you to manage your schedule and keep track of customers, prospects, and vendors. Vendor: Multiactive Software; `www.multiactive.com`.

ecBuilder
For Windows. This trial version of ecBuilder lets you create a commerce-capable Web site quickly and easily. Vendor: Multiactive Software; `www.multiactive.com`.

ACT! 2000 For Windows
This trial version of ACT! 2000 is an application that helps you create to-do lists, schedules, and contacts databases. Vendor: SalesLogix Corporation; `www.saleslogix.com`.

Graphic Converter
For Macintosh. Shareware software. Graphic Converter is a powerful shareware application for Macintosh computers that allows you to open and convert pictures in many different file formats. Vendor: Lemke Software; `www.lemkesoft.com`.

Hotdog Professional
For Windows. Trial version. HotDog Professional Webmaster Suite provides a flexible, text-based HTML authoring environment. Vendor: Sausage Software; `www.sausage.com`.

Telemagic   *Evaluation version.* Contact management software useful for maintaining lists of PR contacts by category; www.telemagic.com.

CD Files

What follows is a list of all the files on the CD-ROM.

Video clips

Illustrations for Chapter 14, "Getting PR on the Tube":

V01	"Hooray It's a Homerun With Cal Ripken" (©2000 The itsy bitsy Entertainment Company)
V02	"Progressive Watercraft Insurance 'Keys Please' Pilot Program"
V03	"IKEA Workers Will 'Kiss Your Feet' to Shop on Oct. 9"

Resource files

CDRF01	Associations
CDRF02	Web sites
CDRF03	Books
CDRF04	Periodicals
CDRF05	Media directories and distribution services
CDRF06	Clipping services
CDRF08	Video production and satellite feed companies
CDRF09	Other resources and suppliers
CDRF10	Conferences, seminars, events
CDRF11	PR code of ethics

Chapter files

CD0302	Sample PR audit
CD0303	Sample PR plan
CD0304	Form for tracking PR expenses
CD0305	Budget for PR campaign
CD0801	Jericho Communications Newsletter
CD0901	Sample press releases
CD0902	Prewriting checklist

CD0903	Press release writing guidelines
CD1001	Sample query letters
CD1002	Sample pitch letters
CD1003	Sample feature article
CD1201	Contact form
CD1401	Sample media alerts
CD1701	Event planning checklist
CD1901	Crisis management plan
CD2001	Sample media impressions report

If You've Got Problems (Of the CD Kind)

I tried my best to compile programs that work on most computers with the minimum system requirements. Alas, your computer may differ, and some programs may not work properly for some reason.

The two likeliest problems are that you don't have enough memory (RAM) for the programs you want to use, or you have other programs running that are affecting installation or running of a program. If you get error messages like `Not enough memory` or `Setup cannot continue`, try one or more of these methods and then try using the software again:

- ✔ Turn off any anti-virus software that you have on your computer. Installers sometimes mimic virus activity and may make your computer incorrectly believe that it is being infected by a virus.

- ✔ Close all running programs. The more programs you're running, the less memory is available to other programs. Installers also typically update files and programs. So if you keep other programs running, installation may not work properly.

- ✔ Have your local computer store add more RAM to your computer. This is, admittedly, a drastic and somewhat expensive step. However, if you have a Windows 95 PC or a Mac OS computer with a PowerPC chip, adding more memory can really help the speed of your computer and allow more programs to run at the same time. This may include closing the CD interface and running a product's installation program from Windows Explorer.

If you still have trouble with installing the items from the CD, please call the IDG Books Worldwide Customer Service phone number: 800-762-2974 (outside the United States: 317-572-3993).

Index

• *Q* •

• *U* •

• *V* •

• W •

• Y •

• Z •

Notes

Notes

Notes

Notes

Notes

Notes

IDG Books Worldwide, Inc., End-User License Agreement

READ THIS. You should carefully read these terms and conditions before opening the software packet(s) included with this book ("Book"). This is a license agreement ("Agreement") between you and IDG Books Worldwide, Inc. ("IDGB"). By opening the accompanying software packet(s), you acknowledge that you have read and accept the following terms and conditions. If you do not agree and do not want to be bound by such terms and conditions, promptly return the Book and the unopened software packet(s) to the place you obtained them for a full refund.

1. **License Grant.** IDGB grants to you (either an individual or entity) a nonexclusive license to use one copy of the enclosed software program(s) (collectively, the "Software") solely for your own personal or business purposes on a single computer (whether a standard computer or a workstation component of a multiuser network). The Software is in use on a computer when it is loaded into temporary memory (RAM) or installed into permanent memory (hard disk, CD-ROM, or other storage device). IDGB reserves all rights not expressly granted herein.

2. **Ownership.** IDGB is the owner of all right, title, and interest, including copyright, in and to the compilation of the Software recorded on the disk(s) or CD-ROM ("Software Media"). Copyright to the individual programs recorded on the Software Media is owned by the author or other authorized copyright owner of each program. Ownership of the Software and all proprietary rights relating thereto remain with IDGB and its licensers.

3. **Restrictions on Use and Transfer.**

   (a) You may only (i) make one copy of the Software for backup or archival purposes, or (ii) transfer the Software to a single hard disk, provided that you keep the original for backup or archival purposes. You may not (i) rent or lease the Software, (ii) copy or reproduce the Software through a LAN or other network system or through any computer subscriber system or bulletin-board system, or (iii) modify, adapt, or create derivative works based on the Software.

   (b) You may not reverse engineer, decompile, or disassemble the Software. You may transfer the Software and user documentation on a permanent basis, provided that the transferee agrees to accept the terms and conditions of this Agreement and you retain no copies. If the Software is an update or has been updated, any transfer must include the most recent update and all prior versions.

4. **Restrictions on Use of Individual Programs.** You must follow the individual requirements and restrictions detailed for each individual program in the Appendix of this Book. These limitations are also contained in the individual license agreements recorded on the Software Media. These limitations may include a requirement that after using the program for a specified period of time, the user must pay a registration fee or discontinue use. By opening the Software packet(s), you will be agreeing to abide by the licenses and restrictions for these individual programs that are detailed in the Appendix and on the Software Media. None of the material on this Software Media or listed in this Book may ever be redistributed, in original or modified form, for commercial purposes.